FARRAR
STRAUS
GIROUX

MORT ROSENBLUM

Chocolate

Mort Rosenblum was a special correspondent to The Associated Press and editor of the *International Herald Tribune*. His books include *Olives* (NPP, 1996), winner of the James Beard Award for Writing on Food, and *A Goose in Toulouse*. He lives in Paris.

# Chocolate

# Chocolate

## A Bittersweet Saga

*of*

## Dark and Light

## Mort Rosenblum

NORTH POINT PRESS

A DIVISION OF FARRAR, STRAUS AND GIROUX

NEW YORK

North Point Press
A division of Farrar, Straus and Giroux
19 Union Square West, New York 10003

Excerpts in Chapter Three reprinted from *The True History of Chocolate* by Sophie
D. Coe and Michael D. Coe copyright © 1996 Thames & Hudson Ltd., London.
Reprinted by kind permission of Thames & Hudson Ltd., London.

The Library of Congress has cataloged the hardcover edition as follows:
Rosenblum, Mort.
   Chocolate : a bittersweet saga of dark and light / Mort Rosenblum.—1st ed.
      p.   cm.
   ISBN-13: 978-0-86547-635-6
   ISBN-10: 0-86547-635-7 (hardcover : alk. paper)
      1. Cacao—History.   2. Chocolate—History.   3. Cocoa trade—History.
I. Title.

   SB267.R67 2005
   641.3'374—dc22                                              2004054734

Paperback ISBN-13: 978-0-86547-730-8
Paperback ISBN-10: 0-86547-730-2

Designed by Cassandra J. Pappas

www.fsgbooks.com

1   3   5   7   9   10   8   6   4   2

*For the Chocolate Monsters:*
*Alexa and Eliza; Louis and Paul;*
*Sam Martin; Elise and Kiana;*
*Carina and even Gianna,*
*who prefers olives*

Nine of every ten persons say they love chocolate. The tenth lies.

—ANTHELME BRILLAT-SAVARIN

# Contents

# Chocolate

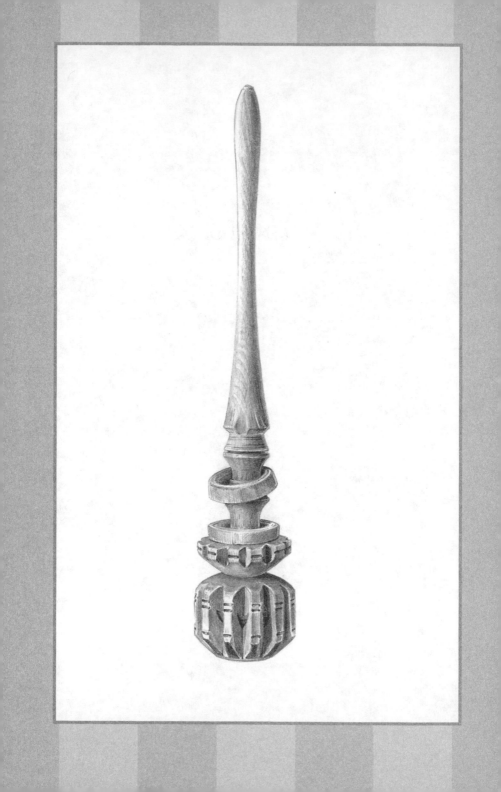

# Chapter 1

## THE GODS' BREAKFAST

A half millennium ago, a canoe full of Indians rowed out to an ungainly floating house anchored at Guanaja, a palm-flecked island off the Honduran coast. Christopher Columbus had stopped by on the way home from his fourth and last trip to America, still hopeful he might find useful riches beyond an expanse of alien real estate. The Indians offered what he took to be a handful of shriveled almonds. He was mystified when a few dropped to the bottom of their canoe, his son reported later, and "they scrambled for them as though they were eyes that had fallen out of their heads." But Columbus's Mayan was no better than the natives' Spanish. He returned to Spain empty-handed.

Chocolate has come a long way since then.

These days, those almondlike cacao beans that the grand Swedish botanist Carolus Linnaeus named *Theobroma*—elixir of the gods—are the basis of a $60 billion industry. From the time laborers scoop them from pods in equatorial jungles until fine chocolatiers massage them into gold-flecked ganaches, the value of a bean might increase several hundred times. But money is hardly the way to measure their worth.

One night in Paris, a friend took me to a tasting of the Club des Croqueurs de Chocolat, a circle of people who believe well-crafted bonbons to be as vital to life as oxygen. We tried one creation after another, noting every nuance from the sheen on their coatings to subtle flashes of flavor that lingered on the tongue. With knowing nods and silent smiles, we made checks on evaluation sheets next to adjectives borrowed from the complex lexicon of wine.

Finally, sated to near stupor, we settled back to hear the tastemaster announce plans for the next session. We would, he said, be sampling the finest *éclairs au chocolat* that France had to offer.

*"Ah, oui,"* one woman breathed from the back of the room. *"Oouuiii,"* another added, with more power, and a third joined in with loud staccato moans: *"Oui, oui, oui."* Suddenly the sedate hotel dining room was blue with the piercing shrieks of passion. Columbus would have loved it.

Like every other American kid, I grew up on Hershey bars and those colorful little blobs that, M&M's claims aside, melted in my hand as well as in my mouth. Over the years, as an amateur food lover and professional traveler, I learned to appreciate other variations on the theme. That evening in Paris, however, showed me I was clueless, a chocolate ignoramus.

Tracing chocolate from its origins to its most elaborate final forms, I suspected, would be a wondrous journey. But only after I followed cacao into a fierce African rebellion and then stood paralyzed with pleasure at the heady scent inside Michel Chaudun's little shop in the seventh arrondissement of Paris did I realize how much chocolate has flavored the last five centuries.

I started out by paging at leisure through Roald Dahl's *Charlie and the Chocolate Factory*. Before long, I was delving into the themes of *War and Peace*.

By the end, I saw why people like my friend Hadley Fitzgerald, a California therapist of reasonable habits, would have to think a moment if the devil offered to buy their souls for chocolate. Hadley's body and being require a daily dose.

Taken to its highest finish, cacao ends up as a *palet d'or*, a simple square or circle of creamy dark filling—the French call that "ganache"—inside a thin, hard covering of silky smooth chocolate, the *enrobage*. At its best, a *palet d'or* shines with a rich brilliance. And it is signed by its maker in bits of real gold, which carry no taste but deliver an unmissable message: This is the good stuff.

I began to catch on when I savored two *palets* made with distinct types of chocolate from the French company Valrhona. One was Manjari, from Madagascar cacao; the other was from Gran Couva plantation in Trinidad. Except for cream in the ganache, both *palets* were pure chocolate.

The Manjari came in a rush of ripe raspberries. It peaked and then settled into a long, lush finish. Gran Couva was flowers, not fruit, a slow-moving cloud of jasmine that carried me away to some very happy place.

Nothing is simple about good chocolate. Some high practitioners prefer the term *palet or*. Either way, the old translation was "pillow of gold." According to the Académie Française des Chocolatiers et Confiseurs, Bernard Serarady devised the name in 1870, in the town of Moulin. But Saint-Germain-en-Laye disputes that claim. In 2004, French chocolatiers convened to argue the point.

Soon I dispensed with the fancy final product and bought bulk chocolate bits from my favorite producers in the Rhône Valley, in Tuscany, in California's Bay Area. In form, though in no other way, these reminded me of those baking chips I used to forage from my mother's pantry.

Beyond industrial candymakers with brands we all recognize, chocolatiers come in two flavors. There are those who make chocolate from beans, from the Swiss-based behemoth Barry Callebaut to such specialists as Valrhona. And there are artisans known as *fondeurs*—the word means "melters"—who turn this base chocolate into high art.

France bestows upon its chosen chocolatiers the aura of philosopher-kings. Pierre Hermé, a hulking bull of a man with a delicate touch, opened his small Parisian shop on the rue Bonaparte and had to hire a press agent to ward off the journalistic swarm. Robert Linxe sold his redoubtable La Maison du Chocolat in Paris to a globe-girdling French industrialist, yet eager pilgrims still come to sit at his feet.

For chocolatiers, "chocolate" implies *un produit frais*, a fresh and living thing that must be consumed within days. Yet that Hershey bar dug up after sixty years from Admiral Richard Byrd's cache at the South Pole is also chocolate. It was made for World War II field rations. According to army specifications, it was designed to taste "just a little better than a boiled potato." That way, soldiers would not wolf it down heedlessly. Having been frozen all those years, it was still edible. In the view of purists who disdain industrial cocoa products, it could have gone right onto a store shelf. Who'd know the difference?

And yet, purists be damned, millions still revere a Hershey bar. In a good year, the world can produce three million tons of cacao, less than half the coffee crop, but still a lot of beans. And how one likes them is a simple matter of preference.

Chocolate, in substance and in spirit, covers a lot of ground. Taken to a fine finish, it is no less nuanced than wine. If there is Ripple, there is also Rothschild.

$\mathcal{H}$ernán Cortés tasted chocolate only sixteen years after Columbus sailed home. Although he noted in his letters that it just might catch on, much about cacao still remains a mystery. From bean to bonbon, the production chain is long. Few people who slave away in steamy heat all their lives to grow cacao have ever tasted chocolate. Hardly any confectioner who does the final fancywork has ever seen a cacao tree. Tropical institutes study the botany. Engineers perfect production. But for all the science around it, fine chocolate still demands a touch of alchemy, masterful sleights of hand bordering on the magical.

In its primary state, chocolate is odd-looking and often forbidding. *Theobroma cacao* can be an extremely picky plant. Young trees seek the dank shadows of tall tropical hardwoods; older ones like more sunlight. They also like their space. They grow only within twenty degrees of the equator but can climb up mountainsides as high as two thousand feet. And they demand a long rainy season, with deep, rich soil and temperatures that never drop below sixty degrees.

Their setting can be heart-stoppingly beautiful, under such towering monsters as *Erythrina*, the coral tree, with its vivid scarlet sprays of blossoms. "The cocoa woods were another thing," V. S. Naipaul once wrote of his native Trinidad. "They were like the woods of fairy tales, dark and shadowed and cool. The cocoa-pods, hanging by thick short stems, were like wax fruit in brilliant green and yellow and red and crimson and purple." (For reasons I could never determine, English usage often prefers "cocoa" for both the plant, the bean, and the drink it produces; I prefer the less-confusing approach of Romance languages: cacao and cocoa.)

By the time a graceful cacao seedling grows to maximum age, about forty years, it can be as tough and twisted as a scrub oak. Its bark is often a patchwork of greenish white lichen. If well pruned, as it must be to produce quality pods, its crown of leathery leaves—most dark green, some in rich colors—forms a canopy about eight feet above the ground. Left wild, it grows three times as tall.

Cacao starts with delicate white flowers that sprout improbably from the alligator-skin trunks and limbs. Most blossoms wither and drop away. They germinate only with the help of a midge, hardly bigger than a pinhead, that lives in surrounding undergrowth. Perhaps four or five in a hundred transform over three months into bright green oval pods, no bigger than a small pineapple. They ripen to painter's-palette shades from yellow to deep purple.

Each pod's thick, fibrous husk protects about forty beans inside. These nestle in a sticky white pulp with the wonderfully sweet taste of an Asian mangosteen. No sensible rodent or monkey misses the chance to steal a ripe pod and spend a day gnawing its way inside. This is just as well. As pods do not fall from the tree, seeds must be transported by bird, animal, or man for a new plant to grow.

Plantation workers harvest the pods with lethal-looking hooks on poles. Using machetes or clubs, they deftly open the pods, careful not to damage the beans. The gooey mass scooped from inside must ferment for days, protected from outside air, until the mucilage drains away and dries.

At first, this was done simply to dry the beans so they could be shipped long distances without spoiling. Over the years, however, growers realized that fermentation begins to unlock the flavors inside. Now this initial step is crucial to final taste. Beans are then dried of most of their remaining moisture, packed into jute bags, and dispatched to Europe and North America.

All of that, of course, is just the preliminary stage of making chocolate.

Those tiny midges are vital to the growing process, but a harrowing range of other insects and diseases can kill the trees or destroy their pods. A plague of witches'-broom beginning in 1989 all but drove Brazil out of the cacao business. Maladies with names like pod rot and swollen shoot can wreak havoc. If trees lack moisture for too long, their leaves drop off and they die.

By the time Cortés discovered the Aztecs' *cacahuatl*, anthropologists say, earlier inhabitants of the Americas had been drinking it for at least a thousand years. What the Spaniards found was a domesticated variety of *T. cacao*, known as *criollo*, which is native to Central and South America. Its slim oblong pods contain pure white aromatic beans that are the source of particularly prized chocolate. But it is finicky. It grows relatively few pods and only under highly specific conditions. It is susceptible to pests and disease. And it languishes in unfamiliar surroundings.

Once established in the New World, the Spanish, Portuguese, and Dutch brought cacao trees to their tropical colonies overseas. But, despairing of the fragile *criollo*, planters relied on a different variety known as *forastero*, which means "foreigner." It is hardier and more productive, and it travels well. Its beans are purple inside, unlike the white centers of *criollo*. And they lack *criollo*'s fragrant richness.

As late as the mid-twentieth century, growers in Mexico tore out old *criollos* to plant *forasteros* that produced a much bigger—but a much inferior—crop.

Spain dominated the early cacao trade. As demand increased for chocolate in Europe, kings in Madrid kept close watch on their lucrative crop. After a century, though, their monopoly was threatened. Portuguese colonizers grew cacao in Brazil, and Dutch sailors also brought trees to Southeast Asia. In 1822, trees were transplanted from Brazil to Portugal's outpost of São Tomé, off the West African coast.

Soon afterward, cacao was also growing in the neighboring Spanish island colony of Fernando Po. Late in the nineteenth century, an African plantation worker smuggled seedlings from Fernando Po to the nearby British colony on the mainland, the Gold Coast, now Ghana. Trees spread to the French Ivory Coast across the border and into Nigeria.

In the early 1700s, a Caribbean calamity resulted in a third variety of *T. cacao*. Something that history records as the Blast devastated Trinidad. Today, no one is certain whether this was a monster hurricane or a deadly blight. Either way, it wiped out the island's *criollo* trees. They were replaced with the hybrid *trinitario*, which has since found its way around the equator.

A fourth variety, *nacional*, was developed in Ecuador, with a distinctive spicy flavor named for the region where it grows, Arriba. It is, essentially, a better sort of *forastero*.

During the first part of the twentieth century, as a new industry fed a fast-growing chocolate craze, England and France muscled ahead in the world cacao market with their African *forastero*. Today, 70 percent of the world's beans come from Africa. Ivory Coast alone produces nearly half of the global crop—the worse half.

Worldwide, about 15 million acres are planted in cacao. And 90 percent of it is grown by families, perhaps with a few hired hands, on holdings of less than twelve acres.

Pure *criollo* goes into perhaps 1 percent of all chocolate, and *trinitario* beans account for about 10 percent. Like vintners and olive-oil makers, chocolatiers have started to examine the raw material they had taken for granted over generations. With a great chocolate awakening that coincided with the turn of the millennium, single varietals were suddenly all the rage. And the most prized was the vanishing *criollo*.

In Trinidad, a gene bank protects some of the oldest forms of *T. cacao*. And some experiments are under way. With Venezuelan government aid, botanists are trying to revive the elusive rich taste that once flavored so much of the Americas. A plantation south of Lake Maracaibo that started with three hundred trees planted late in the 1990s may eventually help bring back a glorious lost flavor.

rcheologists say that the Olmecs, in what is now Mexico, drank chocolate a thousand years before Christ. Only a limited amount has been learned about these enigmatic early people who left behind huge stone gods with high domed foreheads, sad eyes, and fleshy lips. Stunning jade masks and other archeological evidence suggest a complex civilization. Nothing is known about what they liked for breakfast. But, like other Mesoamerican Indians, they must have loved to suck the sweet pulp from ripe cacao pods.

The highly cultured Mayans were the first to make a sacred drink of cacao. They roasted and ground the beans, mixing the powder with chilies, herbs, and wild honey. Cacao was at the top of the list when tribute was offered to their rulers. It went into the tombs of kings. By the time Columbus arrived, cacao beans were the coin of the realm. They were used for trade between the Maya and the Aztecs who settled to the north, in central Mexico, in the thirteenth century.

The beans were money that grew on trees, which explains why those Indians at Guanaja were loath to lose any in the bottom of their canoe. Centuries on, that seems like a noble concept. How can you hoard coins that so quickly dry up and crumble away?

Among tribes in Nicaragua, Francisco Oviedo y Valdés reported, a rabbit cost ten beans and a slave was worth one hundred. Dalliance with a prostitute cost eight to ten of the shriveled edible coins; this was negotiable. The currency system was based on 20. Each four hundred beans were a *ʒontle*. Twenty of those made a *xiquipil*. And so on.

By the time Cortés arrived, the Aztecs had elevated their *cacahuatl* to holiness. The drink was made with complex blends that sometimes added cornmeal to the fiery chilies and aromatic spices. Bernal Díaz del Castillo, the mildly reliable chronicler of the Conquista, reported that the emperor Montezuma faced his harem of two hundred wives only after drinking fifty chalices of spiced cacao. The supposed aphrodisiac effect of the Aztecs' chili-laced chocolate inflamed the Spanish imagination.

"Their main interest in life is to eat, to drink, to debauch, satisfying a wild lust," Oviedo y Valdés wrote, with what seemed like a touch of envy. At another point, he added details: "It is the habit among Central American Indians to rub each other all over with pulpy cocoa mass and then nibble at each other."

While some early Mesoamericans relied on wild honey with a kick of hot chilies to flavor their chocolate, the Aztecs took more trouble. Cortés notes one secret recipe: 700 grams of cacao, 750 grams of white sugar, 2 ounces of cinnamon, 15 grams of pepper, 15 grams of clove, 3 vanilla beans, a handful of anise, some hazelnuts, musk, and orange blossoms.

Mexicans today still grind roasted cacao beans and sugar into a grainy viscous paste that is mixed in a clay vessel, a *jarro chocolatero*. Chocolate and liquid are whipped with a *molinillo,* a wooden stick with rings carved at the end. As this is hard work, the job is left to women, who spin the stick between their palms at a furious pace until delicate froth builds atop the liquid. Purists still use water, but milk is now more popular. Cinnamon is usually added, and some special drinks include corn.

Cacao fascinated Cortés. "The divine drink of chocolate builds resistance and fights fatigue," he wrote to King Carlos I. "A cup of this precious drink permits a man to walk all day without food." He described how, in Montezuma's court, the *cacahuatl* was served in golden goblets with great ceremony. When he came home in 1527, Cortés brought beans to his own emperor. If Carlos I liked the new beverage, he left no word. For two generations, chocolate was a mysterious rarity available only from travelers who brought home their own supply. Then in 1585 a cargo ship from Veracruz brought enough beans in its hold to create Europe's first chocolate fiends.

Cacao was processed in monasteries and nunneries. The Jesuits made a specialty of it, experimenting with new concoctions. They maintained plantations, using the income to build churches and schools. King Felipe II, a man of great appetites, developed a taste for chocolate. By the late 1500s it was the royal rage.

Almost immediately, the church found itself mired in polemic. Was cacao a miracle drug or a sinful stimulant? Was it food or drink? In 1569, Pope Pius V set things straight. Cocoa, as a beverage, was permitted during Lent. And because the pontiff found it so repugnant, he declared there was no danger of its causing moral harm.

Naturally, there were holdouts. One colonial bishop, furious that cocoa-slurping ladies in the back pews were disturbing the Mass, put his foot down. The women refused to relent and moved to another church. And the bishop, inexplicably, died of poisoning.

Physicians and scientists disagreed violently among themselves, but the pro-chocolate faction carried the day. Juan de Cárdenas, in a book called *The Problems and Marvelous Secrets of the Indies*, wrote in 1591 that chocolate's high fat content had a positive impact on the body's "animal heat." Thomas Gage, a Scottish medical missionary, declared, "A glass of good Chocolate restores and, above all, fortifies the stomach."

After the Jesuits, it was the Jews. Expelled from Spain and then Portugal without many options, Jewish artisans settled in the French Basque country, just over the border in Bayonne, where they made the first French chocolate early in the seventeenth century. But, hemmed in by the Pyrenees, they had little commerce with Paris.

The Spanish managed to keep a lock on cacao for most of a century. But then it reached Flanders and Holland, at the eastern edges of Spain's European empire, and the monopoly collapsed. Francesco Antonio Carletti, a Florentine merchant, brought it to Italy in 1606. Soon, chocolate salons opened in Venice and Florence, and then in Perugia and Turin. Italian chocolate lovers added a touch of elegance, devising new ways of preparing cocoa and serving it in specially designed porcelain.

In 1615, a fourteen-year-old Spanish princess named Anne of Austria was dispatched to marry the French king, Louis XIII, who was only a few days older. Refusing to go without her chocolate, she brought cacao beans to Paris in her luggage. Before long, as is their wont with edible items that come to their attention, the French appropriated chocolate.

rance reinvented the exotic import, folding it into a culinary culture that accompanied an enthusiastic mission to civilize a less enlightened world. For late-Renaissance Parisians bent on the good life, cacao quickly established itself as the drug of choice. It was considered an energizer, a mood lifter, and, still, a powerful spur to the libido.

Among the earlier rituals of French royalty was to receive guests for hot chocolate. A chosen few were invited into palace bedchambers at midmorning, and servants poured breakfast from silver jugs.

Cardinal Richelieu was an immediate cacao addict. He drank chocolate to calm his flaring temper. Cardinal Mazarin, an intimate of Anne, was so smitten by the new drink that he employed his own personal chocolate maker.

David Chaillou was the first official chocolatier in Paris. A royal patent in 1670 granted him "the exclusive privilege of making, selling, and otherwise dispensing a certain composition named chocolate." He concocted a range of variations on Spanish recipes. Although he catered mostly to the aristocracy, his customer base was huge.

A year before Chaillou went into business, another cocoa-loving Austrian princess married the next Louis. The wedding took place in Saint-Jean-de-Luz near Bayonne—and all that Jewish-made chocolate. The king preferred red Burgundy, commenting once that the new Spanish drink "fools hunger and fails to fill the stomach." Not so, the queen.

"The king and chocolate were the only two passions of Marie-Thérèse," according to one unsigned biography I chanced upon. It was not clear if that was her proper order of preference.

For the next hundred years, until the French Revolution, every Louis in line found himself involved with chocoholic consorts. Madame de Maintenon insisted that Louis XIV, the Sun King, serve chocolate on all grand occasions at Versailles. Louis XV's favorite mistresses craved the stuff for differing reasons.

The Marquise de Pompadour fed the king chocolate to arouse his passions. Without it, she confided to friends, he was "dead as a cold duck." She sipped cocoa herself to make it through the night. Madame du Barry, unsatisfied by the monarch's panda-like libido, dispensed chocolate to her string of lovers so they could keep up with her.

Marie-Antoinette, she of let-them-eat-cake fame, was yet another Austrian who came to France with chocolate in her baggage train. She also brought her own Viennese chocolatier, whose specialty was a brew mixed with orchid powder, orange blossoms, and almond milk.

Chocolate figured prominently in the letters of Madame de Sévigné, which kept track of a grand and gay seventeenth-century France. At first, she loved a hot cup of cocoa, whipped with water and sugar into lush foam by the servants who attended her as she traveled about the country. When her daughter left Paris to join a new husband as Madame de Grignan, la Sévigné lamented the absence of cocoa in the distant Ardèche.

And then she went off chocolate completely, fearing it might burn the blood. In 1675, Madame de Sévigné wrote to her daughter and favorite correspondent of the misfortune that had befallen a countess of their circle: "She drank so much cocoa while with child that she bore a baby who was black as the devil and died after a few days."

Enthusiasm in France spread across the Continent. Chocolate houses thrived, along with their own special paraphernalia. Porcelain makers produced patterned versions of a cup and saucer known as *la trembleuse*. The cup fitted snugly into a raised ring on the saucer to keep aged, trembling wrists from spilling hot cocoa.

Chocolate, coffee, and tea all captivated Europe at about the same time, and each made its impact. Coffee, the cheapest, was a man's drink, taken in clublike public houses along with another exotic import, tobacco. Tea was twice as expensive as coffee, with a more genteel following among both males and females. But, after all, it was only hot water and wet leaves. Chocolate, at double the price of tea, was the noble newcomer.

About the time Chaillou received his royal patent, a forgotten Frenchman opened London's first chocolate shop at Bishopsgate. Unlike the aristocratic clientele in Paris, his customers included ordinary Londoners, and he started a new trend. Chocolate houses sprang up, rivaling the popular coffeehouses as a place to meet friends, play cards, and discuss the day. White's opened on St. James's Street in 1697, elevating the cocoa ritual to high art. Men in fussy wigs and breeches hobnobbed with ladies in flowing gowns in rooms decorated with sumptuous gilt moldings. Patrons could buy theater and opera tickets as they whiled away afternoons. The nearby Cocoa Tree offered similar fare in an ambiance dominated by Tory parliamentarians arguing about politics.

Samuel Pepys, a denizen of London clubs who was not easy to impress, recorded in his diaries a tepid reaction to his first taste of "Tee." But he later noted his judgment on what he called Jocolatte: "Very good."

The English, as usual, set a different course. In 1674, two different pubs—the Coffee Mill and the Tobacco Roll—offered chocolate to eat. Cacao was not just for cocoa. The prototype candy bars they made were coarse and, by all accounts, not that tasty. But here was a quiet milestone that changed the world. It started a global craving for chocolate in every imaginable solid form, which, three centuries later, grows yet more intense every year.

*E*urope took time out for a revolution in America and another in France. But then, under a Napoleonic calm, artisan chocolatiers lost no time opening up in Paris. Debauve & Gallais was established in 1800 on the rue Saint-Dominique. It is still around. In 1807, the first gastronomic guidebook to appear in France, Grimod de la Reynière's *L'Almanach des gourmands,* raved about a little shop at 41, rue Vivienne.

"We enter the superb store of M. Lemoine, drawn by an ingenious arrangement of liqueurs, chocolates, and bonbons," it began. "The unctuous chocolate owes this eminent quality to new methods that M. Lemoine uses to mix his chocolate." The guide also praised Tanrade, on the rue Neuve–Le Pelletier, for "exquisite chocolate prepared with cacao selected with uncommon care."

But M. de la Reynière had not seen anything yet. The nineteenth-century innovators were still puzzling over their early experiments.

The first breakthrough came in 1828, in Holland. Coenrad Van Houten found a way to extract cocoa butter and then make powder from the remaining mass. By blending some of the separated cocoa butter with sugar and adding it to the powder, he could mold chocolate.

In 1875, after eight years of trying, the Swiss inventor Daniel Peter worked out a way to combine milk with chocolate. He was helped by Henri Nestlé, whose dabbling in dairy science evolved into the largest food empire on earth. No one had been able to mix fat in chocolate with water in milk. Nestlé condensed milk, eliminating the water.

Another Swiss, Rodolphe Lindt, took chocolate to a higher plane. He developed the technique of conching—named for the shell-shaped troughs he used—which brings out chocolate's true texture and taste. A heavy roller moves back and forth through molten chocolate to break down and blend the components while releasing acetic acid and other unwanted volatile elements. Mainly, the process allows full flavor to develop in the mixture. Lindt's original procedure took several days, and serious conching still does.

As confectioners perfected their art, others worked at each step of the complex supply chain that brought raw cacao beans from distant equatorial forests. Growers found ways to coax more production from trees that resisted mass planting. Shippers carried sacks of beans across great expanses of ocean, mindful that a moldy hold or a careless crew could ruin their precious cargo.

At the same time, artists across Europe sought to capture on canvas this exotic, erotic new flavor. Jean-Étienne Liotard's *La Belle Chocolatière*, painted in 1743, depicts a prim serving girl in reverent devotion to her task: delivering cocoa to her mistress. His later *Le Petit Déjeuner* features the mistress, lips almost quivering in expectant pleasure as the tray approaches. Both capture the fashion of the time: Chocolate is served in a lovely Meissen polychrome cup and accompanied by a glass of water.

The eighteenth-century paintings ranged from chaste to downright sinful. François Boucher, in *Le Déjeuner,* showed a happily functional family in a cozy kitchen starting their day with a long-handled silver pitcher of cocoa. Noël Le Mire, in *La Crainte*, portrays a bare-breasted, reclining woman in voluptuous throes reaching for a similar pitcher on a nearby table. An overturned chair suggests something besides breakfast has just taken place.

By the late 1800s, Europeans were used to chocolate, and they wanted more. It was time for industrial advances. Germans were early masters of big chocolate. Five brothers named Stollwerck were obsessed with finding better ways to do things at their fast-growing factory. With great gears and flapping rubber belts, they mechanized each of the crucial steps in production. Chocolate bars were packaged in fancy dress, and colorful posters that touted them are now worth fortunes to collectors of commercial art.

Heinrich Stollwerck quite literally fell into his work. He was adjusting a blending machine of his own invention, in 1915, when it exploded. He lost his balance and drowned in his finest chocolate.

In the twentieth century, the new advances were backed by big money. Large companies shook up the small world of craftsmen chocolatiers. And, at times, the selling of sweets has been just about the nastiest business on earth.

In the United States, Forrest Mars and his sons fought bitterly among themselves before shaping a company that squared off against a common foe, Hershey. Their war was over market share. In England, however, the ugly struggle between Cadbury and Fry was all about beans.

Fry and Sons opened in 1728, the first entrepreneurs to pioneer big chocolate in Europe. Early in the 1900s, Cecil Fry, together with another well-established English Quaker family firm, Cadbury, arranged to import South American cacao. But the Cadburys made secret deals with growers to starve their partner-rival of his supply. Bad blood acquired venom over time.

When Fry died, mourners filled Westminster Abbey for his funeral. His widow watched the Cadbury patriarch arrive late and make his way among the silent pews. She rose to her feet and shouted, words echoing in the great vaulted cathedral: "Get out, Devil."

———

*T*hese days, the company Nestlé built now counts $65.5 billion a year in sales, and about 12 percent of that is chocolate. Nestlé nearly bought Hershey Foods in 2002 for something close to $11 billion. Other candy conglomerates, with roots in the nineteenth century, operate on a grand global scale. Big is not necessarily bad.

Pierre Hermé, for instance, does not turn up his nose at industrial sweet stuff. In a pinch, he says, he'll eat a Hershey bar. He is especially fond of France's red-wrapped Daim, toasted toffee covered in chocolate, on the order of a Heath bar. But Hermé is clear on the subject.

*"Tout ça, c'est ne pas du chocolat,"* he says. *"C'est de la confiserie."* None of that is chocolate; it's candy.

Fine chocolate is made from high-quality beans that have been treated well from the time they are taken from their pods. A slip-up or a shortcut at any of a dozen crucial stages will reveal itself in the tasting.

Chocolatiers agree on a crucial point: As with wine, olive oil, or anything else elaborated from nature, quality depends upon the basic material. Anyone can make a mess of good cacao, but it is next to impossible to produce an excellent chocolate from inferior beans.

As more people catch on to the secrets of good chocolate, demands increase dramatically for a limited supply of what the world market calls "flavor cocoa." Big players swing their weight at every chance. Small ones develop personal ties and nurture them with care. Sometimes buyers simply show up and make a deal. But in most cases, tradition-bound systems lock in the privileges of middlemen who are reluctant to lose their cut.

And the competition can get vicious. One European firm had to recall its agent in Brazil after he sought permission to murder a neighbor who kept moving the stakes that delineated the company's plantation.

Even the best beans arrive from the tropics in an unpredictable state. Producers sometimes load up sacks to cheat on the weight. A thorough sifting removes sizable stones, motorbike gears, barnyard droppings, or the odd pistol. Washing cleans away other contaminants except for microbes killed in later stages of processing.

With all of today's technological advances, the final process of making chocolate still dates back to those nineteenth-century break-throughs.

After roasting and winnowing to remove the husks, beans are broken into cotyledons—nibs—of pure cacao. When ground and heated, nibs turn to molten cocoa liquor. From some of this, cocoa butter is separated out, and the remaining cocoa powder is used for drinking or baking chocolate. But most of the liquor is further refined. Extracted cocoa butter is blended back in to smooth its texture. Sugar is also added, depending upon the sweetness required.

The molten mixture must then be refined. Quality manufacturers use a five-roll mill that progressively breaks down particles until they reach a velvety smoothness. Then they are ready for the conche.

Finally, the chocolate is tempered. The French and Belgians call this last step *tempérage,* and the best of them worship it. Chocolate is heated to a carefully determined degree and then quickly cooled. Temperatures vary according to the mix. This seemingly simple step is what marshals the molecules so the finished chocolate ends up creamy-smooth and shining.

There are, of course, variations. The British Royal Society of Chemistry's primer on the subject runs to 170 pages of fine print, with enough formulas and diagrams to confound a molecular biologist. The venerable factory of Lloveras, near Barcelona, makes to order its Universal, which combines many of these steps. But the basics do not change.

Big producers use complex production chains to ensure clean and consistent repetitions of exactly what is ordered. The Mars family loses no sleep worrying that someone will stamp an off-center *m* on one of their little candies. A Cadbury's bar tastes pretty much the same, anywhere and anytime, over its very long life span.

But these companies cannot use the best of scarce ingredients and still price competitively. Shelf life almost invariably comes at sacrifice to flavor. Expensive chocolate is not necessarily the best. But the best chocolate is rarely cheap.

This is often not obvious. A Hershey bar falls into the category of McDonald's; love it or hate it, what you see is what you get. Hershey's company history is a well-known part of American lore. But much of the world chocolate industry thrives on corporate flimflam. Cachet sells, and names are not changed in order to confuse the innocent. Just because something is labeled Lindt does not mean that Rodolphe's great-grandson is in the back licking his finger to make sure each jug of milk comes from clover-sated cows.

A company that traces its history back 150 years might be technically correct in using the founder's name if it overlooks all of the intervening takeovers and makeovers. But artisan chocolate can quickly lose its quality when kicked into mass production.

In the end, the common boast of lineage—"since eighteen-whatever"—means no more than it does on a restaurant façade. It matters little if some culinary genius started the business generations ago. For people who appreciate good food, all that counts is the chef in the kitchen when they sit down to eat.

Older Belgians fondly recall Joseph Draps, who named his handmade chocolates after the long-haired rich lady who rode naked on her horse through the streets of Coventry to protest a tax her husband imposed on peasants a thousand years ago. But in the mid-1960s, the little family company melted into the American conglomerate of Campbell's Soup.

The success of Godiva is partly because so many people believe that Belgian chocolate is superior to all others. From my first day on the chocolate trail, I was obsessed by this obvious and overriding question: Who *does* make the best chocolate?

Consumption figures suggest Swiss chocolate is the most popular. Switzerland sells the most chocolate per capita, by far, at nearly twenty-four pounds a year. But the figure is high also because tourists buy so much to take home as gifts. Americans consume only half as much; the French, less than that.

Belgium is certainly the most serious about its chocolate. After the New York Fancy Food Show, I went to a cocktail party at the Belgian consul general's home. Six people I had never met cornered me with the same reproach: "I hear you think the French make better chocolate than the Belgians." This, I imagine, came from a remark I'd made several days earlier to provoke a stuffy Belgian.

In Brussels or Bruges, shops with an artisan air seem to dominate every square and street corner. But most sell industrial chocolate under old family names. Belgians made their reputation with the *ballotin*, a brilliant stroke of marketing by Neuhaus. This is a simple domed box, in assorted sizes, which presents the contents within as something of value. A few excellent chocolatiers fill their *ballotins* with real treasures. Others offer little more beyond fancy wrapping.

Pierre Marcolini, an innovative Belgian with grand dreams, shook up staid Brussels with creations that blended subtle teas and pungent fruits with his dark chocolate. In Paris, Pierre Hermé paid him what he considered a high compliment: "Marcolini makes French chocolate in Belgium."

In fact, nationality is not much of a guide. Each country has its traditions. Belgians prefer thicker molded coatings and more fresh cream in their centers. Italians lean toward dark chocolate with hazelnut. Swiss like sweet milk in quantity. Some Americans now make some wonderful stuff that goes a long way beyond Milton Hershey. Even the Spanish, who brought chocolate to Europe but then dropped from the picture, now offer remarkable innovation. But in the end, chocolate making is a personal art, and people like what they like.

All of that said, I'd like to log a simple request: If anyone ever banishes me to a desert island with only one style of chocolate, please make it French.

# Chapter 2

## CHOCOLAT

atrick Roger paused every so often to acknowledge the *ooh*s and *ahh*s of appreciative regulars at his little shop near Paris. Mostly, he was caught up in building his doghouse. With the touch of a master carpenter, he fitted together planks and then added a shingled roof that sloped to rain gutters and drainpipes. He installed window sashes, with shutters and latches. Patrick stopped a moment to cast a critical eye over the architectural chef d'oeuvre. Then he started working on the dog.

This was one of his minor chocolate sculptures, a mere table centerpiece for his brother's wedding. After the first, he made a dozen more, each in a different attitude. The life-size cocker spaniels looked real enough to bark. Every one had a dish of red prime ground beef. Chocolate, of course. And just for good measure, Patrick equipped each doghouse with a brick chimney that emitted clouds of chocolate smoke.

More sophisticated works were scattered about among glass bins of elegant chocolate made for less decorative purposes. One creation, more suitable for the Louvre than for a candy shop, portrays a well-muscled plantation worker in a tattered straw hat slicing open pods, with years of hard labor etched into his face.

Patrick's tiny world near Paris is a galaxy away from Hershey, Pennsylvania, and even farther from the dank jungles where cacao grows. The shop is on a cobbled street next to the appetizing window of a charcuterie; you would find it only with someone's guidance—or damned good fortune.

At thirty-five, lanky, with a lean and hungry look and straight curtains of pageboy hair that flop over his face, Patrick could pass for someone's gofer. But he is a MOF. At home in France, that ranks him with rock stars and philosophers.

The title, *meilleur ouvrier de France,* is referred to affectionately by the one-syllable word formed of its initials. It is given by a government panel in three competitions each decade to artisans in 220 fields. In a society that values its collective stomach, those most honored are the chefs and pâtissiers. From 1990 to 2000, eleven chocolate specialists were chosen.

Competition is brutal. In the final round, Patrick worked for twenty straight days, nearly all of them seventeen hours long. Triumphant MOFs are usually dedicated souls who begin learning their art from fathers and grandfathers before they toddle their first steps. When I asked Patrick if that was true in his case, he laughed.

"I had no idea this sort of thing even existed," he said, referring not only to chocolate sculptures but also to the gleaming *couvertures* and velvety *pralinés* that fill any decent French chocolatier's shop. "I grew up in a tiny farm village, lost somewhere in the weeds."

His village, Le Poislay, is in rolling Vendée farmland southwest of Paris. Its culinary delicacies run to animal parts and tubers. But like any respectable French village, it has a baker, who happens to be Patrick's father. As a kid, Patrick learned the rigors of careful measurement and temperatures. And sometime in his early teens, he discovered that chocolate can be better than what comes out of a printed paper wrapper.

Barely in his twenties, Patrick moved to Sceaux, just west of Paris. He brought his childhood sweetheart, Véronique, the daughter of the village butcher. They found a hole-in-the-wall shop in the old town center near the luxuriant gardens of a grand royal palace. Electronic machinery to conche and temper chocolate runs easily into six figures.

The tradition among ambitious French chocolatiers is to marry a rich wife. Patrick borrowed to his eyeballs. He and Véronique lived in a minuscule room above their shop, pushing aside vats of molten ganache and packing cartons when it came time to bed down at night.

Patrick had a particular flair for *praliné*. Americans mostly know "praline" as hard sugar candy with pecans. To the Belgians and Swiss, a *praline*, with no accent, is a piece of filled chocolate, what the French call a *bonbon*. But in France, *praliné* is a rich blend of ground almonds and chocolate, the reputed result of a fortuitous mishap. In 1731, the chef of the Maréchal Duc du Plessy Pralin accidentally dumped toasted nuts into melted chocolate. He served it as a new creation, and the duke loved it.

After a while, the couple acquired a bit more space, and a lot of new customers. At busy periods, a dozen helpers scrambled around a mountain of shelled nuts, crates of Brazilian limes, and everything else in the tiny back courtyard.

For years, investors did their best to lure Patrick to Paris. But he loved his shop in Sceaux and the freedom it represented. And so, as Mohammed declined to go to the mountain, the mountain came to Mohammed. Véronique could barely keep up with the customers who drove an hour for a taste of Patrick Roger chocolate. During 2005, however, demand finally outstripped his purist tendencies. The full line is also available on Boulevard Saint-Germain-des-Prés.

When the couple married one summer, several of France's great chefs offered their services as wedding gifts. A warm-weather meltdown took a toll on chocolate trappings, but the 160 guests have yet to stop talking about that dinner. The setting was a château of regal splendor. Patrick's father made hors d'oeuvres. Each course was prepared by a MOF. At the end, Christophe Michelak, the chef-pâtissier whom Alain Ducasse chose for his Plaza-Athenée kitchen, brought petits fours too big to eat without a fork. Then the real *après-dessert* appeared. Most of the contents of Patrick's shop was laid out on tables. Guests gorged until few could move.

After the couple enjoyed a brief honeymoon, the little shop in Sceaux was fully stocked and bustling again.

Like any good merchant, Patrick knows his market. "Skip that one—it's disgusting," he advised when I eyed a tray heaped high with tempting bonbons. They were Poire William–infused concoctions with a wide following, and he felt obliged to keep making them. Another bestseller he disliked was a ganache of lemon-laced caramel.

Instead, he offered me his signature *palet d'or*, displaying a gleam of pride that suggested Michelangelo showing off his chapel ceiling.

A *palet d'or* is the basic bonbon, a simple square of unctuous dark chocolate ganache enrobed in thin *couverture*. Although *couverture* means "covering," the term is also used for fine finished chocolate. By tradition, it is marked with a flourish of gold leaf. To satisfy customer demand, a *palet d'or* might be flavored with coffee. But the real thing is *nature*, "plain." With no other tastes to distract or to mask it, it represents the moment of truth.

Patrick's *palet d'or* is simple perfection. Its sheen and delicate shape offer promise before you get near enough for a noseful of rich chocolate. At first bite, the *couverture* snaps almost loudly enough to hear. Your teeth sink into creaminess. Subtle flavors in the chocolate peak and dip among hints of spiced fruit, and then they linger on the tongue. A professional nibbles and pauses to draw out the pleasure. I wolfed and reached for another.

Like most chocolatiers, Patrick is a *fondeur*, a melter. He buys blocks or pellets of chocolate from companies that process beans into ready-to-eat, or ready-to-bake-with, chocolate. The giant among these suppliers is Barry Callebaut, headquartered in Switzerland with plants across Europe. But the gold standard is the small French operation named for its Rhône Valley roots: Valrhona.

After that first visit, I went back periodically for the sheer pleasure of watching Patrick work. There was no secret to it. He did some things according to science, watching thermometers for fluctuations of half a degree. And when flair mattered more than strict measurement, his long fingers flicked ingredients into the mix. He blended his own homemade *praliné* in a giant copper kettle, too big for the kitchen, on a gas ring in the courtyard.

Patrick's pace varies with the season. A quarter of his yearly busi-ness is done in the weeks before Christmas. Perhaps 15 percent of it is crammed into a brief period that starts with Valentine's Day and lasts through Easter. In slow periods, friends drop by. Acolytes come to sit at his feet. Although he chats easily and jokes while he works, conver-sation stays clear of closely guarded secrets.

Early one April, I checked out Patrick's Easter shop window. The display centered on a luscious-looking three-foot-high pear in dark chocolate colored in the yellows and reds of ripeness. A large choco-late mouse had taken a few bites, but plenty was left for anyone with the $2,000 or so to buy what was left. It was, in fact, a work in progress. Each time Patrick created a new element and put it in the window, some eager *ooh*- and *ahh*-er bought it on the spot.

The theme was that old tale of the country mouse and the city mouse. Patrick's rural rodent was mousy gray and skinny, with buck-teeth and a goofy grin. Its urban cousin was sleek, fat, and brown. One country mouse—really a lovable rat—lounged at the business end of an unsprung mousetrap baited with yellow Gruyère that looked good enough to filch. Every element, including the staples and spring of the mousetrap, was chocolate.

I found Patrick in back making *pâte d'amande* ducklings, sixty at a time, with accents of chocolate. In each, he carefully inserted a toasted almond as the duck's bill. "Nope, I get these in France," he replied when I asked if he used the same Spanish almond suppliers that some fine confectioners swear by. He did not say where in France. "They're pretty much perfect, but expensive . . . ?" He shook five fingers to make the point.

In fact, he said, he could buy excellent *praliné* for less than he paid for the almonds in the fresh creamy paste he made himself. But the red, white, and blue collar on his white smock, the mark of a MOF, de-manded excellence, not economy. And more, Patrick does not cut cor-ners, with his ingredients or his time.

His rodents, for instance, came in different sizes, each requiring handmade molds of impossible complexity. It is tricky enough to shape plasticized molds for figures that harden to a solid state. But fine chocolate is brittle and fragile, subject to the most sensitive of temperature shifts. A lifelike mouse with twitching nose and cockeyed ears tested the limits of skill. When I asked Patrick how he did it, he laughed. "Complicated," he replied before swiftly shifting the subject.

Down the counter, Sébastien Potier made ostrich-sized chocolate eggs that would have satisfied Fabergé. Each was made from two delicately molded halves and filled with chocolate pieces. He had worked at La Maison du Chocolat, the Paris-based paragon of prestige. But he preferred to make a long daily trek to Sceaux, where he could exercise his imagination to work and exchange insults with a young boss. (When I rang later to ask Sébastien's last name, Patrick yelled across the shop, "What's my animal called?")

As Patrick poked eyes into his ducklings, we talked about war and peace far beyond Sceaux. But his peripheral vision never faltered. Every so often, he interrupted an excoriation of George W. Bush to lecture Sébastien on the art of making chocolate eggs.

When his assistant finished a batch, Patrick dabbed faces on each egg, using food dye and a rapier paintbrush. Then with molten chocolate and a shot of cold air from a pressurized can, he affixed them to a chocolate base. Each egg was set at a different angle, and every one gleamed as if made of polished glass.

"I'm lucky because I've got cold hands," Patrick said, brushing my wrist with chilly fingers. "I can touch the edges without leaving prints." Even so, it takes a surgeon's steadiness not to mar the sheen, the result of carefully applied cocoa butter.

Patrick works without a plan or a pattern. Whether it is a silly brown bunny or a voluptuous nude woman in white chocolate, things just take shape as they might in a sculptor's studio. When he perfects something he likes, he repeats it, again and again. Somehow he finds reward in what to others might be deadly drudgery.

An adventuresome spirit helps. Patrick was about to accompany agronomists to the Pacific island of Vanuatu, where planters were experimenting with a strain of *trinitario*.

These days, young artisan chocolatiers are a rare and dying breed; they face the same economic facts of life that stifle haute-cuisine chefs. With a French workweek of thirty-five hours, it is hard to enlist apprentices for dawn-to-dusk crush periods. When times are hard, pricey chocolate is not a priority.

In France, people who can perform miracles with food manage to do well. Not long before my Easter visit, a rich Moroccan had commissioned Patrick to dazzle his wedding guests. The man ordered eighteen eggs, each three feet high, to be flown to Casablanca. That cleaned up some bills. Yet Sceaux is still a trek from the capital, with a limited customer base. The Rogers may find themselves forced to move into Paris and go big-time.

In the meantime, Patrick concentrates on his chocolate. For a change of pace that April morning, he decided to make cans of sardines. He had already started two of them as an experiment. Each was twice the size of the real thing, with rounded corners and a carefully shaped rim around the top. Half of the lid was rolled up on a sardine-can key. Three fish—one of them headfirst and two of them tailfirst—poked out of the opened part. Everything, crinkled tin lid included, was chocolate.

"Let's make these look like sardines," Patrick said, smearing silver food dye into melted cocoa butter and dabbing just enough to give a fishy impression. He reached for a lovely emerald shade of food dye and then stopped. "Hmm, a green ocean? I don't think so." A few quick strokes of blue did the job. With more silver, he outlined a tall-masted ship and then stopped to muse again. "Which way do the sails go?" he asked. "I've been in here so long I can't even remember what a boat looks like."

Within minutes, he had finished the two sardine cans, milk chocolate sardines, and dark chocolate sardines.

"So, what should I charge?" he asked. "Maybe twenty euros?" That was about $21.50.

"More," I said. "And whatever you charge, I want to buy the dark ones. But only next week when you're done using them in the display."

Shortly thereafter, I went out front to buy some assorted ganaches and *pralinés* for friends. Patrick came up in a hurry. "If you want those sardines, you'd better claim them now," he said. I looked over to see an English tourist poised to pluck them from the window display. Poor guy never knew what hit him.

*I* first found my way to Sceaux thanks to my principal guide to all things cacao, Chloé Doutre-Roussel. Early on, I realized I would need an official taster to supplement my unpracticed palate. A friend led me to Chloé. I explained my project to her, and for the simple love of chocolate, she signed on for the duration.

Chloé is a chocolate lunatic. The French would call her *une choco-dépendante*, which means, roughly, a chocoholic with class. This is no literary exaggeration. She wears dresses with discreet kangaroo pouches in front so she can sneak bites of chocolate during long business meetings. At ninety-nine pounds, she is an open-and-shut argument against killjoys who insist that chocolate makes you fat. Chloé does not discuss her private life, but she smiles a lot.

Chloé taught courses and set up a consultancy, *Carrément Chocolat*. Her notes, those not circulating among her friends, fill a substantial basement. Chocolatiers fight over her remarkable taste buds. Pierre Hermé, who worked with her at Ladurée, a Paris restaurant, hired her to critique his new creations. Pierre Marcolini imported her periodically to train his staff. Though she is a pillar of France's chocolate haut monde, her circle includes little-known geniuses who shun the limelight.

For all her red-haired, freckle-flecked air of shyness, Chloé is never reluctant to say what she thinks. When Hermé named his popular raspberry bonbon Chloé, she said, "I was touched by his gesture of complicity, but he *knows* that I hate ruining the taste of good ganache with red fruit flavors." At the Salon du Chocolat, where the fashion is to fawn over the fare, she horrifies stars with blunt assessments of what needs fixing in their otherwise notable line of wares. Most seem to appreciate it.

Her knowledge is encyclopedic. Growing up in Mexico, she learned the old lore of cacao. At university, she studied tropical agronomy. Working for the United Nations in the Caribbean, she absorbed developmental economics. In London, living on a meager budget, she was accepted dues-free into a circle of devotees, the Chocolate Society, on the strength of an enthusiastic letter.

Back in Paris, Chloé supported her habit with a day job as Web site manager for L'Oréal. But she used weekends and vacations to tour plantations, poke into factories, stand at chefs' elbows, and hang around researchers. Every free moment went into the real love of her life, to a degree many found amusing—or disconcerting. Robert Steinberg, a retired physician of staid demeanor who is part owner of Scharffen Berger chocolate makers in Berkeley, California, visited her tiny apartment and found himself quietly edging toward the door as she darted about producing chocolate samples from all of the cool, dark corners where she had squirreled them away.

"I thought she was a madwoman," Steinberg told me later. "She had chocolate everywhere: in the hall closet, under the bed . . ." Chloé loves that story. In fact, she says, she keeps her bedroom at 59 degrees F (15 degrees Centigrade). If it is a choice between protecting her chocolate or catching pneumonia, she has her priorities.

When we first sat down to plot my approach, Chloé revealed her A-list of favorite chocolatiers and their products. These included a man who turned out to be my choice to provide my stash of chocolate should I be marooned on a desert island.

*J*acques Genin was in the middle of Paris, but he was harder to find than Patrick Roger. An address was not enough. Chloé had given me a street number, but when I got there, I was sure I had taken it down wrong. It was the dingy back end of the fifteenth arrondissement, across the street from some sort of low-rent government office building that might have been a bankrupt tire factory. The battered white door, unmarked, had neither a handle to turn nor a bell to ring. The opaque front window prevented a peek inside. I shrugged and knocked hard.

The door opened only a few inches, and I knew this was the place. A first whiff of warm fresh chocolate nearly lifted me off the ground. Then the door swung open, and I knew what young Charlie must have felt when he followed Willy Wonka through his factory gates.

Two gleaming stainless-steel machines, each looking capable of a *Star Trek* voyage, dominated the single small room. They were Savy Goiseau *enrobeuses* for coating ganache with thin *couverture*. A marble-topped island filled the center space. One wall was stacked with tin canisters and boxes bearing the names of the fanciest eateries in Paris. And piled high on every spare surface, one atop the other on racks or teetering from shelves that reached the ceiling, were trays of delicate chocolates.

Jacques darted back and forth, slipping past his helpers with practiced grace. With a shock of sandy hair, an impish twinkle, and a sharp nose of generous dimension, he looked like Roman Polanski in a good mood. He beamed a greeting and, without much preamble, launched into chocolatespeak. Talking rapidly while he worked, he punctuated sentences by plucking samples from passing trays and handing them to me. This posed an existential dilemma. Finally, I abandoned duty and put aside my notebook to keep both hands free to accept heavenly bounty.

"Try this," he said, pausing to lend a certain gravitas to the occasion. It was his new favorite. The delicate Valrhona *couverture* cracked as I bit it. Creamy ganache melted as it settled on my tongue. A subtle but unmistakable *parfum* of fresh mint flooded my mouth, and a peppery undertone sent happy pinprick signals to corporeal outposts. It was moments old, still warm from tempering.

All of this registered on my face, and Jacques scrutinized me with a creator's pride. After waiting a long time until the lingering taste abated, I made some superfluous appreciative remark. "Peppered mint," he announced, just as superfluously. If chocolate gets any better than that, I never found it.

Jacques's guerrilla factory is the result of obsession, passion, and an allergy to working in someone else's shadow. Like almost every other chocolatier, he started as a pastry chef. Soon he was a rising star at La Maison du Chocolat. Chafing at working long hours for low pay, he was less than happy with conditions. He felt hemmed in by what he called arbitrary practices. A dispute over management's treatment of a fellow worker pushed him over the edge. With no clear plan in mind, he struck out on his own.

Jacques did not mess around with molded dogs and silver sardines. With no retail business beyond the occasional connoisseur who knows what is behind the clouded window, he made chocolate to order.

Toward Christmas, the tiny room might suggest Santa's workshop if le père Noël ever shouted obscenities at a wayward elf who did something dumb that could endanger quality. The pace is beyond frenetic yet curiously under control, like the final moments of an Olympic bobsled run. Easter is nearly as crazed. In calmer times, the mood is upbeat, and long hours are punctuated by peals of laughter. At the end of a good year, the little shop on the rue Saint-Charles will have handled eighteen tons of chocolate.

Just before one Christmas, I dropped in to see the operation in full panic. Jacques flashed a quick smile and tossed me a white apron. For the next hour, I was plucking bonbons off the conveyor belt and setting them onto wax-papered trays. The high-tech *enrobeuse* left a high sheen on the top and all sides, but that was not enough for Jacques. He flipped over each tray and painted by hand the last touch of perfection. For another hour, we packed red-ribboned round boxes for Alain Ducasse's three-star restaurant at the Plaza-Athenée. I suppose you could call it hard labor, but the endless supply of rejects to be eaten seemed a fair-enough wage.

The time to catch Jacques is on a rare break when he settles into a wooden chair at the Portuguese lunch joint on the corner. When we first met there, he sucked hard on a taste-bud-frying cigarette, ingested thick black coffee, and waxed poetic about his favorite subject. On my last visit, there was a change. He had had a heart attack at age forty-four. The cigarette was gone, and he ordered fizzy water. But the poetry was as undiminished as his enthusiasm.

"Vanilla," Jacques said, letting the word hang in the air as he savored it. "I met this person. A woman from Madagascar, about thirty, and she has taken over her parents' plantation. She is heartbreakingly beautiful, and her vanilla is even more beautiful than she is. I've never seen such perfect quality."

He took me back to the shop for some more of my favorite game of "Try this." The first sample was rich in Madagascar vanilla. That must have been some woman. The second was accompanied with such a wide impish grin that I knew Jacques had found a new favorite. It was a simple ganache flavored with a lovely, subtle tea that came slowly to the tongue and then would not leave. "Butterfly of Taiwan," he said. "Want another one?"

Jacques was having a bad day. While preparing for heart surgery, he learned that his eleven-year-old daughter, whom he loves more than chocolate, had developed a serious leg problem as she trained for competitive figure skating. He wondered aloud if he should give up the business for something that took a mere sixty hours a week. It was plain that he wouldn't. In fact, he was already hatching plans to open a shop and restaurant in Paris.

"Our profession is making happiness, pleasure," he said, "and that's how we should look at it. What is there better to do with your life? When I see these chocolate makers who are so competitive, so negative, who think only about their profit-and-loss situations, I wonder. If you're going to cut corners, if you're not ready to do all the hard work and pay attention to the slightest detail, you might as well be making sheet metal."

Working in anonymous isolation suits his temperament. He answers the phone when he feels like it. Much of his product goes out under someone else's name, but that does not seem to bother him. He knows who he is.

"If somebody manages to find my door and knocks on it, of course I'll sell him chocolates," Jacques said. "We're not really a retail business. But if people do me the honor of wanting what I make, how can I say no?"

We talked more about basics. "Chocolate is a fresh product," he said, using the phrase *un produit frais*, which also applies to crème fraîche or strawberries. "It should be eaten quickly." He was speaking practically as well as philosophically. Some cream-based ganaches spoil faster than others and must be eaten within a week or so. But, Jacques explained, all good chocolate has a limited life span.

"You can wrap it in foil and keep it cool to prolong its flavor, yet something is always lost with time. The longer the time, the greater the loss. Chocolate is never as good as when it first rolls out of the *enrobeuse*."

Over time, I found that any conversation with Jacques quickly starts and ends with a basic essential point. Good chocolate is about pleasure, about comfort, about love. And this was not exactly a surprise.

*B*ack in my callow-youth days, some campus Casanova passed along that old saw of dating philosophy: Candy is dandy, but liquor is quicker. Whoever the poor fool was, I hope he has caught on by now. If drunken fumbling counts, and speed is of the essence, I suppose he had a point. But for reasons that no savant has yet to satisfactorily explain, nothing melts the heart like good chocolate.

Casanova himself used to eat chocolate on his way out for the evening. Not only did it fire his libido, he believed, but it also prevented the dreaded pox. Countless others, before and since, have sworn by chocolate to enhance a romantic mood. Back in 1861, Richard Cadbury put chocolate in a heart-shaped box for Valentine's Day; these days, on February 14, people around the world give each other $1 billion worth of chocolate. A half a millennium after Cortés, chocolate still evokes the aphrodisiac notions that pervaded those first fevered accounts of conquistadores and missionaries.

Early European scientists offered conflicting explanations about body humors and blood heat. As cacao made its way across the Continent from Spain, social commentators chimed in. The French, of course, delivered weighty judgments on matters of chocolate and love.

In the early days, morality monitors based their judgments on a simple premise. If licentiousness was bad, anything as exotically dark and steamy as hot cocoa aroused suspicion. More recent research in a dozen countries has added useful analysis. Still, it has failed to come up with anything much more conclusive than early guesswork.

Cacao contains phenylethylamine, a molecule produced in the hypothalamus that triggers the same giddy warm glow one feels when a lover enters the room. It has serotonin, which can excite the senses. But the amounts are limited. If some toga-party clod tried to ply his date with enough chocolate to enflame her passions, he would likely find her in the bathroom long before the bedroom.

Regardless of all of these uncertainties, there is no doubting the spell chocolate casts on its addicts. Take, for example, the stir created when the renowned London emporium Fortnum & Mason revealed that it had an opening for a chocolate taster. The brief announcement triggered sighs heard round the world. The job description was something like this: Travel everywhere in search of the best possible chocolate and, in the meantime, sit at a desk while chocolatiers try to seduce you with their latest delights. News agencies carried the story. E-mails from friends who knew of my project clogged my computer. Within days, three thousand people had applied for the job, most of them women who listed their main qualification as "I love chocolate."

The job was quickly filled. Turning down 2,999 others, Fortnum & Mason hired Chloé. The centuries-old hidebound house of taste had decided to revamp its approach to chocolate. Its ground-floor confectionery display was about as romantic as English sensible shoes. The store offered some good chocolate, but the overall tone reflected that popular watchword: No sex, please, we're British.

In a public-relations blitz, Fortnum & Mason selected *The Observer*'s weekly food magazine to break the story. There was Chloé, posed as if for *Penthouse*, leaning forward to reveal serious décolletage, in a sultry I-love-chocolate attitude. A flip of hair covered one eye, but the other reflected pure sensual pleasure. Both hands fondled chunks of dark chocolate.

"Meet Chloé, a woman with a very dark secret," the headline read. And a boldface caption offered an extract from the text: "She rubs a tiny piece of chocolate against her cheek lightly, and lets the heat of her skin melt its surface."

But in conversation, Chloé adds some serious thought. Chocolate is no aphrodisiac, she explains. That is, it does not enhance sex. Instead, it goes a very long way toward helping people fall in love.

"Chocolate is an extremely sensual material, so it has always been associated with sin, something pleasurable, which is why so many religions look down on it," she said. "You just have to give yourself permission to enjoy it. As the bouquet of melting chocolate perfumes your palate, it spreads a feeling of well-being. Each of your five senses is excited, and they all interact with each other."

(What she actually said in French was *"embaume le palais de son bouquet."* I struggled to capture that verb in translation. It is a direct cognate for *embalm,* but its use among the sensory-attuned French extends beyond dead bodies. Finally, I went to my Harrap's bilingual dictionary. It offered an example of usage: "*le chocolat embaume,* there is a delicious smell of chocolate.")

This is not a bad start. And when good chocolate is packaged with style, the effect can be overwhelming.

"Everyone, no matter who, associates chocolate with the best part of childhood," Chloé said. "Pronounce the word, and people become kids again. It is something precious, a reward. It is warm and humid, and when it melts in your mouth, it inspires a sense of well-being. Just receiving the box, you're already prepared for the experience. Somebody cares about you. Even before you smell the chocolate, you're in a high state of excitement and sensuality because your body has kept the memory of past pleasures."

The impact is physiological. "Before you start eating it in these conditions, your body is already making more phenylethylamine," Chloé continued. "And then you bite into it, your hypothalamus is stimulated and sends yet more phenylethylamine into the body. You're in mild shock. This amounts to deep feelings of desire."

In such circumstances, you'd need a heart of stone not to edge toward love at least with the chocolate if not with the person who gave it to you.

Beyond romance, there is an indefinable quality that takes people away from the moment and back to some pleasant memory. While working at various business-suit jobs in the past, Chloé amused herself with experiments along this line. Deep into serious meetings, as frowning men and pursed-lipped women pondered grave matters, she would plunk down a box of chocolates. Invariably, every face around the table remade itself into a goofy smile. Tension would ease, and agreement seemed easier to reach.

"Everyone suddenly turned into a child, with a face that said, *'Merci, maman,'*" Chloé said.

Chloé's passion dates back to her childhood of bouncing around chocolate-unfriendly places with her diplomat father. In Latin America, only bulletproof industrial candy made it to store shelves. Any good chocolate sent from home melted before it reached the mailbox. Whenever something memorable managed to present itself, she treasured it as a rare gift.

She turned up her nose at milk chocolate or other candy, even cake. She wanted only dark chocolate. From her own experience, she believes there is a universal craving among the chocolate-deprived. One friend of hers, a painter from the Dominican Republic, concurs. As a child in a poor school, he remembers a classmate who kept the wrapper from a chocolate bar for weeks after its contents were gone. He sold sniffs of it in exchange for buttons, all the young buyers could afford. Some of his customers were desperate enough to rip off a button, risking their mother's wrath.

Chloé was amazed at her first Fortnum & Mason chocolate evening, an annual event when people mob the store to sample various wares. The hit, as always, was a fountain that burbled molten milk chocolate. "We offered twenty different samples of unusual and interesting chocolates," she said, "but most people waited half an hour in line for some of the crappiest stuff. It was familiar to them."

And she was flabbergasted at the fuss reporters made over her job. "They kept saying, 'Now you can eat chocolate for free,'" she said. "But long before I came to Fortnum & Mason, I was already eating a pound a day. In fact, to my regular pound of chocolate, I now add another pound that I usually spit out. If journalists go on too much, I give them an off-the-record comparison. It's like selling your body by day and having a boyfriend at night."

Chloé's basic philosophy is simple: Forget the meaningless catchall word *chocolate* and find out what sorts of chocolate speak to your soul and body. Everyone's personal "package" is unique, she believes. Once you know what you're after, the rewards are beyond measure.

"For me, the two most important things about chocolate are that it can improve your quality of life and bring you easily available pleasure," Chloé said. "It helps you enjoy living, and that's why we are here. At least that's how I look at it. I've found that even people who think they don't like chocolate find new pleasure; even they develop a technique."

Chloé has put a lot of thought into perceptions and realities. In her tastings, she crusades for the noble bean in a manner that would have gotten her burned at the stake in Joan of Arc's day. Most people, she has found, feel so much unconscious guilt that even if she puts chocolate in their hands, they cannot enjoy it. "It is such an immense relief when you can rid yourself of any guilty feelings," she said. "The main thing is not to inhibit the senses, so you can appreciate chocolate one hundred percent."

Even if chocolate does not actually fire the libido, she adds, it can be an important part of happy sex. "I've found that the only people who can really enjoy chocolate without being gourmets are mostly those who believe it has an aphrodisiac effect."

Chloé believes that, as with wine, the more you learn how to taste and appreciate chocolate, the more you intensify the reaction. And if it is good chocolate, you will intensify the pleasure. You can learn to smell, even hear, the chocolate. As you educate your senses, you broaden what Chloé calls "your database of available chocopleasure." This helps you discover what suits you best.

She plans each tasting like a military campaign, starting with styles familiar to the group. She tries to determine their past experiences, and she guesses at how adventuresome they are likely to be. People raised on sweet milk chocolate tend to run screaming from hard-core dark stuff with only hints of sugar; preferences evolve over time. She limits a tasting to seven or eight chocolates. Otherwise, senses are overwhelmed.

People break each piece into four, which allows them to move slowly from aroma to mouthfeel, while leaving a bit to compare later with other samples. The exercise can be frustrating.

"People always laugh at me when I first tell them to taste only one-quarter of a small chocolate square," Chloé says. "But when they realize that they are hardly able to interpret what they feel from a first impression and need to try again, they take it more seriously. They can spend ten minutes on a single little piece."

Tasters nibble their tiny corner of chocolate and then, enduring *cacao interruptus,* pause to discuss it. It gets easier. The more people write down impressions and identify differences, the more nuances they begin to notice.

"You can increase your pleasure by four or five times simply by learning how to taste chocolate," Chloé says. "When you determine your favorite sorts and styles, it gets even better. You always know which one will please you the most at any moment. And if you listen, your body will tell you how much you need."

Even after some experience with straitlaced British tastes, Chloé remains convinced that fine chocolate will be appreciated, more and more, for its sensual qualities. She sees new attitudes toward chocolate not as some passing wave but rather as a fundamental change.

"I think the growth will be explosive," she said. "More and more people will be sensitized. The designations of *appellation d'origine contrôlée* will follow the same course they did with wine and then olive oil. Laws have to be passed, and the rest will follow. How can it be otherwise? Good chocolate brings so much pleasure. And, *en plus,* it is extremely good for health."

Chloé fumes at the bad rap chocolate gets for making people fat. If by "chocolate" one means heavily sugared candy, she says, it will likely contribute to the rounding of an overeater's lines. But cacao itself adds up to few calories. And any chocolate worth eating, she insists, has a limited amount of simple sugar that easily burns away.

"The popular myth is that those who eat a lot of chocolate are over-weight women who lounge around at home," Chloé says. "This is totally false. Mostly, real chocolate fiends are busy, active, and slim."

In the end, Chloé concludes, the question is whether "chocoholic" is more than a figure of speech. "When good chocolate works its full effect on you, you're totally stoned," she says. "That's why the real controversy over the last ten years is not whether chocolate is an aphrodisiac, but rather whether it's an addiction."

*B*ack in 1985, a toxicologist named Chantal Favre-Bismuth at Fernand Vidal Hospital in Paris studied thirteen men and nine women with what she described as *chocolatomanie*. She picked people who normally ate dark chocolate with at least 50 percent cacao content to weed out sugar addicts. Over three months, her subjects ate 100 to 400 grams per day; that is, some wolfed down nearly one pound daily.

At the end, she had raised as many questions as she answered. But she demonstrated that while chocolate perked up general physical and mental performance, it created no suggestion of dependency. If some people described it as a drug, it was no addictive narcotic. Even though it was cheap and easily available without some back-alley dealer, none of her subjects exhibited antisocial behavior, or loss of mental or physical function, from chocolatomania.

In conclusion, Dr. Favre-Bismuth noted: "Man remains an excitable and fearful mammal, and the absence of anxiety among heavy consumers of this stimulating food could have a biochemical base that is still to be determined."

I found Dr. Favre-Bismuth on her flowered balcony in the sixteenth arrondissement. She was still teaching toxicology but was more concerned with cheap crack than with dark chocolate. Almost a generation after her research, she believed her thesis more strongly than ever. After publishing her findings, she found another forty people who supported the conclusions. No one had proven her wrong. Or, more accurately, no one had proven much of anything.

"This kind of research is very expensive, and universities use their limited resources for things that have an obvious negative impact on health," she explained. "If there were major studies done, the chocolate industry would have to finance them, and that has not happened yet."

And it may not happen anytime soon. Chocolate is selling briskly. Apart from the widespread, and untrue, belief that it makes you fat and gives you pimples, it is not suspected of harmful effects. Why rock the boat?

Beyond her scientific observations, Favre-Bismuth had strong ideas on the subject. To start with, she loved chocolate. "It is one of the most delicious and noble factors of our whole existence," as she put it.

"All of our lives amount to a fight between boredom and anguish," she said, "and chocolate has a role." Dark chocolate is preferred by active, intellectual, or sporty types, she said. The classic image of a depressive overweight woman gorging on chocolate has some basis in fact. Cravings can appear seven to fourteen days before menstruation. "But in such cases," she added, "it is sweet milk chocolate, and the crucial element is sugar."

She ticked off a range of compounds, hormones, and assorted substances in chocolate that affect the human body. The actions of dopamine and phenylethylamine are clear enough, she said, but those are just the beginning. Seventeen amphetamine receptors play a part. So do opioids linked to cacao. Scientists are only now starting to understand the chemistry involved. Most scientific knowledge of *T. cacao*'s effect on the human body still remains based on hypothesis.

Psychological aspects also figure in. "For some, there is a connection to the maternal breast, the way chocolate melts in the mouth," she said. "This partly explains why people like soft ganaches and don't like irregularities in their chocolate."

But she dismissed the idea of chocolate as an aphrodisiac.

"I don't think it has an effect on sexuality," she said. "At least I have not observed it. I don't think the human body needs any outside stimulants, but if people want to believe chocolate helps, good for them."

Later, she finished the thought with a throaty laugh: "Chocolate lovers talk a lot about sex, but those who eat a lot of it aren't particularly active."

Favre-Bismuth had found some interesting cases. One twenty-five-year-old anorexic woman ate more than a pound a day and swore that her body never stopped secreting the aroma of chocolate.

In the end, however, Favre-Bismuth found chocolate failed both tests of addiction. It is not dangerous to the human organism. And no symptoms of withdrawal appear when consistently high consumption is abruptly stopped.

In reviewing the mountain of research devoted to the subject, I found some intriguing material but no clinical trials to refute Favre-Bismuth's conclusions. One study came from the University of Arizona medical school in Tucson, where I first gorged on Hershey bars. In 1999, Kristen Bruinsma, with Professor Douglas Taren, wrote a master's thesis that ended up in the *Journal of the American Dietetic Association*.

"Although addictive behavior is generally associated with drug, alcohol or sexual behavior, it is becoming apparent that certain food substances, most notably chocolate, may effect similar physiological and psychological reactions in susceptible people," she wrote. "Although chocolate is not clearly established as an addictive substance, it is, by a large margin, the most commonly craved food in North America, especially among women. In fact, one classic study by A. J. Hill and L. Heaton-Brown in 1991 documented chocolate-specific cravings as constituting almost half of all food cravings."

In a map of the brain, Bruinsma listed eleven biogenic amines in chocolate, besides phenylethylamine, that "potentially induce drug-like neurophysiological effects." In addition, caffeine and theobromine are methylxanthines, "stimulants that may contribute to the addictive nature of chocolate." Then there are cannabinoid-like fatty acids, the N-acylethanolamines, as well as neuropeptides and endogenous opioid peptides. Also, hormonal functions may increase chocolate cravings.

Beyond any physiological impact, Bruinsma adds, a simple fact feeds chocolate addiction: You can self-medicate to your heart's content without breaking any laws or risking sloppy, dangerous behavior. If the term *addiction* has complex definitions, she says, "chocolate cravings appear to exist in 40 percent of females and 15 percent of males, three-fourths of whom claim that no other substance will appease their desire."

Bruinsma cites studies across the United States and Canada that reach a similar conclusion that up to half of all women experience chocolate cravings.

Like the others, she did no actual trials to disprove Dr. Favre-Bismuth's contention: Chocolate does not create an observable physical dependency, that is, actual addiction. In fact, the American Psychiatric Association publishes a thick manual on substance abuse, regularly updated, which lays out the definitions. As Dr. Favre-Bismuth found, chocolate does not meet any of the criteria for physical or psychological dependency. But considering all the passion and pleasure clearly attached to the love bean, such definitions may be splitting hairs.

*C*hocolatiers, by and large, are enthusiastic about romancing the bean. Whatever their own sentimentalities, it sells. Jean-Paul Hévin scored a hit in Paris with his *chocolat dynamique*, ginger-laced ganaches to which he attributes aphrodisiac properties. The scientists may quibble with his sweeping assumptions, but the sleek bonbons in lush wrappings suggest a voluptuousness that passes the Chloë test. And if the effect is only in the head and the heart, that is not a bad start.

Chocolate lovers, I learned, share a secret life, with its own lore and literature. My California pal, Hadley, sent me a book she keeps close at hand, next to her astrology tables and psychology texts: *Bittersweet Journey*, by a New York photographer and romantic named Enid Futterman. It bills itself as "A Modestly Erotic Novel of Love, Longing, and Chocolate."

Futterman defines her purpose in an epigraph by Carl Jung: "One does not become enlightened by imagining figures of light, but by making the darkness conscious." She starts with the story of Charlotte, a child in Brooklyn, who eagerly awaits her father's return from work.

Each night he smuggles a chocolate bar, hidden in his coat pocket, past the reproving gaze of an unenlightened mother. Charlotte takes it to bed and eats it under the covers:

> It quieted and excited her at the same time. Everything about it was a relief—its flavor, color, fragrance, even its name, which was so like hers. Sometimes she would whisper it, like a magic word, as if by saying, she could taste it. It was a word of consonants, a collision of hard and soft sounds. She would utter them slowly, savoring even the tiny silence between the two syllables, and the almost inaudible *t*. Chocolate.

And that was only a Hershey bar.

As a grown-up, Charlotte leaves her husband for a Sacher torte, flying to Vienna to begin a chocolate pilgrimage across Europe. "Paris was the last stop. Mecca, Jerusalem, Oz." She speaks in percentages of cacao content in her favorite chocolate and repeats the hallowed Valrhona names like a mantra: Manjari, Guanaja, Caraïbe.

Charlotte finds her bliss:

> She could hear the names in her head like a song. The names and the words of chocolate are French. *Couverture, Truffe, Bonbon*. In France, chocolate has depth and chocolates are pure. Food is art, and chocolate is food, regarded with the respect given to cheese and wine. But chocolate does not improve with age; *ganache* ought to vanish somewhere between the tongue and the palate. Why did she want to possess what could be consumed?
>
> She consumed it all. Michel Chaudun's truffles. Jean-Paul Hévin's *pralinés*. Christian Constant's exotic, erotic perfumes. Ylang-Ylang. Verbena. Vetiver. Charlotte never met any of these Frenchmen, but she knew them all, and they knew her.

If you keep your eye out for it, chocolate pops up everywhere. In Michel Faber's epic of nineteenth-century London, *The Crimson Petal and the White*, straitlaced Emmeline Fox labors in the Rescue Society to save fallen women. But in a moment of fantasy, luxuriating over a steaming cup, she conjures up a different self-portrait: "Emmeline Fox: cocoa fiend. She can imagine herself on the cover of a tuppenny dreadful, a masked villain dressed in men's trousers and a cape, evading police by leaping from rooftop to rooftop, her superhuman strength deriving entirely from the evil cacao seed."

A classic paean to the love bean is the film script for *Chocolat*. In the novel by Joanne Harris, Vianne Rocher's sweet-smelling little shop, La Céleste Praliné, is the setting for human drama in rural France. In the film, however, Swedish director Lasse Hallström makes chocolate itself the principal character.

Vianne—in fact, Juliette Binoche at her most upbeat—appears one morning on "the clever north wind" in the village of Lasquenet, with her young daughter, Anouk. Something mystical is afoot; both wear Little Red Riding Hood cloaks in the swirling mist, and neither struggles with her luggage. It is Lent, but Vianne declines to join everyone else in church. She is not a believer, she explains to general horror. To further horror, she stipulates that, daughter notwithstanding, she is Mademoiselle Rocher. For weeks, she and Anouk labor behind the blinds of an abandoned shop on the square. When it reopens, villagers discover Chocolaterie Maya, filled with the heady magic of ancient American roots.

One by one, tradition-bound villagers fall under the spell of Vianne's *confiserie*. By spinning a stone Mayan wheel, she divines what each chocolate will do for whom. Each time someone ventures into the shop, against the injunctions of a stern mayor who speaks with God, she smiles and says, "I can guess your favorite."

Yvette Marceau, for instance, says her husband, Alphonse, has lost his sex drive. Her job of scrubbing toilets hampers her ardent efforts to restore it. Vianne smiles and hands her a packet of chili-laced chocolates.

"You've obviously never met my husband," Yvette says.

"You've obviously never tried these," Vianne replies.

From then on, in the interstices of the plot, Yvette and Alphonse rut like weasels.

At Anouk's constant urging—"Tell the story of *grand-père* and *grand-mère*"—Vianne reveals the mystery. Her grandfather, a pharmacist who sensed life beyond pounding compounds in a mortar, ventured to Guatemala on botanical studies. He married a Mayan princess. To his grief, he found that the gods compelled her to move with the clever north wind, enlivening benighted places with the magic of cacao.

With the appearance of Roux and his river gypsies, there are tender scenes of love and chocolate. The ending has its surprises, but some parts are easily guessed. Lasquenet comes alive. Children find their childhood. Chocolate happily carries off an aged grande dame played by Judi Dench. It leads a young priest to true Christianity. And it undoes the pious and pitiful Comte de Reynaud.

To someone other than a chocolate fanatic, it is only a movie. But the freelance writer Hilary Brand, for one, was moved to use it as an inspiration for a book called *Christ and the Chocolaterie*, a cacao lovers' approach to Lent. All in all, the film script went a long way toward explaining why the Patrick Rogers and the Jacques Genins work ungodly hours with smiles on their faces.

And in the end, *Chocolat* is a timeless tale of good and evil, with a happy twist: One zealot's evil can, to others, be awfully good.

Chapter 3

# ORIGIN OF THE SPECIES

New York Botanical Society team excavating Mayan ruins at the village of La Joya de Cerén, El Salvador, in the spring of 2002 found some revealing evidence under three meters of lava. The archeologists believed that the settlement buried beneath the volcano that had erupted there fourteen hundred years ago ought to be remembered as the Pompeii of the Americas. It must have been something to see. Villagers fled in such maddened panic that they left all their cacao beans behind.

New research in Central America adds more evidence that, for all the reverence early Mexicans attached to their chocolate, cacao was also the food of earlier gods.

The Mayans' dazzling civilization, going back nearly two thousand years, treasured a sacred foaming brew made from toasted cacao. Beans were ground and mixed with water, along with maize gruel, chilies, vanilla, and honey. Dye from annatto-tree seeds—achiote—colored it red.

Scientific detectives, such as those at La Joya de Cerén directed by Dr. David Lentz, piece together chocolate antiquity with scant clues. Their new evidence adds to generations of earlier work. Lentz, a scientist from the Chicago Botanic Garden, was fascinated to note that the hardened ash preserved impressions of plants growing in the center of town. This seemed to counter the belief that only royalty had access to the treasured beans. "They had cacao immediately growing around their households," Lentz later told a *New York Times* reporter.

By now, Mayans are fairly well documented. The earlier Olmecs, however, are still mostly a mystery.

It is hard to miss the twenty-ton stone statues the Olmecs left behind in the Veracruz lowlands of eastern Mexico, but they reveal little. Their high domed foreheads and thick, fleshy lips suggest no similarity to other ethnic groups of pre-Columbians. A few fortunate museums display smaller Olmec pieces, sophisticated carved heads in jade and obsidian. These pieces, too, offer few clues.

I sought guidance from James Beck, a Columbia University art historian who thrives on such ancient mysteries. He is fascinated by the Olmecs, but he only shook his head when I asked about them. "Sometimes I think they arrived on a rocket ship from outer space," he said. "I'm not kidding."

The Olmecs' civilization dates from 1500 to 400 B.C. They recorded time with an elaborate system of bars and dots while ancestors of the Romans were still counting on their fingers.

Clearly, the Olmecs had a highly developed system of agriculture. They most likely came up with the process known as nixtamalization of maize: cooking corn kernels with white lime, wood ash, or burnt snail shells to make them easier to grind into dough. Without this vital step, Spaniards later found, the corn lost much of its protein.

Linguists believe the Olmec tongue was related to the Mixe-Zoquean family. One word attributed to this group was pronounced *kakawa*. Most anthropologists are convinced that these advanced but enigmatic people were the first to domesticate *Theobroma cacao*.

*B*ut most of what we know about the origins of *T. cacao* is guesswork. The plant is widely believed to have appeared first in Amazonia, between the Orinoco and Amazon rivers. Although the genus *Theobroma* has roots millions of years old, the species could be as young as ten to fifteen thousand years. These dates coincide with human habitation of northern South America. According to some theories, two other species were crossed to produce the sweet white pulp.

Alain Barel and his fellow scientists at the prestigious International Center for Agricultural Research and Development (CIRAD) in Montpellier, France, believe that the original cacao trees were on earth before human beings. The first variety to appear, they contend, was actually *forastero*, which means "foreigner." Confusion arises because the first cultivated cacao variety was *criollo*, meaning "native." This is logical enough: It was the only one the Indians knew.

Since cacao pods do not fall to the ground, the seeds are spread only by birds and small mammals. Or by larger mammals, humans, who carried them to favorable climes.

Cacao seeds were most likely brought to Central America during Preclassic Mayan times, between 1500 B.C. and A.D. 200, Mesoamerica's first great agricultural period. By 1000 B.C., extensive maritime trade routes stretched from Ecuador to Mexico in Mesoamerica. There was also traffic from the coast of Venezuela to eastern Central America and the Yucatán beyond.

No one can say when the first Indian toasted those beans over a fire and released the same aromas that today captivate an entire world. The modern history of chocolate starts five hundred years ago with fragments from lost-then-found logs of Christopher Columbus. A great deal was written about the Aztecs' passion for chocolate after Cortés reached Tenochtitlán in 1519. As a result, common wisdom dates chocolate back to Montezuma. But those able to decipher Mayan hieroglyphics and interpret ancient art have much more to say on the origins of cacao.

Arturo Gómez-Pompa, professor of botany and plant sciences at the University of California at Riverside, has spent decades tracking the mysteries. In the journal *Latin American Antiquity*, he reported on the evidence of cacao in the Yucatán, just as conquistadores had noted, despite generations of belief that the soil and climate could not have supported it. The cacao, Gómez-Pompa surmises, was from sacred groves the Maya cultivated in sinkholes known as cenotes. Or maybe, he adds, cacao trees grew wild.

"Whatever the case, the discovery of this cacao lends support to the notion of the Mesoamerican origin of the domestication of local wild populations of *Theobroma cacao*," Gómez-Pompa wrote. His ethnohistoric research raised more questions than it answered. But he reached an intriguing conclusion: "Ancient and modern Maya have preserved germplasm that could prove useful for the genetic improvement and protection of one of the world's most important forest products, cacao."

Michael Coe, in a prodigious labor of love, put into a book the work of his wife, Sophie Dobzhansky Coe, who died of cancer in 1994. The book sets out what she learned over the hundreds of hours spent tracking down centuries-old texts in the libraries of Europe and America. Its title, *The True History of Chocolate*, is a play on *The True History of the Conquest of Mexico*, that turgidly classic sociopolitical travelogue completed in 1572 by the aged and nearly blind Bernal Díaz del Castillo. Yet the Coe book is scientifically sound and a pure pleasure to read, the product of two Mesoamerican anthropologists with a shared passion for food.

The Classic Maya flourished between A.D. 250 and 900, when their civilization collapsed. Their culture was presaged by earlier primitive farmers, contemporaries of the Olmecs. These loosely knit pre-Mayan tribes lived in the cool highlands of Guatemala and what is now the Mexican state of Chiapas before moving to the Petén plains of northern Guatemala in 1000 B.C.

"If they did use the wild cacao that they found growing in the lowlands," Coe wrote, "they must have had some other name for it, since it was not until some time between 400 B.C. and A.D. 100 that they received the word 'cacao' (by now pronounced the way we do today, to rhyme with 'cow') from Mixe-Zoquean speakers; 'cacao' meant then, as it still does, domesticated *Theobroma cacao*, and not any wild form or other species of *Theobroma*."

An Olmec-derived culture of Mixe-Zoqueans, which archeologists call Izapan, probably brought cacao to the Classic Maya. They settled at Izapa on the Pacific coastal plain of Chiapas, at the heart of the rich cacao region of Soconusco where fragments of old *criollo* plantations still survive. The domesticated trees they left behind, Coe reports, later made Soconusco "the diamond in the crown of the Aztec empire."

By the time their culture waned, the Izapan had spread along the Pacific coast from Chiapas to the Guatemalan foothills and across the Isthmus of Tehuantepec. Part of the Mayans' Popul Vuh, or "Book of Counsel," can be traced back to carved stone stelae at Izapa.

The Popul Vuh was written down in Spanish soon after the Conquista; Mayan scholars believe it was transcribed from now-forgotten hieroglyphics. The grand saga begins with the creation of the cosmos and, with poetic mythology, carries the epic of life up to the Spanish invasion.

In the beginning, the old couple who created the universe produced a set of Hero Twins, who meet separate gruesome ends in the Mayan underworld. One twin is later revealed as the Maize God. An illustration painted on a Classic Maya vase depicts the tragic finish of this Hero Twin who gave his people corn, their staff of life. His severed head is suspended in a cacao tree. The young god's other great gift was teaching people how to make chocolate.

The Classic Maya built dozens of cities, with magnificent art and architecture. Despite incessant warfare, they covered temples and palaces in delicate relief, working in stone and jade, and creating polychrome murals. Incised ceramic pots and gold jewelry added elegance to the court. They also left a rich literature written in elaborate glyphs on bark paper made from wild fig trees. Only four volumes survive today, and they are from the Post-Classic period just preceding the Spaniards' arrival. They are books of folding screens, with Classic-style calligraphy and illustration.

The Dresden Codex, the most beautiful of these old works, deals with the sacred 260-day cycle. In it, seated gods hold pods, and plates are heaped with roasted beans. "We know that this is cacao, since the text written above each deity states that what is held in the hand 'is cacao (*u kakaw*),'" Coe notes. "And on a Dresden page dealing with the New Year ceremonies so important in Post-Classic Yucatán, the Opossum God travels a sacred road to the edge of the town carrying the Rain God on his back, while the associated text tells us that 'cacao is his food (*kakaw u hanal*).'"

The Madrid Codex, if less artistic, is rich in cacao lore. In one panel, a young god grasps limbs of the familiar tree, and a quetzal flying above him holds a cacao pod in his beak. Another panel shows four gods piercing their ears with obsidian blades, and their blood showers onto cacao pods. "This is especially interesting," the indefatigable Coe explains, "since our ethnohistoric sources tell us that there were strong symbolic associations between chocolate and human blood among the late post-Classic Maya and the Aztecs."

There are more clues from the Maya, mostly scenes painted or carved onto vessels that were buried in tombs. No one knows whether common folk who tended the trees could afford to sample chocolate. But cacao routinely followed the highborn nobility into the afterlife.

Archeologists found a spectacular tomb at Río Azul, near the Petén region of Guatemala. A fifth-century ruler was buried there on a wooden litter, covered in cotton kapok, along with fourteen clay vessels. Six of these were cylindrical vases with tripod feet and covers. One of them, a painted and stuccoed pot with a stirrup handle, a locking lid, and an ornate base, bore two hieroglyphs reading "Cacao."

Hershey Foods laboratories in Pennsylvania found that the unusual pot had traces of theobromine and caffeine, definite evidence of cacao. Several others contained theobromine alone, but one of the tested pots had no trace of either alkaloid.

"It sounds as if the Hershey chemists adhere to the theory that there was one chocolate drink possible among these ancient Maya," Coe wrote. "It is just as possible that the dead lord began his voyage through the underworld with sustaining portions of several different chocolate drinks by his side."

Everything else suggests the Mayans had wide variety on the menu. A painting from A.D. 750 shows a palace servant making a lush cap of froth by pouring chocolate from a small vessel held chest-high to a larger one on the ground. Like the Aztecs later on, the Mayans loved their foam. Colonial dictionaries of the Maya language from the Yucatán had entries for *yom cacao,* meaning "chocolate foam," and *takan kel,* translated as "to roast cacao well in order to make lots of foam on the chocolate." There was also a term for what the palace woman was doing. *T'oh haa* meant "to pour chocolate from one vessel to another."

Cacao was made into a range of drinks, gruels, and powders. It was possibly even eaten solid. The range of flavorings ran from sweet wild honey to blazing hot chili. Mostly, the beverage was consumed cold, but some liked it hot.

On the sweltering coast of Guatemala, Mayans drank the nectar straight out of the pod. Antonio Fuentes y Guzmán, a Spanish chronicler of the seventeenth century, detailed how the Mayans piled fresh beans and mucilage into a small beached canoe. Gravity did the rest. The run-off juice was "an abundant liquor of the smoothest taste, between sour and sweet, which is of the most refreshing coolness." Because the juice ferments with exposure to air, the stuff was also strong enough to blister paint.

By the tenth century, Toltecs appeared in Mesoamerican history. Later Aztec accounts described them as supermen, skilled in the arts and fearsome in battle. But within two centuries, internal dissension collapsed the empire. Their capital of Tula, in today's Mexican state of Hidalgo, fell into ruin. Small Mayan nation-states again reclaimed their old territories.

The Yucatán coast is too swampy and wet for cacao. Guatemalan highlands are too cold. For warring chieftains, the grand prize was rich cacao-producing lands: Soconusco on the Pacific; Chontalpa in Tabasco; sections of the Guatemalan foothills. Statesmen negotiated trade agreements with leaders who controlled these crucial territories. Before the Spaniards appeared, great battles were fought to control Boca Costa, a rich stretch of land straddling Chiapas and Guatemala. Victorious Mayan kings exacted heavy tribute in cacao from conquered tribes who harvested the trees. In essence, these cacao belts amounted to the Mayans' mint, where money grew on trees.

Historians find cacao marbled through early Mesoamerican societies. Among the elite, chocolate was the Dom Pérignon of engagement parties and weddings. Dennis Tedlock, a Quiche Mayan specialist, notes the verb *chokola'j*, which means "to drink chocolate communally." That may have been the original source of the word *chocolate*.

Sir Eric Thompson, the renowned expert on the Maya, cites a colonial report on the Chol Maya of the Chiapas forests:

> The form of marriage is: the bride gives the bridegroom a small stool painted in colors, and also gives him five grains of cacao, and says to him, "These I give thee as a sign that I accept thee as my husband." And he also gives her some new skirts and another five grains of cacao, saying the same thing.

In the end, Coe leaves no doubt about who pioneered in chocolate:

> We may conclude by reiterating that chocolate and the remarkable tree from which it derives were thus *not* the invention of the Aztecs, as most books on the subject would have us believe, but of the remarkable Maya and their distant predecessors, the Mixe-Zoquean-speaking Olmecs. It was the Maya who first taught the Old World how to drink chocolate, and it was the Maya who gave us the word "cacao." They deserve recognition in the culinary history of *Theobroma cacao*.

*B*ut it was the Aztecs who made cacao a holy fetish and incorporated the gods' elixir into their grand ceremonies. And, even more than for the Mayans, it was their coin of the realm.

In his second letter to King Carlos I, Cortés reported: "Cacao is a fruit like the almond, which they grind and hold to be of such value that they use it as money throughout the land and with it buy all they need in the markets and other places."

Cortés and his small band landed at Yucatán early in 1519 and then worked their way up the coast to Veracruz. In those first years of conquest, they paid little attention to chocolate. The march to Tenochti-tlán was swift and brutal, a few hundred ironclad Spaniards against a warrior nation regarded by its enemies as invincible.

Among the best accounts is Hugh Thomas's weighty *The Conquest of Mexico*, which examines reports by Cortés's chroniclers in the light of present-day reflection. Thomas explains how the Spanish exploited tribal enmities, Aztec superstitions, and the obvious edge afforded by gunpowder and horses. He is no foodie, but he has a sharp eye for de-tail. Cacao is never far from the narrative.

In 1520, Cortés took his main force back to Veracruz to head off an expedition sent by the governor of New Spain to arrest him. It was a complex matter of jealousy and intrigue. Pedro de Alvarado, left be-hind in Tenochtitlán with only a few Spaniards, quickly lost control. Afraid of an uprising, he abruptly canceled an Aztec celebration that Cortés had approved. For good measure, he murdered half the dancers and seized Montezuma as hostage. Outraged, the Aztecs gained the up-per hand. And, Thomas relates, an unnamed warrior told Alvarado: "If you do not free Montezuma soon, you will be properly killed and cooked with chocolate."

Jacques Soustelle's *Daily Life of the Aztecs* offers a more leisurely look at the society Cortés managed to obliterate. True enough, the Aztecs had their bloodthirsty side. Each year, thousands of people— prisoners of war, unfortunate nobles, young virgins—were sacrificed to the gods. Hearts were extracted with obsidian knives to appease a range of deities: to improve the rains, to ward off curses, to keep the heavens in balance. Priests flayed the victims and made ceremonial cloaks of their skins. But the Aztecs knew how to party.

"Night-long banquets began with a washing of hands, followed by cigars and cocoa," Soustelle wrote.

> The feasts went on until the dawn, with dances and songs, and the party broke up only in the morning, after a last cup of scented co-coa, redolent of honey and vanilla. Rich men and dignitaries could drink cocoa, a luxury imported from the Hot Lands, sweetened with

vanilla-scented honey or mixed with green maize, with octli (fermented agave sap) or with pimento.

*Octli* was pulque, the mildly alcoholic brew that Mexicans still love. The Aztecs used it in moderation. Drunkenness was usually punished by death. Far more popular, for those entitled to it, was chocolate.

Colorful accounts of the Aztecs' cacao craze were sent back to Spain by various adventurers and travelers who sailed to Mexico in Cortés's wake. Not everyone loved it.

Chocolate, Girolamo Benzoni wrote in 1575, "seemed more a drink for pigs than a drink for humanity." The Milanese historian recorded his mixed reaction in his *History of the New World*:

> I was in this country for more than a year, and never wanted to taste it, and whenever I passed a settlement, some Indian would offer me a drink of it, and would be amazed when I would not accept, going away laughing. But then, as there was a shortage of wine, so as not to be always drinking water, I did like the others. The taste is somewhat bitter, it satisfies and refreshes the body, but does not inebriate, and it is the best and most expensive merchandise, according to the Indians of that country.

Gonzalo Fernández de Oviedo noted with some horror that when Indians drank the obnoxious brew mixed with annatto, which they called achiote, it turned their mouths red as if they had been drinking blood.

These early accounts are often distorted by Spanish pride and prejudice. With the advantage of scholarly detachment, Michael Coe adds some context.

Perhaps the most widely repeated detail in histories of chocolate is how Montezuma drank fifty cups of the stuff before entering his harem of concubines. This comes from an eyewitness account by Bernal Díaz del Castillo of a banquet prepared for the emperor. More than three hundred dishes were laid out, he wrote, and from time to time they brought him some cups of fine gold, with a certain drink made of cacao, which they said was for success with women; and then we thought no more about it; but I saw that they brought more than 50 great jars of prepared good cacao with its foam, and he drank of that; and that the women served him drink very respectfully.

One should keep in mind, Coe cautions, that Bernal Díaz was a doddering octogenarian when he wrote his account, a half century after the fact. And, Coe adds, the emperor was not likely to need a sexual stimulant. "This was a Spanish obsession," he wrote, "as was the chronic constipation with which the invaders were afflicted, through a diet which was almost all meat and lard, with few if any fruits and vegetables. The conquistadores searched for native Mexican laxatives as avidly as they did for aphrodisiacs."

That all-too-familiar diarrhea known as Montezuma's revenge, it seems, would follow only in later generations.

Coe sheds light on just how valuable cacao was to the Aztecs. According to an account by Francisco Cervantes de Salazár, Coe notes, Montezuma's warehouse held more than 960,000,000 beans. These were measured in "loads" of 24,000, the standard weight of a backpack carried by Aztec porters from the plantations of Chiapas.

Some of the beans were ground into chocolate. But the rest made up the national treasury and the military payroll. According to Bernal Díaz, two thousand containers of foaming chocolate drink were prepared regularly only for Montezuma's guard.

Coe also unearthed a text published in Venice in 1556 by a man who scholars know as the Anonymous Conquistador. He is described as "a gentleman of Hernán Cortés," but his name is lost to history. He wrote in detail how beans are ground into powder, which is added to water and whipped with a spoon. The mixture is then poured from one basin to another to raise thick foam.

"When they wish to drink it," Anonymous wrote (in Coe's translation), they mix it with certain small spoons of gold or silver or wood, and drink it, and drinking it one must open one's mouth, because being foam one must give it room to subside, and go down bit by bit. This drink is the healthiest thing, and the greatest substance of anything you could drink in the world, because he who drinks a cup of this liquid, no matter how far he walks, can go a whole day without eating anything else.

Perhaps the most useful reports on chocolate come from early Spanish missionaries who saw their role as restoring some of God's grace after the bloody excesses of the conquest. They learned the Aztecs' Nahuatl language, local customs, and New World agronomy. Their goal was to restore what they could of Mexico's civilization, bringing the Bible to the Aztecs while protecting them from brutal Spanish sinners who got Christ's message wrong.

Fray Bernardino de Sahagún, a mendicant Franciscan, may well have been the world's first field ethnographer. His twelve-volume encyclopedia, *General History of the Things of New Spain*, sumptuously illustrated, accurately set down every aspect of Aztec life. The encyclopedia stayed in manuscript form until the nineteenth century, suppressed by the Spanish king, Felipe II. In the 1950s, Arthur J. O. Anderson and Charles E. Dibble translated it from Nahuatl.

Above all, Sahagún gave us the setting. Beyond the grisly aspects of their religious practices, the Aztecs had put together a complex civilization to rival anything the world had yet seen. They numbered perhaps ten or eleven million in all. Their dazzling capital of Tenochtitlán with its twin city, Tlatelolco, had more than two hundred thousand inhabitants, making it one of the largest metropolises of its day.

As the legend has it, the Aztecs lived a simple life in mud huts somewhere in the hills of northwestern Mexico, a homeland they call Aztlan. A vision directed them to build a city surrounded by water in a place where they found an eagle perched with a serpent in its talons. On the site of today's Mexico City, they found their spot. Charged with fresh spirituality, they built great pyramids toward the sun and vast temples of astounding intricacy.

Aztec engineers mastered hydrology to a point that still baffles scientists today. They divided off a portion of the vast salty lake around their capital to ensure fresh water for irrigation and drinking. Causeways with drawbridges allowed them to build a magnificent city of canals and gardens that was all but impregnable to invading armies. Had Montezuma been more decisive, and less confused by ancient prophecies that their lost great god would return in a shape somewhat resembling the light-skinned Spaniards, history might well have worked out differently.

Ordinary people were essentially free, organized into landholding bodies called *calpoltin*, each with its own leaders and lords. Education was universal for boys and girls. Families had their own fields, as long as they worked them. But there was also a hereditary ruling class, with rights over commoners and a substantial stock of serfs to work their lands. This, more or less, was the Aztecs' chocolate high society.

The grandest of lords had the title of *huei tlatoani*, or great speaker. That is, the emperor. A high council chose him from the few eligible royal candidates. He ruled for life and was succeeded by a son or brother. His person was sacred, and no one was allowed to gaze upon him, let alone touch him. Cortés did both, of course, scandalizing the pious Aztecs.

Priests were celibate and probably more chaste than the missionaries who came to convert them. Their beliefs were highly complex, centered on dozens of gods and goddesses that represented natural forces. Tlaloc, the god of rain, loomed large. And there were the two mortal adversaries: Tezcatlipoca (Smoking Mirror), patron of wizards and warriors; and Quetzalcoatl (Plumed Serpent), lord of the sacred clergy. Huitzilopochtli was an ancient stalwart, not only the supreme deity of war but also the Aztecs' Sun God.

Gods and their omens defined the Aztec meaning of life, which was fortunate for the Spaniards. The Toltecs worshipped Quetzalcoatl, who, they believed, descended to earth in human form to teach them science and the arts. Among other things, he brought them cacao from the garden of Paradise. Tlaloc kept the tree watered. Xochiquetzal, goddess of love, adorned it with fragrant white blossoms and gave it her spirit.

But Quetzalcoatl ran afoul of Tezcatlipoca and fled to the east on a raft of woven snakes. He promised to return in a year of the reed, as 1519 happened to be. After a comet blazed in night skies and earthquakes shook Tenochtitlán, the priests forecast the Plumed Serpent's return on April 21. That was the day Cortés reached Veracruz.

Beyond the grand structures of Aztec belief, Sahagún's fine strokes etched in daily details of life. One volume covers the *pochteca*, long-haul merchants who kept the royal palace stocked with vital luxuries. They supplied quetzal feathers, jaguar skins, amber, and, of course, cacao.

Sahagún reports that fine chocolate was known as *tlaquetzalli* (precious thing). He describes a market woman's preparation as follows:

> She grinds cacao; she crushes, breaks, pulverizes them. She chooses, selects, separates them. She drenches, soaks, steeps them. She adds water sparingly, conservatively; aerates it; she makes it form a head, makes foam; she removes the head, makes it thicken, makes it dry, pours water in, stirs water into it.

That is not so different from what Mexicans do today.

In 1570, Felipe II dispatched his royal physician, Francisco Hernández, to find medicinal plants in the New World. Over the next seven years, this accomplished naturalist catalogued more than three thousand species. He noted the Aztecs' name for the cacao tree: *cacahuacuauhuitl*. This combines the Nahuatl words for *cacao* and *tree*.

Hernández listed four separate cultivated varieties, from the large-podded "eagle cacao" to the "earth cacao," with fruit so small that it had the same Aztec name as peanut. Modern botanists believe these were all *criollo*.

Today, surviving Aztec artifacts give a notion of the role cacao played. The Brooklyn Museum of Art, for instance, has a volcanic stone statue of a man grasping a pod big enough to reach from his neck to his knees. His face, painted red, suggests a generous smear caused by a satisfying drink of annatto-laced chocolate. He is smiling happily. Then again, that expression may be trepidation.

When priests made their routine human sacrifices to ensure the gods delivered a new day, victims were given cacao pods to make them worthy. It was perfect symbolism. The pod's shape was close enough to that of the human heart, which would soon be held up, steaming, to the sun. And the thick, rich chocolate, colored red, looked like nothing so much as fresh blood.

In recent years, philological detectives have worked hard to track down the root of the word *chocolate*. Writers today refer authoritatively to a Nahuatl word—*chocolatl* or *xocolatl*. Even Webster's legitimizes this etymology. But no early source uses the term. As Hernández and Sahagún both note, the word was *cacahuatl*.

Ignacio Dávila Garibí, the great Mexican language historian, suggested that Spaniards coined the word *chocolatl*, using the Mayan *chocol* and then replacing the suffix *haa* (water) with the Aztec *atl*. Coe consulted Miguel Leon-Portilla, the eminent Nahuatl authority, and both agreed that this explanation made the most sense. After all, the Iberians who settled Mexico needed a different term for the sugared version they preferred over the cold and bitter original-formula *cacahuatl*.

And, of course, Coe adds a final thought. Back then, the four-letter root of *cacahuatl*—caca—meant what it still does today. Old Spanish-English dictionaries, for instance, define *cacafuego* as "shitfire." It was hardly suitable for the noble new drink, which faced enough resistance because of its color and consistency, to be weighted down with scatological overtones.


*C*acao reached Europe for the first time in 1528, most likely as an afterthought in Cortés's baggage. Among all the other treasures and curiosities that accompanied his eastbound voyage, Cortés brought dried cacao beans to Carlos I. He likely had a foaming cup of *chocolatl* prepared for his monarch. But Carlos, who was also the Holy Roman

Emperor Charles V, had imperial collapse on his mind. He did not make much of it.

The first cacao came back in dribs and drabs. And then in 1585, six decades after Spanish colonization began, a heavily loaded fleet left Veracruz for Seville to begin commercial trade. Soon after, Europe's chocolate craze took off with a furor.

Joseph Bachot, a French physician who loved his meals, referred to cacao as "food of the gods" as early as 1662. Its first Latin name was *Amygdalae pecuniariae*—the money almond—until Linnaeus, an ardent cacao drinker, came up with the genus name *Theobroma*.

As the New World took lasting shape, colonial authorities began looking around for new sources of cacao. Chiapas and Tabasco grew a basic supply for Spain, but their *criollo* trees were meager producers. And the finicky variety did not like to travel.

Plantations spread to islands in the West Indies and onto the South American coast. Dutch sailors managed to carry *criollo* trees from Venezuela to Celebes, now Sulawesi in Indonesia, in 1560. But another two centuries passed before cacao trees—*forastero*, mostly—were widely planted in Asia.

Portugal's American footprint was in Brazil, where settlers planted large cacao plantations. In 1822, Portuguese sailors carried cuttings of *forastero* across the Atlantic to the small island of Príncipe, south of Nigeria. From there, trees were planted on the sister island of São Tomé. These were a hardy varietal called *amelonado* because of their melon-shaped pods. Soon the trees spread from the Portuguese colony to Spain's nearby island of Fernando Po.

In 1879, an enterprising African had plantation workers sneak some cuttings from Fernando Po across the Gulf of Guinea and planted them in the Gold Coast, now Ghana. A statue still stands to this farsighted Ghanaian thief. His first trees grew into the rich crop that underwrote much of Britain's colonization of Africa.

But even earlier, in Ivory Coast just to the west, the French were already at it. Cacao, like coffee and tea, had implanted itself well beyond its points of origin.

———

*T*he little studio where I had installed my chocolate base camp was awash in maps, old agricultural reports, and history texts. I had learned where to find good chocolate, and how to look for more. But I was also starting to recognize the general misconceptions and historical inaccuracies that came from too many people dipping into the same few sources. It was time to get on the road.

*Chapter 4*

# CHOCOLATE FOR TURKEYS

artina Tlacoxolat looked a bit troubled when I asked if she could whip up a batch of mole, and I couldn't figure out why. As accommodating as people come, surely she would comply with this simple request from a visitor sent by her son in New York. That this was a three-day job should not deter her; life in San Juan Huilico Atlixco offered its spare moments. Then I realized the problem. After she and her family and I tasted some of the mole, where would she find another fifty people to finish it?

Growing up in Tucson, I considered myself a Mexican food gourmet of the highest order. That is, I studied the textured intimacies of tacos, enchiladas, and tamales, unbothered that they were no more than *antojitos,* the snack street food so close to the hearts of us sons of the Sonoran Desert. I knew only that mole—pronounced *mo'-lay*—was chocolate chicken, and I did not want to go there. But, mole and all, the chocolate trail starts in Mexico.

Real Mexican food, of course, is infinitely complex, as regionally based as French cuisine, with just as much pain in the preparation. And if there is anything to rank with *gigot d'agneau* as a defining dish with festive connotations, it is mole. Though this dish is mostly made with chicken these days, the old recipes call for *guajolote*, the tasty if tough little Mexican turkey. Properly done, mole does not come in small batches.

Anyone invited to a fiesta can determine whether it is a casual gathering or a serious celebration with the simplest of questions: *¿Hay mole?* That is, will they serve mole? A priest and a ring are required to consecrate a marriage in Mexico, but everyone knows no union is consummated until the families dish up mole to the immediate world. Done properly, mole is not thrown together on a kitchen range but rather assembled over days, with friends and family all working to soak, pound, chop, roast, or stir gently atop an outdoor charcoal stove.

*Mole* usually refers to the whole dish—fowl included—but the word specifically means the thick sauce itself. I had a rough idea of what went into it, but I needed an up-close lesson. Lucky timing and the kindness of friends landed me at Martina's door, which was shaded by banana leaves and opened onto an immaculately swept dirt patio in a little village south of Puebla. By then, I had spent more time than I had planned looking for the perfect mole mama.

Things seemed to have fallen into place when I mentioned my search to Sara Jenkins, a young New York chef of amazing skills learned in Italy at the knee of her mother, Nancy Harmon Jenkins. "Talk to me," Sara said. "My entire kitchen staff came from Puebla."

Sara was jammed with work at a new restaurant, which had outdoor tables in lower Manhattan but no one from Puebla on the new staff. She would get back to me as soon as she could. In the meantime, I brushed up on the subject.

Since the Aztecs, the chocolate time line follows a trail of mole. The word means only a complex chili-based sauce. But when modified with *poblano*—coming from Puebla—it means a chili-based sauce with a nuance of sweetened chocolate to balance the other flavors.

Chocolate mole is also made in Oaxaca, in different and more varied versions, and Oaxaca is now the real chocolate heart of Mexico. But the old colonial metropolis of Puebla, eighty miles southeast of Mexico City, with as many churches as there are days of the year, seemed like the original source.

According to historically based legend, or legend-laced history, seventeenth-century nuns at the Santa Rosa Convent in Puebla cooked up chocolate mole in their convent kitchen to impress a visiting viceroy. There are various versions of what transpired. One has a clumsy sister dropping chocolate into the sauce, the way a slippery-fingered cook in France accidentally put almonds into chocolate for the Duc du Pralin, thus inventing what the French call *praliné*. Another has it that a flustered nun, chattering in Spanish as she pounded away at her stone mortar, mispronounced the verb for what she was doing as "mole" instead of "meule." This, for some reason, launched her companions into fits of laughter, and the moment was immortalized with a new name.

Etymologists offer a simpler explanation: the Nahautl word for sauce is *mulli*.

Puebla was a jewel in colonial times, a lovely city built along Spanish lines but laid out and landscaped by people with a sense of proportion and grandeur. I had last seen it forty years earlier as a summer student in Mexico, and it had stayed fresh in my mind. Mission-style churches faced grand buildings with rich tile and iron-grille balconies. Bracing mountain air and reliable rainfall produce lush flowering plants that fill public squares.

The proud city of Puebla was where Mexican forces overran Emperor Maximilian's troops on May 5, 1862. The French took back Puebla a short while later, but that historical detail does nothing to dampen joyous celebration all over Mexico each year on Cinco de Mayo.

Mostly, I remembered the restaurants. Every corner seemed to have a few, if not proper caterics with sturdy tooled-leather chairs and silverware, then at least holes-in-the-wall exuding come-hither aromas.

Driving in on a Saturday morning, I found the Malthusian nightmare. Population growth on top of a systematic flouting of any sensible rule of planning had blotted out the charm. The narrow lanes built for horse and carriage were choked beyond belief with cars and trucks. Ahead of my taxi, someone paused to take a rare parking spot. A driver was maneuvering out of a tight space. Within a nanosecond, an earsplitting storm of horn noise impelled us forward. Not that the drivers' impatience sped up traffic. We spent fifteen minutes on that single block.

Spanish-era buildings had been carved into shops selling second-hand auto parts, ugly furniture, and junk tin kitchenware. And the restaurants were gone. On the main square, the zocalo, the ubiquitous golden *M* marked an overlit hangar full of kids. There was homegrown fast food: greasy fried meat or *tortas*—sandwiches. A few dubious places offered "Continental" fare.

Asking around, I decided my best chance for good *mole poblano*, outside of someone's kitchen, would be at the Hotel Colonial.

It was a perfect setting, the ornate home of some early grandee, and it dominated a well-kept pocket of old Puebla. During Mexico's early years, visiting presidents inflamed the masses from its balconies. Broad staircases edged in blue and yellow ceramics curved between floors, their dark wood railings worn smooth over the centuries. Narrow, cranky elevators had been added, but no one seemed certain where they went, or if they ever got there.

Dining areas meandered across most of the main floor, and additional alcoves, a story higher, looked onto an indoor patio and an outdoor fountain. A kindly waiter took me through the kitchen, brought toward modern times in fits and starts but otherwise just as the old artisans had built it. Tiled ceilings arched over blackened fireplaces and monster stoves. Dishes towered above stone sinks. The Colonial was no architectural masterpiece; it was simply old Mexico the way tourists like me loved to picture it.

I ordered mole and waited. It was good, all right, but no better. As the chicken is boiled, its bland taste puts heavy responsibility on the sauce, which is supposed to be slightly hot, and not sweet enough for sugar in the chocolate to be noticed. The two dozen ingredients must blend to the masterful mix that Mexicans treasure. The Colonial's came close. It had none of that hint of burned tire that overpowers bad mole. But I knew I had to keep looking.

After lunch, I stopped at the Santa Rosa Convent to see the now-famous kitchen where those nuns reportedly discovered mole. My trusty copy of Frances Toor's *New Guide to Mexico*, published in 1944, makes no mention of the incident. It merely notes a "beautiful all-tile Colonial Kitchen." This whole nun-mole business might, in fact, be one of those instant legends that are always so good for tourism. I was curious to find out.

Modern guidebooks commend the convent as a high point of Puebla, but no one seems to have told the people in charge. A ratty little room marked TICKET OFFICE announced frequent times for guided visits. I waited all morning and saw only a few mystified tourists. Finally, a disheveled man bustled in to collect ticket money and then led us off with all the warmth of a coyote taking illegal aliens to Arizona.

The kitchen is breathtaking. Handmade tiles cover every wall, window seat, vaulted ceiling, floor, and fireplace. Centuries have added a warm patina to the tones of blue, green, and cream on the old glazed tiles. Starbursts are set into each flat plane. Alternating patterns decorate work surfaces and hearths. I am fairly sure of this, at least. The guide whipped us through before I could set an f-stop.

I tried to stall a moment by asking questions. The guide answered each on the trot. I started to reach into my pocket to rent more of his attention. But something warned me not to believe a word he said.

Frustrated, I sat down to regroup by a broken fountain under dead palm trees. I was beginning to have enough of Puebla. Rather than stay the night, I returned to Mexico City. Late the next morning, still puzzling over Plan B, I checked my e-mail. Sara had scored. She had dashed off a message in such haste that half the words were scrambled. Her friend Sergio Tlacoxolat had given her his mother's number, although he had not yet warned his mother. When I called, a confused but accommodating Martina gave me directions. Moments later, I was headed back toward Puebla, bound for a small village under the volcano.

The Tlacoxolats' farmlet nestles at the edge of San Juan Huilico Atlixco, down a track off the highway south of Puebla. The backdrop is Mount Popocatépetl, a conical mountain of brooding beauty in shades of purple with a white mantle of snow. Sometimes it smokes and gurgles. That day, it just sat there, the perfect emblem of a Mexico that I remembered.

A solid little house anchors the family compound, a ragtag collection of open sheds, mud huts, and verandas shaded by flowering vines. A rooster that had lost its watch was crowing its head off at one in the afternoon. Burros brayed, and birds made a racket in the mango trees.

In nearby fields, Martina's husband, Tirso, grows corn, beans, tomatoes, and cucumbers, as well as enormous gladioli. He has a pickup, a horse named Horse—Caballo, actually—and a lot of work. She makes a little money selling chocolate she brings from Oaxaca.

Glancing around, I saw signs of recovery in the American economy up north. A concrete-block barn was back under construction. A new scooter leaned against a fence. Family fortunes rise or fall according to help from the six of their eight children who work across the border.

On Sundays, the Tlacoxolats try to take it easy and appreciate life. But they were gracious to my importuning visit. By the time I arrived, Sergio had telephoned from New York to explain the circumstances. Martina plunged into the assignment. She showed me her normal mole pot, a blackened clay cauldron the size of an industrial waste container. We would use a smaller one.

Tirso, Martina, and I drove to a town market down the road. Rosa Rosas was in her usual spot, behind a mountain range of chilies. Mexican cooks depend upon a dizzying variety of peppers, from the basic green *guajillo* to small red habaneros that can double as rocket fuel. Rosa had them all, but Martina's mole recipe requires only three: the long red poblano, which Mexicans elsewhere call *mulate*; the flat, wrinkled *pasilla*; and the workaday *guajillo*, which is like an Anaheim chili.

Martina sorted carefully among the mounds, hefting each likely pepper to examine its pulpiness, texture, and ripeness. Meantime, Rosa rhapsodized about mole.

"We always make a lot when we cook it, because we never know how far it will have to go," she said. "That is what is so wonderful about Mexico. It's our tradition. If someone shows up, we feed him. He is a welcome guest, part of the family. He could be a cabinet minister or a barefoot campesino who happens to wander by."

And, she added, making mole is always a social event. "There is so much to do that we share the labor," she said. "Everyone helps, passing the time with gossip, jokes, songs. When you make mole, you have to have fun."

The chicken was selected with equal care from another philosopher-vendor. *Mole poblano* was first eaten with wild turkey, which was what people found centuries ago when they took their muskets out to the woods. The taste for turkey grew stronger after the bird was domesticated and fattened to party-size proportions. These days, the butcher said, a lot of people still demand turkey for mole as it should be. But chickens are so much easier to handle.

After a while, Martina's load was substantial. She trotted down the street with bulging bags in each hand. Tirso walked behind, unburdened. I started to reach for a bundle but thought better of it. Every culture has its ways. Instead, I helped the man of the house protect his wife's flanks.

Mole starts with chilies. We worked over each pepper with our fingers, removing stems and veins and then scraping any remaining seeds into a dish for use later as seasoning. For our small batch, Martina used twenty of the poblanos. These, along with a handful of *guajillos*, were for flavor. She added four of the longer red *pasillas* for heat. As we hurried along, I focused hard on the first rule of Mexican kitchens: When your eyes start to water, as they will, for God's sake do not rub them.

When the charcoal in her courtyard brazier burned down to glowing coals, Martina quickly roasted each chili. One by one, she dropped the peppers onto the fire until their skins blistered and blackened. For tongs, she used her fingers until they, too, were blistered and blackened. Mostly, Martina smiled at my obvious concern. Two or three times, a heartfelt "Ouch!" blew her cover. She dumped each roasted chili into a bucket of water to cool, soften, and shed its singed skin.

Martina poured sesame seeds onto a plate, and we plucked out the bad ones. She toasted the rest in a heavy iron skillet and put them aside. Then she poured sunflower seed oil—just some supermarket stuff—into the pan and deep-fried slices of those large green bananas that are more properly called plantains.

When the plantains were removed, golden brown, Martina dropped several handfuls of raisins into the bubbling oil until they puffed up into fat little globes. Next, she spilled the chili seeds into a colander and toasted them in the oil. Each ingredient, in turn, was added to a large clay olla. She tore up chunks of bread and old tortillas and left them to toast in the oil in the skillet. Then she scurried to the kitchen to check on the chicken she had simmering on her stove.

As I watched her, Martina might have been my Jewish grandmother making soup: a pot, a chicken, salted water. But there would be no celery, carrots, or garlic, and certainly neither kreplach nor matzoh balls. She wanted only simple broth to add to her mole. The bird was meant as mere backdrop, bland enough to absorb all the other flavors and not get in the way of their blended bouquet.

Suddenly, a screech called her back to the fire. Her teenage daughter, still far from mole mama status, had forgotten to equip herself with a spatula. "Run! Run!" she yelled as she watched helplessly. The tortillas were black. Edges of the bread had burned to carbon. Martina only chuckled. Scraping off a token bit of char, she tossed the bread and tortillas into her mix. "You'll see," she said, with an unsettling trust-me grin.

One by one, other components went into the clay pot: almonds roasted in oil; a head of garlic left on the stalk, charred briefly in the flames; cloves and cinnamon sticks pop-toasted in the colander over the fire; grilled raisins that had been softened in boiling water; anise and black pepper. Mexican lore demands twenty-seven ingredients in a *mole poblano*. But Mexican reality is that rules are subject to change according to a cook's inspiration and the contents of her larder.

Finally, it was time for the chocolate. Martina spilled some chicken broth through a strainer into a dish in which she melted a sizable chunk from one of the brown hockey pucks she buys in Oaxaca. Each disk of chocolate, molded in a simple tin circle, is composed of two and a half parts of sugar to one part cacao.

This last step—the addition of sugary chocolate—is crucial for the right balance. If there is too much, the final result cloys. If too little, the mole has a powerful kick to it, and you've missed the point. The problem, of course, is that few decent Mexican cooks actually measure. Martina simply senses how hot the chilies might be and how much blackened char got into the mix.

We had reached the stage where the real work was supposed to start. By tradition, the well-stirred contents of the olla are spilled onto a metate, a flat stone on four stubby legs, and worked over for hours upon hours with a stone roller. This is women's work, naturally, backbreaking labor done on bended knees. As Rosa had said in the market, women who make mole have got to have a sense of humor about it all.

In our case, we took the sensible shortcut. We carried the olla down the road to a crumbling adobe shack. Inside, a cheerful old woman turned on her milling machine, which looked like a cross between Gutenberg's printing press and a torture device from the Spanish Inquisition. Within minutes, we had our mole.

Still warm from the fire and creamy from the mill, it defied all description. Martina was right, of course. That bread and tortilla char was just another happy nuance that could not be placed. It was spicy enough to bite back but also richly mild. If any flavor dominated, it was sesame and almonds, bringing to mind happy moments in the best of Sichuan restaurants. If there was chocolate, you could not prove it by me. Still, I could sense it.

The real test came at Martina's table, when she ladled the thick hot mole over a boiled chicken drumstick and thigh. I had a flash of my early days in the Congo when I first tasted *mwamba*, chicken in spicy peanut sauce. But this was something else entirely.

That plate of perfect mole linked Montezuma's empire to a modern-day Mexico with new values that often do not jibe with its old roots. Maybe Spanish nuns did devise this dish long after the Conquista. But as I sat with the Tlacoxolats under the volcano, that seemed like superfluous detail. I felt very near the heart of chocolate.

_J_n the village of San Pedro Atocpan, a short drive northwest of Mexico City, it is hard to find anything that is not mole. During the 1950s, an enterprising villager from Puebla found a market among Mexico City housewives who had to have mole but were too busy to make it. Atocpan went collectively crazy for the stuff. Today, a generous handful of shops grind it to order by the kilo. Even more restaurants serve it in a variety of forms. Just about everyone in town has family mole secrets locked away in a safe place.

The best time to visit is during October, when Mexicans from everywhere jam into Atocpan for its three-week mole festival. I went in spring, hoping to find the place in a more relaxed state. The mole fairgrounds were deserted, but gardeners kept the grass and trees in perfect shape, awaiting the annual bash. A sign at one end read DON'T THROW GARBAGE HERE—THINK OF YOUR FAMILY'S IMAGE.

I stopped at La Casa de Buen Mole, where Genaro Ortíz and a young helper labored away in spite of the slow season. Ortíz told me that Atocpan has ten thousand residents, and they are all mole millers. I took this as a slight exaggeration, although by the end of the day I began to wonder. As he explained it, it wasn't one man but rather a movement of settlers from Puebla generations ago who brought fresh blood to Atocpan. Naturally, the newcomers brought their own recipes. Either way, the whole village went nuts for chocolate-flavored fowl.

Ortíz's customers often want him to go heavy on the almonds, hazelnuts, pecans, and peanuts. Many cooks use prunes, but he doesn't stock them. It is too much work to remove the pits. For thickener, instead of the bread and tortillas that Martina uses, he crumbles in stale cookies.

I asked Ortíz where I might find a restaurant serving good mole. He gave me that look. I might have asked where to find a lobster on the coast of Maine. I had been told about Don Pedro, but it was closed. Instead, I chose a place called Los Cípreses del Rey David. It had towering King David–type cypresses in a lush garden of bougainvillea, oleanders, and gladioli. Muscular geraniums rose high above their clay pots. Besides, it had a sign announcing "the best mole in the world."

Inside, I found a spot at a brightly painted table and looked at the menu. I chose flat enchiladas made with blue-corn tortillas and topped with a rich brown mole. Tender boiled pinto beans came on the side. As I ate, Vicente Fernández wailed *"Volver, Volver"* from the jukebox, an old classic about lost love that goes straight to the nostalgia glands. Cooking noises echoed from the kitchen, wafting on a cloud of pleasant aromas. I got up to investigate.

Valente Espíndole, the owner, was forty-eight and had been cooking at his restaurant for fifteen years. He wore a T-shirt of some experience over a respectable belly. Cast in a film, he might have had a toothpick in his mouth. When I asked who made the best mole in Mexico, he eyed me narrowly. *"Pues, yo,"* he said. Well, me, of course. I should have remembered the sign out front. I said I meant the question in a more general sense geographically.

"Puebla is the capital of mole," he said, "but some of us improve upon the *poblanos'* skills." I asked about Oaxaca, which also claims title to superior moledom. *Oaxaqueños* boast that they make seven different kinds of mole, although only two of them have chocolate in it.

"If there is no chocolate, it is not mole," Espíndole said. "To make it right, you must use twenty-seven different ingredients." That number again. I asked him if he could list the components.

"I can't tell you," Espíndole replied. He smiled slyly, eschewing all persuasion. "After all, you *norteamericanos* keep your secret to making fried chicken."

In Oaxaca, there was no missing the chocolate. At the downtown corner of Las Minas and Bartolomé de las Casas, I could follow my nose in any direction to shops that ground cacao to order. In the Mercado Benito Juárez nearby, stalls were stacked high with those cinnamon-scented hockey pucks. A dozen restaurants offered old-style moles. And, in any case, I had come to town with a secret weapon.

Weeks before, I had visited some old pals, Yvette Mimieux and

Howard Ruby. Yvette, having retired from films, now roams the world from a home in Bel Air. Her French surname and tinkling all-American voice are misleading. She is half Mexican, and her beloved late *mamacita* was a killer cook. I started to explain my project, but she stopped me after the first few words. "Of course," she said. "Estela Luna."

When Estela first showed up in Los Angeles, she spoke no English. In fact, she had barely finished struggling her way to fluent Spanish. Her home was a Chinantec Indian village high in the mountains north-west of Oaxaca. You can drive there in an afternoon these days, but it used to take four days if you traveled on foot as she did.

By happy coincidence, Estela was on vacation from her job as Yvette's housekeeper. She was headed for the mountain, and we over-lapped in Oaxaca. Estela was with her daughter, Minerva, trendy at twenty-one, a university student with a bent toward foreign affairs. Minerva walked hand in hand with her mother as a dutiful Mexican daughter does.

Estela has that Oaxacan ability to keep one foot in two separate centuries. She is ready for anything a space-age world tosses at her, but her roots go deep into traditions that date back long before Columbus. After Puebla, I was nervous about what I would find in Oaxaca. I should have had faith in its Estela-style character.

"We love our old ways, and we take care of them," she told me as we threaded our way through the jammed markets. As our theme was chocolate, she carefully pointed out its various manifestations: huge clay jars of ancient potions that blended cacao with cornmeal and pungent local herbs.

"At the same time, we have to live in the world as it is," Estela con-tinued, while shaking her head vigorously to a woman offering deep-fried grasshoppers spiced with chili, on which she correctly guessed I would pass. "I've always told my children, if you want something, you go after it. If you sit and wait for a dream to come true, it never will."

As if on cue, her twenty-four-year-old son, Carlos, showed up. Handsome and athletic, he spoke in the gentle, almost grave manner of his mother. Like her, he punctuated his tone with flashes of humor. He wanted to enter government, hopeful of finding ways to improve life for poor families. When he said his eventual ambition was to be president of Mexico, I was ready to put money on his chances.

Mexico had to modernize, Carlos said, but not at the expense of giving up what made it Mexico.

"I hate to see us losing our traditions," he explained. "We're letting go of things we've built up over the centuries. It's the influence of television, travel, of people who come back from the United States and open pizzerias. Old ways inevitably fly off into oblivion when the world turns too fast."

Mexico's problems, he said, come from big talk and unbridled greed. Leaders seldom do what they promise and too often amass riches at the public's expense.

"Real wealth is helping others," Carlos said. "I don't want to get caught up in all this fancy Mexican talk about unrealistic goals. Mostly, I want my neighbors and my friends to do better than I do."

Glancing at Estela, he added a final thought. "You know, if someone offered me the choice of a million dollars or the best mother in the world, I'd take the money. I already have the best mother."

Feeling grateful to Yvette and good fortune, I followed the Lunas on our objective of finding good Oaxacan chocolate. We started with a good look around.

Until 1976, Oaxaca was headed the way of Puebla; old buildings were razed in the small historic center. Only poverty deterred developers from erecting some monstrosity in the heart of town. Then city fathers, dogged by alarmed local residents, passed strict codes to protect the singular style of the town's colonial architecture. Fuming, honking traffic still chokes narrow downtown streets by the old markets. But Oaxaca has been saved.

Oaxacans and foreigners who love the place have made it better than ever. Today, you can visit an Internet café to probe far reaches of the twenty-first century. Then a Zapotec woman seated outside on the cobblestones will sell you a cup of *nicuatole*, the same foaming corn elixir her ancestors drank long before Columbus learned to sail.

Low-rise colonial buildings in green-hued stone, with iron grillwork and vibrantly painted shutters, line the recobbled old streets. Markets overflow with luscious fruits and fiery chilies. Churches recall the pious grandeur of Spain's early missionaries. And at the center, the leafy zocalo thrums with life, a swirl of music and color scented with roasting fiesta food.

Heavy carved doors lead to hotel courtyards ablaze in tropical bloom. Water murmurs in tiled fountains. From one cantina, a Mexican voice from the past wailed about dying for love to the backdrop of tortured guitars. From another, a young woman jazz singer from Los Angeles belted out a more upbeat message.

Funky old shops displayed mounds of hand-hewn hardware or bundles of herbs meant to ward off any malady short of massive heart failure. Others offered high-tech and high-fashion goods in a laid-back manner that suggested they had been in business for two hundred years.

Coming back after so long, I found the party in full swing, with happy new notes to the old beat. The seventy-piece Oaxaca state orchestra, still up on the wrought-iron bandstand where it has played for 134 years, blasted brassy Rossini across the zocalo. I sat next to a dour Mixtecan Indian in homespun and a straw cowboy hat. His substantial wife, wrapped in a woven *huipil* of many colors, smiled indulgently at passing tourists who wore considerably less.

And, smack in the center of it all, those spiced chocolate smells wafted from the corner of Mina and Casas.

At Chocolate Guelaguetza, I found León Pedro Cortés Zacarias grinding chocolate exactly as he had for most of four decades. At sixty-eight, he was theoretically retired. But he was reluctant to give up the heady aroma of warm fresh chocolate oozing from the old metal mills. Cortés had a bristly gray mustache and wrinkles around his eyes that suggested years of good humor.

"No, this is how we've always done it," he replied when I asked if the process had changed over the decades. He seemed amused by the question. "If people like it this way, why do anything different?" Except for electricity, which powered the rubber belt that turned old stones inside in the mill, not much had changed since his ancestors made chocolate for the Mixtecan contemporaries of Montezuma.

Seven mills stood in a row like old-style job printing presses. They would probably do fine with corn, for which they were designed, but cacao came out as coarse as the granular sugar that went in with it.

The process is simple. A miller dumps everything into a metal hopper at the top of the ungainly apparatus. After a brief bit of noise, dark brown chocolate softened with its own cocoa butter oozes out the bottom onto a short semicircular chute and slides into a tin pan. That's it.

Most customers tell the miller how much sugar and cinnamon to put into the mix. Some people also ask for vanilla. The standard order is two and a half kilos of sugar for a kilo of cacao beans. Those who prefer their chocolate "semi-bitter" cut the sugar down to two kilos.

As Cortés explained the proportions, I thought briefly of the French chocolate purists who insist that 5 percent sugar is heading too far into sweetness. I asked for only a kilo and a half of sugar with my kilo of cacao. It still came out cloyingly sweet, coarse enough to sand a plank.

People usually pay a handful of pesos per kilo and walk away with brown sludge in a transparent plastic bag. For deluxe service, they can wait half an hour for their chocolate to be molded into those pucks I saw in Puebla. Hardly anyone eats the chocolate. Instead, it is dissolved, spun rapidly with water or milk in a clay pitcher, a *jarro chocolatero*.

Oaxaca has at least 150 small mills to choose from, but none is like Chocolate Mayordomo. Like all the others, it started as a shop-front family operation. But it expanded rapidly into a local empire that ships its products north across the border and beyond. It is the obsession of Francisco Flores Concha, a silver-tongued swashbuckler straight out of an old Pancho Villa movie.

We found Flores's secretary in a cubbyhole office, which rented its computers to passersby in search of Internet access. In the time it took the secretary to track down her boss, Minerva checked her e-mail and launched her mother into the brave new world of the Web.

The secretary fixed a 3:30 p.m. meeting for the next day. That left

Estela and me time for a quick two-hour lunch beforehand. We showed up at the main shop as instructed, but no one knew where Flores was. He would turn up eventually, we were assured. An hour later, the manager bundled us into a taxi. Flores and his wife were awaiting us for lunch at a restaurant across town.

If these scrambled plans bothered Flores, he did not let on. This was Mexico. We settled in for a second meal that turned into a four-hour, mezcal-lubricated discourse on the glories of Oaxacan chocolate.

My notes grew steadily less legible as the meal went on, but most of what I remember was flamboyant flimflam. Mexico's army is great, Flores explained, because it has so many Oaxacan soldiers whose diet is corn and chocolate. Mexican cacao is superior to any other because of its pure origins. Chocolate cures cancer. Europeans, and most especially the French, are mad for his Mayordomo chocolate.

"Oaxaca is really the center of chocolate in Mexico, and our moles are much richer than the ones in Puebla," he said. "What kills us is the distance. Puebla is closer to Mexico City, so it got all the attention."

Warming to the subject, Flores offered a popular verse, playing on the way Mexican chocolate is ground on a metate and stirred with a stick spun between open hands:

> So holy is chocolate,
> That you make it on your knees;
> You mix it with palms together
> And you drink it looking at heaven.

Flores had worked for a small chocolate maker until 1990. Going off on his own, he opened Mayordomo as a small shop, like all the others, and then built it into an empire. He has ten outlets in Oaxaca and elsewhere in Mexico, with others in Los Angeles and Chicago. His factory at the edge of town turns out six tons of chocolate a day, working two twelve-hour shifts. At each store, employees in brown baseball caps and yellow shirts scurry around to serve the Mexican regulars and enthusiastic tourists who throng the counter.

At his favorite hangout, the store on the corner of Mina and Casas,

I watched Flores enthrall a crowd of first-graders on a school outing. Each left with a chocolate-smeared smile. Unlike Oaxaca's other no-frills chocolate mills, the place is decorated with cacao pods hanging in nets and a mural in vivid colors showing Indians harvesting a stylized tree with a symbolic snake coiled at its roots.

Mostly, I wanted to see the factory, and this would not be easy. No way, Americans who did business with Flores had warned me. I'd have a better chance penetrating Mexico's intelligence headquarters.

Flores never said no. It just did not happen. But one night I caught him in an ebullient mood. It was the company's anniversary, and he had brought cake—chocolate, in fact—for the staff at Mina and Casas. At one point, he threw an arm around me and announced, "This man has come all the way from France just to see Mayordomo." Soon after, he introduced me to an aide, who told me to come to the shop the next morning at 8:30.

When I appeared on time, my friends of the prior evening shrugged noncommittally. The appointed guide had come and gone some time ago. Maybe he would be back. Then again, maybe not. Flores showed up at 11 a.m. and found me still there, my usual sunny smile fast fading to a glower. Fifteen minutes later, I was at the gates.

If the Mayordomo factory held some secret mystery, I didn't find it. Luis Hera, the manager, met me with some wariness. But soon his good humor and professional pride kicked in. We followed his beans, in bags from Tabasco and Chiapas, along conveyor belts to the roaster and then into huge grinders. Essentially, it was a king-size version of all those little mills in downtown Oaxaca.

Hera's plant was clean and efficient. He led me upstairs to his stocks of mole makings—bundled chilies, sacks of nuts and seeds, and all the rest. The final product, packed in glass jars, was surprisingly good for factory-made mole.

On the way out, I found a surprise. Tucked among the grinders and ovens, a conching machine paddled molten chocolate slowly back and forth. The process takes days. It breaks down particles and releases harsh flavor elements, producing a smooth texture for fine confection. I had been told no one in Mexico conched chocolate.

"This is our special stuff," Hera said, happy that I had noticed it. "We make it with vanilla." He handed me the finished product, a flat yellow box wrapped in cellophane. It read, "Mayordomo Chocolate, the sweet gold of Oaxaca."

Later, I tasted it. The chocolate was smoother than the rest. If it would not sand a plank, however, it would certainly buff a fingernail. Because of all the granulated sugar, it crumbled when I bit into it. Conched or not, this chocolate was for whipping into a frothy drink. And that was oddly comforting. In a place that revered its old ways, not much had changed over five centuries. Even if Montezuma might have preferred hot pepper to all that sweetness, he would have felt right at home.

*C*hocolate runs so deep into the roots of Mexico that its role today seems impossible to define. For help, I turned to Laura Esquivel, whose book *Like Water for Chocolate* captured the elusive Mexican spirit. The novel is not really about chocolate. It is the story of a young woman, the daughter designated to care for her parents and siblings while her sisters find husbands to marry. At her stove, simmering under surface cheer, she plots revenge built on her culinary craft.

When I finally reached the author by telephone, after tracking her without success across two countries, I asked why she had chosen her title.

"It's a very old expression, I think from colonial times, for when someone is so angry that they are about to boil over but are still contained," she said. "This is how you heat water for chocolate. It bubbles at the edges."

That summed up Mexico neatly enough. As a final step, I decided to find a modern yet traditional kitchen to see how the old chocolate roots were weathering the twenty-first century. This, of course, was another challenge. I was after precise recipes. And when it comes to preparing complex dishes by the numbers, about the last person to talk to about Mexican cooking is a Mexican cook. But then I found Iliana de la Vega.

Iliana owns El Naranjo restaurant in the heart of Oaxaca. The name means "orange tree," and, with potted citruses in a glassed-in courtyard, tables are set in a pleasant orangerie. The draw is not décor, however, but Iliana's style of cooking.

"I am very Mexican, and I love my country," she said. "I'm not about to do anything radical, like putting red wine in mole. But I want to do my own thing, which is not everything exactly as my mother did. People here are afraid of evolution. You can improve recipes as long as you are respectful of the basics. If you talk to me about authenticity, I don't know what you mean. If you say tradition, then I'm with you."

When she makes chiles rellenos, for instance, Iliana sneaks in hints of sweetness and fire, experimenting with different flavors she finds in the markets. Some diehard Oaxacans cry heresy. But it is wise to reserve a table early in high season.

Iliana bans lard from her kitchen, preferring instead to use a neutral vegetable oil. Even an admirer such as Rick Bayless, the Chicago chef whom many Americans regard as the arbiter of gringo-friendly Mexican cooking, fights her on this point. But there is something comforting here. Wherever you stand on the question, lard or no lard is not a bad controversy in a world that faces larger issues.

One morning I joined Iliana's cooking class; it was *mole coloradito* day. Smoky Oaxacan-style *pasilla* chilies set the tone. But, just as in Puebla, one ingredient quickly followed another and lost itself in a complex and balanced blend. At the end, a dash of chocolate brought it all alive, adding a touch of sweetness and a sharp whiff of honest Mexican roots.

Back in France, I tried to duplicate the blend and gave up with a frustration I found oddly reassuring. Some things aren't meant to be duplicated or transplanted. I had the recipe down pat. But the trick was in fine touches, such as wild avocado leaves that grow in the Oaxaca valley. That, and a thousand years of practice.

# Chapter 5

## THE BITTERSWEETEST TOWN ON EARTH

aul Kay, charging toward his second birthday with the chipped teeth of a devil-may-care toddler and a sunny grin for just about everything, frowned at the six-foot-high silver foil blob with a long white tag on top. As it walked unsteadily his way, gloved hands extended, Paul stepped back and plumbed his embryonic vocabulary for comment: "Don't like that Kiss."

Chocolate is one thing, young Paul figures, and he loves it in just about any form. Still, he prefers not to be mauled by ambulatory candy.

I had taken along Paul and his six-year-old brother, Louis, to Hershey, Pennsylvania, as expert witnesses. If Mexico was where chocolate was first treasured, this was where the world's richest, most can-do nation had taken it after four millennia of evolution. Since I think Hershey's chocolate tastes like sugared wax, the end result of monster mass production with all corners cut, I recused myself from pronouncing on the most popular chocolate in America. Their parents—my sensible nephew Henry and his sensible wife, Beth—came along as friends of the court.

After two days of gorging on milk chocolate and attempting to digest it while lurching around on Hersheypark roller coasters, we thought the verdict seemed clear. Who cared whether chocolate snobs preferred something that suggests the presence of quality cacao nibs elaborated by skillful artisans? After a century of genius branding, Hershey's was as American as Old Glory. It was not the chocolate itself but rather the whole idea of chocolate that Milton S. Hershey sold to a vast nation.

In the Pennsylvania Dutch farmlands around Harrisburg, the plucky son of a ne'er-do-well Mennonite dreamer still looms in legend and lore. And, I found, tracing the Hershey mystique to its roots in reality and tracking its evolution reveals as much about the United States as it does about chocolate.

Only days after our July 4 visit in 2002, we realized that Paul might have sensed an unwanted goodbye Kiss. Word leaked out that the guardians of Hershey's legacy were putting his dream on the market.

*B*orn in 1857 on his family's homestead farm, young Milton Hershey had no taste for scrabbling in the dirt. From his first years, he was torn between a no-frills mother, a frugal minister's daughter who wore a white prayer cap under a black bonnet, and a Shakespeare-loving father who dismissed his dour Swiss Mennonite fellows as sticks-in-the-mud.

Milton apprenticed as a printer and hated it. He went west to Denver to follow his father but found the rough and raucous city in the midst of a post-boom bust. Back east again, he built up a candy business in New York, which collapsed when his father, Henry Hershey, showed up with grandiose ideas. Milton lost money borrowed from his aunt and for a while survived as a manual laborer. In Philadelphia, he opened a sweet shop that did fairly well until his impractical father showed up once again.

The young man returned home to central Pennsylvania and started a caramel factory in Lancaster. While out west, he had learned to make caramels rich and chewy, with a longer shelf life, by adding fresh milk instead of the wax and tallow that his competitors still used. But he needed capital. One day, a visiting Englishman placed a huge order to sell in London. Hershey went to the bank. He borrowed seven hundred dollars over ninety days, but when the due date arrived he could not repay it. Instead, he asked for another thousand dollars. It was then that an English banker named Frank Brenneman changed the course of American confectionery history.

Brenneman followed his instinct and paid a call on Hershey's plant. He was so impressed that he put the loan in his own name, knowing the bank would otherwise refuse it. Barely a week before the money had to be repaid, the Englishman paid his bill in full. Hershey's Lancaster Caramel Company was launched. It expanded to four plants and a retail store in New York. At thirty-three, its barely schooled proprietor was rolling in money, touring Europe for months at a time and returning with enough art treasures to fill his grand new house.

At the 1893 Columbian Exposition in Chicago, a sort of world's fair, Hershey came upon the booth of J. M. Lehmann, who built chocolate-making equipment in Dresden. He smelled the roasting cacao beans and watched as Lehmann hulled and ground nibs into the heady syrup known as chocolate liquor. Lehmann added sugar, vanilla, and more cocoa butter to form a velvety mass he poured into molds. Milton Hershey tasted his first chocolate bar.

Hershey bought Lehmann's entire display and shipped it to Lancaster. Hershey Chocolate Company set up shop in a corner of the main caramel factory. Official company history has it that the intrepid founder proclaimed at the outset something like "Caramels are a fad; chocolate is forever," and plunged into his new métier. There is more to it than that.

In 1898, a decade after the caramel factory took off and five years after his chocolate epiphany, Hershey married Catharine Sweeney, his beloved Kitty. He went on a long break from candy. Kitty, an Irish Catholic beauty with lush dark curls and a sparkling smile, loved to entertain. Even more, she loved to travel. Together, they toured Europe, South America, and the Orient.

Joel Glenn Brenner, in *The Emperors of Chocolate*, digs deeply into why Hershey set his next course. True, she acknowledges, chocolate was hardly known in America, and it offered the master innovator-creator a blank canvas. Milton Hershey knew it would be wildly popular. But at the same time, he was caught between his feuding mother and father. To ease the growing tension, he decided to sell his candy business and take his wife far away from Lancaster.

Hershey sold the company for a million dollars in 1900 at a time when $950 was a decent annual wage. He sailed off with Kitty for what was planned as a lifelong cruise around the world. Before long, he turned back.

"It wasn't chocolate that beckoned him to return, however," Brenner writes. "It was the voice of Henry Hershey still rumbling about in Milton's head—the voice of a dreamer who had seduced Milton, the child, with fantastical visions of Eden."

That million dollars could bankroll any dream. "But," she concludes, "he wasn't about to reinvest that money in business; his vision was an industrial utopia, a real-life Chocolate Town, where anyone who wanted a job could have one, where children would grow up in celery-crisp air, where mortgages would dwindle in perpetual prosperity. Clear water and clear consciences. This was Hershey's vision of home *sweet* home."

*P*eople born long after Hershey died in 1945 are raised on the old stories. Soon after leaving Pennsylvania, I ran into Miriam Weaver, who wore her Mennonite lace cap amid the elaborate hairdos at the New York Fancy Food Show. With her husband, Paul, she runs a nut company in Ephrata, which is part of Hershey's magic kingdom in Derry Township.

"He is very much loved," Miriam said. "He really built the town." Paul nodded vigorous assent. His own great-grandmother was a Hershey cousin. "He gave a lot to the community," Paul said. "He always thought about people. Have you seen the hotel restaurant? He designed it so that no one would have to sit in the corner."

Hotel Hershey was inspired by the Mediterranean palaces that Milton and Kitty frequented on their grand tours abroad. When most of America scaled back in fear during the Great Depression, Hershey blasted forward with new projects to buoy spirits. He imported Italian stonemasons and hired an army of local workers. His architect studied a postcard Hershey gave him. The result is fine Americana: a Europeanesque hodgepodge of Italy, Spain, and Greece.

Manicured gardens frame a splendid reflecting pool. The spa offers baths in—what else?—foaming chocolate milk. In the Iberian Bar, by a walk-in fireplace under high ornate ceilings, guests can light up cigars in chairs where Hershey chain-smoked his Cuban Corona-Coronas. In the kitchen, Rory Reno, the self-taught chef, tries to blend old-world cuisine with the local spirit. One specialty, which I neglected to try, is *foie gras au chocolat*.

The hotel's crowning touch is its dining room, a grand circular hall with towering windows and glass walls all around. Hershey liked to look outside while he ate, the story goes, and he had the room designed so that everyone in the house could share his pleasure.

This was Hershey's way. True enough, he saw greater profit in a satisfied workforce. But the town seemed happy enough with his largesse. He provided free medical care, subsidized electricity, water, trolley service, a theater, a dance hall, a swimming pool, a junior college, and a hockey arena. He ran the town's department store, the pharmacy, and—a mixed blessing—the newspaper. He built homes for executives and workers, each different in design to avoid the look of a company town.

At the heart of it, Hershey Park was a great swath of green, with an outdoor bandstand where employees' families and townsfolk spent summer evenings enjoying pleasures at the limits of Mennonite license.

Kitty died in 1915, only forty-two at the time, and Hershey spent thirty years mourning her. He gave his mansion to the freshly formed Hershey Country Club, keeping only two upstairs rooms where he sat for hours at a time smoking Corona-Coronas and playing chess with an old friend.

The old chocolate factory itself is something to see. Structural steel and metal siding make up the working part, but the front end, facing the town, was built of cut limestone block that gives the place an air of old Jerusalem. Two smokestacks rise high above the row of cacao silos, proclaiming a prosperity that is visible for miles.

Of all of his projects, the school Hershey founded for troubled orpans was his real love. Kitty had come up with the idea. The couple deeded 485 acres of farmland, together with their homestead, outbuildings, and livestock, as the nucleus of what was to be a model institution for scores of underprivileged boys.

Three years after Kitty's death, Hershey quietly signed over his entire fortune to the Hershey Trust to keep the school going. The gift included not only thousands more acres of land but also his stock in the company, worth more than $60 million. At sixty-one, with two and a half decades left to live, Hershey had given away everything he had. Five years passed before *The New York Times* got wind of it.

Today the town's main attraction is Hersheypark, a modern-day version of the old patriarch's gardens. Hershey had offered boat rides and then a wooden roller coaster, which still holds its place among the metal monsters of a new age. But now, fenced in behind ticket booths, it is something entirely different, reflecting an America that likes its attractions big. Hershey Entertainment and Resorts Company manages the mystique for two million visitors a year.

Towering flumes send delighted kids and terrified parents looping through the air before plummeting into pools of water. On the Roller Soaker, spectators below can blast away with water cannons, dousing people in the open cars above. There are uncounted places to load up on fat and calories. Souvenir shops squeeze the last drop out of the Hershey motif.

At Tudor Square Mercantile Company, a ye olde schlock shoppe by the main gate, I found Erma Morgan running the cash register. She was on the late shift, folding sweatshirts and chatting happily with customers. Erma had spent most of her eighty-seven years within a buggy ride of Hershey but still spoke English with the hammer-edged accent of Pennsylvania Dutch. That is, German.

"I like it here, and I like coming to work," Erma said, pausing for an indulgent glance when some kid knocked over a tall stack of books. But, she added, she sure missed Mr. Hershey.

"If he came back today, I think he would take a look and leave right away," she said. "He was a simple man who believed in doing things for people, and they did things for him. He never did any advertising, and he made all the money in the world. Everyone liked him a lot. He never snubbed anyone. That was the whole atmosphere around here. He always came out and talked to the working people. They were his pride and joy."

Erma also missed the old park, where people strolled and danced and saw their friends. "Well," she concluded, "maybe it's not better for us who remember the old park, but maybe it is for the younger ones."

A short walk away, Beth Kreider scurried about with a walkie-talkie mike pinned to her collar as she found seats for hungry crowds at the Chocolate World restaurant. At seventeen, she was seventy years younger than Erma. Training as a dancer, she said she might travel with a ballet company but was not eager to leave.

"I'm a purebred Hershey girl," Beth said. "This place is a little bubble. Everyone is so cheery. It's so clean. You don't see any litter. Education here is excellent. And people aren't fat. When I travel and see all these obese people, I wonder what everyone else eats."

But, she added, "it is really fading fast. Money has a way of changing people's minds and habits. I think Mr. Hershey would be very disappointed if he came back today and saw what we waste, what we spend so foolishly."

The park somehow retains some of its organic sense, kept clean by teams of custodians and watched over by roving junior executives in jackets and ties. Lordly oaks grow among walkways that in summer are ablaze in the pinks and purples of petunias spilling out of their hanging pots. Small sections offer impressions of Arizona's Sonoran Desert or the Everglades. There is a modest and tidy zoo. Atop it all, a monorail skirts the park's edge, giving visitors a good look at Hershey's original plant near the corner of Chocolate and Cocoa streets.

Kathy Burrows, a town native who reveled in her job as Hersheypark public relations manager, hustled between visiting Japanese television crews and rock stars arriving for nighttime concerts. She is often so busy she mutes the ring of her cell phone. But she believes the high-tech hoopla and commercial overlay are no more than a logical evolution of the old dream.

"All these people who say Milton Hershey would turn over in his grave if he saw this, I mean, gimme a break," she told me. "How do they know?"

That July, just after I visited, Hershey was likely doing backflips in his grave. His legal heirs, the trustees of his dream to use the profits of chocolate for social good, set about trying to unload the company. They controlled enough shares to do it. In "the sweetest town on earth," here was irony most bitter. It seemed as if those underprivileged kids—via the corporate board that was acting on their behalf—were running Milton Hershey out of the paradise he built for them.

The old man's magic had long since passed into the hands of Hershey Foods, a public company listed on the New York Stock Exchange. But in 2002 the Milton Hershey Foundation, which succeeded the old Hershey Trust, still had more than half of its holdings in Hershey Foods and controlled 77 percent of voting shares. For the foundation directors, selling in order to diversify was the next logical step in an inevitable evolution.

After Hershey's death in 1945, a series of corporate leaders clung to his old ways in the face of fierce new competition. They refused to advertise or even use modern marketing techniques to hold on to their markets.

Hershey's management could only grit their collective teeth at a popular jingle that Americans seemed to love: "The sweetest things on earth come from Mars."

The slogan was well chosen. Even today, when most people hear the name of America's other great chocolate empire, they think of a planet, not a family. The company built by Forrest Mars, Sr., and passed on to his sons and daughter, was the philosophical antithesis of Hershey's. Over decades, a single-minded sales force had muscled aside the old favorite in markets across the country. Mars was number one. But change came in the 1960s, when Hershey's hired away two senior executives, William Suhring, the head of marketing, and Larry Johns, head of sales.

In *The Emperors of Chocolate*, Brenner put it this way: "Together they introduced the aging, stately Hershey Chocolate Corp. to the cut-throat world of candy that Forrest Mars had created, where Willy Wonka is motivated by greed, rivalry, secrecy and paranoia and will do anything to get you to eat just one more of his chocolate bars."

As time went on, Hershey and Mars settled into a standoff that occasionally veered into mere gentlemanly competition. Mars, Inc., observed a stony silence on Brenner's reflections. With no stockholders to demand explanations, there was no need for comment. But later, a senior Mars executive told me with a merry laugh: "Let's just say reaction was mixed. A lot of what Brenner said was true. And some of it was exaggerated."

The *Forbes* roll of billionaires for 2003 listed Forrest Jr. and John, together with their sister, Jacqueline Badger Mars, as tied in the fifteenth place. Each was worth $14.5 billion, an increase of $5.5 billion over 2002. But all three have retired. The company is often known by its larger umbrella, MasterFoods. But those who run Mars still seem to enjoy the shroud of mystery.

Marlene Machuti, the company spokesperson, is amused when people note that the McLean, Virginia, headquarters is just down the road from U.S. Central Intelligence Agency headquarters. "Yeah," she said, "we're known as the candy equivalent of the CIA. Sure, we don't give public tours of our plant. But does anybody? Guests are in and out of here all the time."

Machuti pours passion into Mars's place in the chocolate galaxy. As a private company, it spends heavily on scientific studies, with laboratories that contribute substantially to the world's knowledge of chocolate. Its funding also supports rain forest research, which helps planters restore abandoned plantations, fight pests, and grow cacao of better quality.

Mars's all-chocolate Dove bar, in dark and light, has given Hershey a run for its money since 1992. And, after all, those lovable little M&M's are still the most popular candy in the world.

Still, MasterFoods lumps its chocolate products in the category of "snack food." Machuti speaks with equal passion about the Sheba and Whiskas so dear to my cat. Or Uncle Ben's Rice and the company's vending machine system. Hershey Foods is also a conglomerate. It is America's largest pasta maker, and it dabbles in restaurants and products far afield from its original purpose. But, in the end, America's chocolate icon is Hershey.

By 2002, when the great chocolate tremor shook central Pennsylvania, Hershey had spent thirteen years as the largest candymaker in the United States. It dominated 48 percent of the American chocolate candy market, with an ever-widening reach overseas. A barely evolved version of the old brown-paper-wrapped bar is still the company's flagship product. The Kiss, which dates back generations, is a major seller, as are Hershey's chocolate morsels, its baking chocolate, and those same cans of Hershey's Syrup that our grandparents used.

If less hermetic than Mars, and forced as a public company to reveal basic financial figures, Hershey Foods also chooses to operate in the shadows. In Milton Hershey's day, parents drove their kids across America to smell the chocolate up close at the 1,500,000-square-foot main plant. By 1950, annual visitors to the factory numbered in the hundreds of thousands. During the 1970s, Hershey Foods closed its doors. The company said that too many people dropped trash; that crowds traipsing through distracted workers; that traffic congested the town.

The unexplained reason was likely more significant: Industrial espionage is a curse of the candy business. Even the lovable Wonka fired all of his workers when competitors mysteriously copied his wondrous products. He had to import Oompa-Loompa pygmies from Africa to keep his secrets safe.

Brenner recalls how a few journalists were allowed inside the Hershey plant for a product launch in 1993. They watched Hershey's Hugs roll off the end of the line, but white plastic sheets covered all the machinery used to make them. At the New York Fancy Food Show, I ran into two gentlemen with Hershey Foods name tags and decided to try a shot in the dark. I outlined my purpose, suggesting it might be useful to have a look at the factory innards.

"You can't," one of them replied. "But have you been to Chocolate World?" I have to admit that my peal of laughter ranged deeply into the unprofessional.

Chocolate World was my nephew Louis Kay's favorite part of our trip to Hershey, Pennsylvania. We climbed onto tiny cars for a lurching ride through the chocolate-making process, past a colorful cardboard cacao plantation and into a comic-book version of a chocolate factory. Louis loved the short ride through a roasting oven, where the temperature rose to suggest reality. At the end, the car delivered us to what had to be the world's biggest candy store, with row upon row of every product Hershey makes and every sort of kitsch doll, mug, and T-shirt that marketing minds could devise.

In fact, that executive was probably right. Chocolate World was a useful insight into the corporate minds of modern-day Hershey Foods and the foundation trustees who minted money from childhood enthusiasms.

Trouble in Hershey went public early in 2002, months before word leaked of the sale. In the first strike in twenty-two years, workers protested cuts in health benefits by a new chief executive, an avowed cost-cutter and the first head of the company ever brought in from the outside. After more than a month, workers went back to their jobs. They kept the health plan but in exchange for other pay concessions.

The strike left a bitter taste, as labor trouble always does in Hershey. Back in 1937, a new union closed the plant with a sit-down strike over matters of seniority. That was during the Depression, when Hershey not only built his grand hotel but also financed the Milton Hershey School buildings and paid off all church mortgages from his own pocket. Thousands of angry townsfolk marched with signs that read, BE LOYAL TO MR. HERSHEY. HE WAS LOYAL TO YOU.

Hershey's original gift to the Milton Hershey Trust had grown to be worth more than $5 billion by 2002. The school had 1,200 students, from kindergarten to twelfth grade, no longer only inner-city boys and girls from broken homes. It spent $96,000 per year on each student, and did not suffer for it. The Milton Hershey School had a richer endowment than the University of Pennsylvania, Columbia, or Duke.

Defending their position on the sale of the company, foundation directors said their fiduciary duty required them to diversify holdings. Financial experts, they argued, advise that foundations should hold no more than 5 percent of any one company. Sound advice or not, that line of reasoning brought the town up in arms. In emotional conversations with reporters, people decried the idea of a Cadbury or Wrigley logo looming overhead. For many, everything around them of value traced back to one remarkable man and his chocolate factory. And Milton Hershey was not one to ask directions from his broker.

To most lovers of fine chocolate, Hershey's is nothing to fight over. Europeans tend to dismiss its taste with evocative words ranging from chalk to cheese. Some call it "barnyard chocolate." One grand old man of chocolate, Hans Scheu, a Swiss who retired as president of the Cocoa Merchants' Association of America before he died in 2004, termed it "sour" and "gritty," without the feel or smell of real chocolate.

Critics can get downright virulent. Émile Cros, a French cacao expert at the world-renowned agricultural center in Montpellier, CIRAD, commutes to Venezuela to help restore original strains of *criollo*. He is known for his sensitive taste buds. When I asked him for a single word to describe a Hershey bar, he replied, "Vomit."

Those sound like fighting words. Someone is obviously enjoying all the Hershey bars and Kisses that after all these years continue to sell in the millions. But this was not about national pride or cultural preference. The deeper I researched, the more I appreciated the pronouncements on inferior chocolate I kept hearing from high practitioners: It is all in what you let yourself learn to appreciate. Wine offers a clear enough illustration.

As a kid, I developed a fondness for Mogen David. After all, I could belt it down at my bar mitzvah, eight years ahead of the Arizona drinking age. It was only later that I picked up those overpowering notes of cough syrup. Now that I have spent some time in Burgundy, it seems plain enough that Morgon, let alone Montrachet, outranks Mogen David. This is not because the former is French. Even middling California wines put to shame most run-of-the-mill European *vins de table*.

Like it or not, Hershey's has its own distinctive taste. The beloved founder was no chemist, and he spent little time studying the experiments of others. Unable to learn the closely guarded secrets of the Swiss, he came up with his own trial-and-error formula for milk chocolate, which left a strong note of sour. His conching process, shorter than most, produced a peculiar grainy texture. He was generous with sugar but tightfisted with cacao, and he was not always picky about where he bought his beans.

But Hershey managed to inure a country to his particular style. For most Americans, Hershey is synonymous with chocolate. They still prefer it to anything else, regardless of what many might dismiss as European prejudice. They pour it on ice cream, flavor milk with it, and ingest bits of it by the handful.

The old man built his chocolate empire with care. Pursuing his philosophy—and assuring a reliable source of beans—he ran his own plantations in Cuba and elsewhere in the Americas. The poorest pod cutter was part of his extended family.

In the end, most defenders and detractors agree, one can only expect so much from anyone's industrial candy. At the mass-market level, things like shelf life, melting point, and that ever-popular watchword economics weigh too heavily in any decision.

Two obvious bidders for the company were among the corporate sharks that schooled around Hershey. Both were giant companies that grew from the backroom beginnings of single-minded men. There was Cadbury Schweppes, the British giant that emerged triumphant from an ugly chocolate rivalry between the Cadburys and the Frys, those two Quaker families in England. And there was Nestlé of Switzerland, the largest food company in the world, which was founded by the German pharmacist who invented milk chocolate in Switzerland alongside Daniel Peter.

Following the financial newspapers in the fall of 2002 was like watching the internecine perfidies of daytime soaps.

Hershey's asking price was reported to be $11.5 billion, which figured in a 10 percent premium over market value. It looked at first as if Nestlé and Cadbury Schweppes might jointly buy the company to carve it up. But Cadbury was in a bind. If anyone else bought Hershey, Cadbury stood to lose a $750 million windfall because it was stuck with a fourteen-year-old contract that allowed Hershey—even if its ownership changed—to sell Cadbury's Almond Joy, Mounds, and Crème Egg products in America.

Nestlé had done a similar deal for Hershey to market its KitKat and Rolo brands, but this contract stipulated that rights would revert if Hershey was sold. And that meant the company was worth a billion dollars less to Nestlé.

When the story broke, the likely buyers backed off a bit. Beyond the numbers, some European executives were not sure what to make of a little town that got so emotional over a simple commodity and a brand name. During the thick of it, a letter to a friend from Hershey Foundation board member William Alexander found its way into *The Patriot-News* in Harrisburg.

"The board is not committed to sell," Alexander wrote.

It is only one of several options being explored. Once and for all we are going to find out if anyone exists who will pay a sufficient premium to justify the sale . . . My best guess is that the supposed premium for control will be offset by discounts for the KitKat license and social constraints.

By "social constraints," Alexander referred not only to angry marches in the streets of Hershey but also to a political storm up the road in Harrisburg. Mike Fisher, the Republican state attorney general who was running for governor, filed a motion to block the sale, at least temporarily. As the defendant was a charitable trust, jurisdiction was under the Orphans' Court of Pennsylvania.

"We think it's time the court put a halt to this sale," Fisher said in a written statement. "We are concerned about the speed in which the Hershey Trust seems to be moving forward with their plans."

Richard A. Zimmerman, a former chief executive of Hershey, testified for the state. Any buyer would cut spending to make up for the cost of the purchase, he said, adding: "There's no doubt in my mind there would be some massive changes."

Foundation lawyers responded that although the trust might be registered in Pennsylvania, Hershey Foods was incorporated in Delaware.

The London *Times*, meanwhile, calculated the cost that Hershey's ghost would cast over the deal. Under generous employment conditions, 14,000 employees qualified for severance benefits that could add $400 million to the deal. Benefits were thought to give a broad range of workers up to three times their base salary for two years after a change in ownership.

And then there were passionate people such as F. Frederic "Ric" Fouad, the forty-one-year-old president of the Hershey School Alumni Association. Fouad, born in Chicago to Iraqi parents, visited Baghdad with his father in 1963 when not yet three years old. His father was shot and killed because, the family says, he was openly critical of the Iraqi government. His mother, an American, moved to New York but fell ill. Fouad, often alone, was a terror in public school. At the age of eleven, he ended up in Hershey, and his life turned around.

In interviews with reporters, Fouad left no doubt about how former Hershey kids viewed what he called a shameful scandal. He vowed to block any sale with all the resources he could muster.

In the end, the ghost of Milton S. Hershey prevailed. Buyers balked not only at the inflated price per share but also because of the controversy swirling about the company. Townsfolk kept up the pressure. Lawyers and regulators hovered in the background. Who could calculate the impact of a protracted struggle over an issue of such vague dimensions? Sale-minded directors threw in their cards. Ten members of the humbled foundation board resigned their seats. Another followed later. And fresh directors exerted unusual Hershey chutzpah.

New plans and products were announced. And then one night, New York City looked up to see HERSHEY'S blazing in lights in Times Square above a store devoted to all-American chocolate. A second huge retail store was planned for Chicago.

An energetic but unsuccessful lobby sought to sanctify the name Hershey by, after all these years, having it replace Derry as the township name. Regardless, they had made their point. Yet another Christmas approached with Hershey as America's synonym for chocolate.

The tumultuous candy war that autumn surprised a lot of people who had never given the subject much thought. For an industry that so heavily traffics in the word *sweet*, things can get extremely bitter.

As these were matters of food and world-shaping import, the formidable French daily *Le Monde* wrote a fitting epilogue in 2003, a full page that was headlined HERSHEY: LA VIE EN CHOCOLAT.

The writer, Sylvie Kauffman, noted that the school's new director was John O'Brien, of the class of 1960, who grew up with neither father nor mother.

She concluded:

On campus, O'Brien, at work on his first day, visits his new domain among the students, busy in their deluxe ghetto, portable computer on his shoulder. Ric Fouad foresees going back to being a lawyer after three years "of a crazy man's life." A bus marked "Christian Tours" disgorges visitors in front of the Chocolate Museum . . .

And everyone in this small world is stocking up with chocolate for the holidays—only Hershey's. Michael Weller, alumni director, takes three bars from his drawer; they owe everything to this chocolate. It may not be the best in the world, but who dares to say so? This is still Hershey's best-kept secret.

# Chapter 6

## THE CHOCOLATE COAST

*A*s I sped down a jungle road at the edge of a West African rebellion, I caught a glimpse of twisted, lichen-blotched branches poking out from under a canopy of leafy hardwoods, banana and kola nut trees crowded in among them. Tangled vines on the ground gave the impression of virgin rain forest. No sign or structure suggested otherwise. But it is hard to miss a cacao plantation.

My discovery was no accident. I had gone to Ivory Coast to find out what war might do to the world's principal cacao crop. Fine chocolate depends mostly on pampered beans from small-production plantations in South America and Madagascar. But that was a small part of the picture. The big factories, like Hershey, consume nearly a million tons a year of *forastero* from West Africa's chocolate coast.

Not far from Yamoussoukro, about ninety miles north of Abidjan, a narrow dirt track took me to a clearing flanked by a ramshackle hut. Léopold Ouegnin emerged to see who had come to call. At forty-two, with a tall hulking frame and a limp, he looked like a gentle boxer who had had enough of the ring. He wore faded shorts and the remains of a football jersey. Unperturbed by the surprise visit, he sat me down under a straw lean-to for a palaver.

We spent the afternoon together, but a quick glance around revealed a single image that said it all:

Back in the trees, a '57 Chevrolet sat on blocks in the sun next to a '56 Rambler. Rust had eaten gaping holes in each. Both were gutted, with snarls of wires where the engines had been. A charcoal brazier had replaced the backseat of the Rambler, and chickens squatted in the Chevy. When Ouegnin's father grew cacao in the late 1950s, a single good year could buy you a Detroit sedan with a radio, whitewall tires, and all. In 2002, Ouegnin had a bumper crop. The world price was higher than it had been in decades. And he would at least earn enough to replace the broken straps on his clapped-out leather sandals.

Since this was Ivory Coast, the source of nearly half of the world's cacao, that seemed an alarming state of affairs.

In the best of circumstances, an Ivorian cacao farmer is lucky to earn one-hundredth of the price per pound that the chocolate in his beans eventually fetches from retail shoppers at the highest end of the line. When he is stuck in a remote jungle at the mercy of rapacious middlemen and a corrupt class of civil servants eager for their own taste of the government's cut, this gulf widens considerably.

Damned bad luck had dumped a civil war at Ouegnin's doorstep on October 1, by coincidence the first official day of the cacao harvest. Seasonal workers from neighboring Burkina Faso (the former Upper Volta) were scared off by antiforeigner diatribes. Even where farmers picked their own cacao, few truckers were prepared to risk roadblocks to collect it. On top of all this, the chaos of African revolution had shut down banks, and no buyers had cash to pay for sacks of beans.

But it was always something. The small producers who grow most of the national crop have suffered decades of exploitation. They depend upon Lebanese brokers and giant multinationals to carry their cacao to a tough world market of which few have much understanding, let alone any control. And worse, price policy is set by intermediaries who manage to pocket a substantial cut without doing much of the work.

Ouegnin detailed his woes with the stoic air of a man used to annual disappointment.

"Sometimes we do all right," he said, politely skipping over the financial details. "All right," I was able to determine, meant he could pay his bills, buy a few essentials, and send money to relatives who looked after his kids in school at Bouaké, a hundred miles to the north. "And sometimes we have trouble."

Ouegnin spoke the perfect, mellifluous French he had learned in school and as a professional soldier in an army that sent its officers to military academies in France. As a youth, he had had no intention of growing cacao.

"When my father died, I decided to come back here and take over the plantation," he said. "Who else would do it? And really, it's not such a bad life. We're far from the city's miseries. Who needs all that crime, traffic, craziness? When I go to Abidjan, I can't wait to get away. Here, it's always quiet and peaceful."

Looking around his little compound, Ouegnin concluded, "After all, here you decide what you do with your day."

Up to a point. Even without war in the neighborhood, he had little time for lounging in the bush. He owns 120 acres in all, 35 of which are planted with cacao. The rest are in coffee, another demanding crop. That comes to about twelve thousand cacao trees, each of which he knows personally. With no money for machine-driven equipment, and little with which to hire extra hands at harvest time, he barely keeps up by working six days each week, from first light to nightfall.

Cacao farming is hard enough on orderly plantations, where crews can work methodically, with some gasoline-powered help and facilities for drying the beans. For dirt-poor African farmers, conditions range from primitive to prehistoric.

Not that Ouegnin was complaining. The plantation seemed to amuse his philosopher's soul. As he trotted through the underbrush in his broken leather flip-flops, for instance, he chuckled when I asked about snakes.

"Oh, yeah," he said, "we have them all. Green mambas, black mambas, the Gaboon viper." Either mamba is deadly, but that particular viper's bite is enough to kill a man before he could find his car keys, even if his car had an engine. Or if a doctor lived anywhere within reach.

"We keep some herbs around that are supposed to be good for snakebites," Ouegnin said, chuckling again as though he was not overly convinced. "You can buy serum to counteract snakebite, but who can afford that? It's cheaper to watch where you step."

I didn't have to ask about the mosquitoes that dive-bombed us as we walked. Eradication programs had all but collapsed, especially deep in the bush, where efforts were only spotty in the best of times. Now, virulent strains of cerebral malaria are endemic in Ivorian cacao country. Visitors can slop on repellent and take preventive antimalarial drugs. Africans, however, either get by on their low-grade immunity or die early.

Most of Ouegnin's trees, planted by his father, have reached their forty-year limit. He spends much of his time cutting shoots and nurturing young plants to replace trees he must uproot. In a country short of agricultural extension agents, his prodigious knowledge came the hard way. But it has its gaps. He grows two types of *forastero* varietals, which he refers to as "the Ghana tree" and "the other kind."

We stopped by an other kind, which Ouegnin had begun to harvest. He whacked open a yellow-orange pod so I could sample the juicy white pulp inside. It was as sweet and delicate as an Indonesian mangosteen, which is up there with black truffles and sevruga caviar as a taste for which I'd be tempted to sell my soul. I could see why marauding monkeys and bush rats could be a worse scourge to cacao growers than armed rebels.

Cacao trees produce pods all year long. Each takes six months to develop from a small white flower that sprouts on trunks and branches. On the West African coast, pods ripen in greatest numbers late in the year. The Ivorian harvest season starts on October 1, with a smaller advance crop. Work builds to a final flurry in early spring.

Ripe pods are sliced off with a sharp steel hook on a pole and are gathered in waist-high stacks. Within a few days afterward, each pod is cut open with a careful whack of the machete. If any of the forty or so beans inside is damaged, the whole batch could go bad. The beans and their sticky mucilage are then piled on banana leaves, which are lashed into an airtight bundle.

For six days or so, the tightly wrapped beans ferment. This process not only kills the tiny embryo in each bean but also begins the fermentation process that produces the flavor of cacao. When the banana-leaf bundles are unwrapped, the beans are a pinkish tan, with all of the mucilage dried away. Beans are then dried, and the fermentation stops.

Like nearly every other cacao farmer on the West African coast, Ouegnin dries his beans in the sun. He spreads them onto cement slabs in his compound, shooing away chickens and the neighbors' toddlers to make room.

Depending upon the weather, beans dry in six to nine days. By then, they are dark tan. Their moisture content has dropped from 70 percent to below a government-decreed maximum of 7 percent. In a final step at the plantation, the beans are inspected and then poured into jute sacks to await the buyers' truck. Sometimes farmers' cooperatives pick up the crop. Ouegnin sells his to a Lebanese dealer.

In theory, the rains are over by October. But that, of course, is a notional concept. Every night, whatever the weather, Ouegnin scoops up his beans and stores them under cover, safe from early-morning dew if not a surprise overnight downpour. And every morning, he studies the sky to determine whether he will spread the beans out again for another day of drying.

These early stages are fundamental to the eventual taste of finished chocolate. However much alchemy goes into the complex processing chain, no one can make good chocolate from bad beans. A careless whack of the cacao hook can damage beans inside a pod and trigger a tainting spoilage. As with apples and olives, a bad one can ruin the lot.

Nothing suggests chocolate in Ouegnin's jungle. The overriding aroma reminded me of my uncle's general store in upstate Wisconsin, a wheaty scent of Purina animal chow. Rotting husks added a whiff of putrid sweetness.

Unlike most everyone else in cacao-growing country, Ouegnin had actually tasted chocolate. "It was about ten years ago, I think," he said, trying hard to recall. "I had a piece of one of those chocolate bars made in Abidjan, in a blue wrapper. Pretty good. But we don't much go for luxuries out here."

It had occurred to me to bring a few Cadbury bars from a supermarket in Abidjan, but I thought better of it. Unless I also brought a portable refrigerator, they would have melted into a gooey mess by the time we reached the highway out of the city.

Driving back to town, I saw variations on the theme. Smaller producers simply spread their beans to dry on the edge of the tarmac, paying little attention to the black stains left by passing cars with leaky crankcases. If Ouegnin had built a life around his quality crop, others simply picked what they could in order to earn a few extra francs that would help them get through the year.

In the end, it really didn't matter who grew good cacao, and who did not, in Ivory Coast. Most of the crop got bundled together in freighters for shipment to Europe or the United States. Some of the big players, like Cargill, Archer Daniels Midland, or Barry Callebaut, did some basic processing; they separated out cocoa butter and cocoa powder. One small company made finished chocolate.

But this was for the mass market, different from what international traders referred to as "flavor cocoa." It was all about squeezing profit out of brute labor.

*In 2001, the labor behind Ivorian cacao began to make headlines around the world. It started with a brief documentary on Britain's Channel Four, produced by an independent company. A reporter interviewed boys as young as fourteen from Burkina Faso who had been taken by traffickers to Ivorian cacao plantations. At the end of the season, they said, they were refused pay.

In one piece of dramatic footage, a youth looked into the camera and said, "Whenever you eat chocolate, you are eating my flesh."

A four-part series ran in the thirty-two Knight-Ridder newspapers in America and was circulated to several hundred other subscribers to the chain's news service. The opening dispatch, by the Knight-Ridder reporters Sudarsan Raghavan and Sumana Chatterjee, began:

"There may be a hidden ingredient in the chocolate cake you baked, the candy bars your children sold for their school fund-raiser or that fudge ripple ice cream cone you enjoyed on Saturday afternoon.

"Slave labor."

The series said that 43 percent of the world's cacao came from Ivorian farms, and on some of them, "the hot, hard work of clearing the fields and harvesting the fruit is done by boys who were sold or tricked into slavery." Despite nuanced connotations of the term "slavery," the reporters were correct. But while the series mentioned "some" farms, it gave no indication of scale.

In a later article in *India Today*, the journalist Lavina Melwani, who knew both reporters, wrote:

"There are over 600,000 farms in the Ivory Coast, and the Knight-Ridder report found slavery on just four farms. Asked about this, Chatterjee says, 'We are not scientists or data gatherers or researchers—we are reporters. It's useful for the U.S. government and the chocolate industry to find out how widespread the problem is. Our role was to put a light on the problem that a lot of people were denying was going on.'"

As often happens in such cases, other newspaper and media reports quickly followed. Some gave unquestioning credence to vague estimates by international organizations. Many failed to note that indentured labor was even more common on coffee and cotton plantations.

*The New York Times Magazine* carried a heartrending story in February 2002: "Is Youssouf Male a Slave?" But editors had to follow it up with an embarrassed apology. The writer, Michael Finkel, admitted that Youssouf was a composite figure.

After the initial reports, journalists from *The New York Times* and *The Washington Post* traveled together for a week as far into the cacao belt as they could hike. Neither found more than a handful of youngsters who might have been brought by smugglers. In their separate dispatches, they concluded that the stories about child slavery were exaggerated.

Léopold Ouegnin had missed the details, but he knew of the furor over "the chocolate slaves" in Ivory Coast. Most alleged abuses were far to the west in the cacao belt around the city of Man, so he had no firsthand knowledge either way. But he was dubious.

"A kid can't do this sort of work, even if you want him to," he said. "I guess you can put him to work clearing brush and carrying things around, but growing cacao takes strength and size and experience. It is no different from anything else in the African bush. Children and old people help their families with the chores. Everyone does something if he can. But slavery?"

The disputed facts had no effect in dampening down reaction in the United States and Europe. Stinging rebukes from international organizations brought calls for a boycott of Ivorian cacao. One world-saving organization got so carried away that it announced on its Web site that 40 percent of the world's chocolate—that is, all the Ivorian cacao—was produced by child slaves.

Well-meaning activist organizations such as Global Exchange, a group of Americans who have performed admirable work, waged energetic campaigns against Ivorian cacao.

Governments issued statements. Trade groups took a stand. In a wired age, unchecked accounts flew around the Internet. One report of a report, relayed by Gambia Tourist Support, estimated that 90 percent of Ivorian plantations used slave labor.

The controversy was put into focus on May 31, 2002, in a Washington-dated Dow Jones dispatch by Elizabeth Price. It reported that the International Labor Rights Fund (ILRF) threatened legal action to require the U.S. government to consider a ban on cacao imports from Ivory Coast. In a letter to U.S. Customs Commissioner Robert Bonner, the ILRF demanded an official investigation and enforcement action under the 1997 Sanders Amendment to the U.S. Trade Act of 1930. This prohibited the import of products tainted by "forced or indentured child labor."

The ILRF had dispatched an economist named Marx-Vilaire Aristide to Ivory Coast. After two weeks, he concluded, "Child slaves are used on cocoa plantations all over [the country] without any observable programs to stop the practice." Aristide suggested the problem would be solved if large multinational processors offered to pay more for beans produced on farms certified free of indentured child labor.

Price added the other side of the argument, quoting Larry Graham, president of the Chocolate Manufacturers Association: "This petition is really counterproductive. There are 600,000 family farms in the Ivory Coast alone, and there is no evidence from anyone that [forced child labor] is going on in the vast majority of them." Graham added, "The few farms out there who are abusing their workers will do so if the price is high or if the price is low."

Price's report concluded with a remark from Bama Athreya, the ILRF deputy director: "Whatever the Chocolate Manufacturers claim to be doing about this, we cannot leave a problem as serious as child slavery to voluntary private efforts, particularly when there is a federal law on the books to combat it."

In August 2002, a broadcast by Mark Doyle, BBC's Africa affairs analyst, began, "New research says that reports of children being traded as 'cocoa slaves' in West Africa have been heavily exaggerated." He cited a detailed study by David Mobray of the respected International Institute for Tropical Agriculture in Nigeria. None of the more than two thousand child workers questioned said they had been forced to quit their homes.

I decided to look around for myself. Before leaving Paris, I asked a journalist friend from Burkina Faso, Habibou Bangre, to track down teenagers and young men who had just returned from Ivory Coast. Her range of interviews produced no dominant theme.

A seventeen-year-old named Adama worked for a cruel man who withheld water until the work was done. "I thought about leaving, but my employer blackmailed me," he said. "He told me that if I left he wouldn't give me the money I earned. At the end of the year, I was paid 500,000 CFA francs [about $2,000]. I could buy a bike and help my parents build their house."

But Amaidou Sawadogo, now twenty-seven, would go back like a shot if the security situation improved. He and his brother have worked on Ivorian plantations for more than ten years, with kindly bosses who gave them extra food when they worked well. Now Sawadogo has his own small plantation.

For me, the question was settled in a morning-long chat with Dominique Kramo, a young Ivorian who coordinates Red Cross help for kids in trouble. He works from a tiny ill-equipped office in Abidjan, struggling to do something useful for an enormous population of youngsters whose survival depends on what they can cadge or steal.

In fact, Kramo said, along with a traditional movement from Mali and Burkina Faso, organized gangs now traffic workers to Ivorian plantations. Some are children sent by desperate parents. Demand is highest on cotton and coffee plantations, he said. As Ouegnin noted, cacao farming takes more skill.

"The answer is to attack the overall economic conditions so that everyone can live a better life," Kramo told me. "I get crazy when I see outsiders who don't understand anything use a simplified approach. What happens then is that people don't buy Ivorian cacao, and the whole situation is worse for everyone, especially kids in a fragile position. We have enough problems as it is."


*T*he controversy is part of a far larger picture, a holdover from old European empires. France and Britain had each built a showpiece colony, side by side on the Gulf of Guinea. The French Ivory Coast was a wealthy expanse of plantations etched into rain forest and linked by all-weather roads to the glittering mini-Manhattan capital of Abidjan. The British Gold Coast was funkier. Accra, its capital, had the tin-sided, vine-choked feel of storybook Africa. But it also hummed with prosperity. Both had grown rich on cacao.

In the Gold Coast and Nigeria, Africans planted the first cacao plantations on their own initiative. In Ivory Coast, a French administrator handed out imported seed to farmers, but most resisted planting it. One early colonial report noted: "After much persuasion, they planted the seed, but such was their resentment at having to do so that they used to go out at night and pour hot water on it in the hope of killing it. Nevertheless, some of the seed survived and in due course cocoa became a popular crop."

The Gold Coast was set free in 1957 as Ghana, in a blaze of new-Africa fervor. President Kwame Nkrumah erected monuments with pharaonic panache. He built a grand port and filled it with Soviet ships bartered for cacao. He scrapped the Westminster-style parliament that Britain left behind and squandered London's other goodbye gift of a fat budget surplus. Nkrumah was soon overthrown. And over decades of military coups and thwarted elections, cacao plantations dwindled to a fraction of their former glory.

Ivory Coast was different. An upcountry paramedic with the title of doctor, Félix Houphouët-Boigny had a political party in place when Charles de Gaulle turned loose France's African empire in 1960. Some leaders of former French colonies asserted their new independence, as Nkrumah did. Houphouët-Boigny kept a shadow cabinet of French advisers. His currency, the CFA franc, moved in lockstep with the French franc. French military bases and a sweeping defense treaty spared the leader the cost of an army.

Houphouët-Boigny was a pragmatic man. As long as he remained in the pocket of Paris, his own pockets swelled to bursting. Cacao, his country's main crop, was good business. For years, Ivory Coast reflected light on the darkening continent around it. How could Africa be doomed with such a hopeful example?

Kids had their teeth fixed and went to school. A university turned out scientists and thinkers. French businessmen whisked up and down in air-conditioned elevators, each with fresh money or some new hustle for a fast-expanding economy. At night, Abidjan's golden youth joined European tourists for starlit dinners by the lake-sized pool of the Hôtel Ivoire. In poor parts of town, people ate spicy fish grilled at countless *maquis,* open-air restaurants. Dance clubs, awash in beer, throbbed until dawn. This was what people meant by "developing country."

But Houphouët-Boigny, obsessed with grandeur, seemed determined never to die. Rather than name a successor, he diverted yet more money from Ivorian cacao receipts and dwindling French aid. By the time he actually did stop breathing in 1993, well into his eighties, he had squandered millions on a tragicomic monument to himself.

The president's native village of Yamoussoukro is today still a village. But now it has a basilica with a marbled cupola that dwarfs the dome of St. Peter's in Rome. Gone gray in the tropics, it is nonetheless an emblematic white elephant to replace the long-gone pachyderms whose tusks gave the country its name. Four-lane freeways to nowhere, brightly illuminated at night, bisect virgin jungle and a few patches of squalid homes. Rooms stay empty in the towering hotel that InterContinental dropped from its chain. Few golfers brave the heavy hot air to play on its world-class course.

At the center of Yamoussoukro, a fortified fence, miles long, surrounds Houphouët-Boigny's palace and tomb near the old family compound. And in a greenish black moat, several hundred crocodiles of mystical repute guard the memory of Ivory Coast's aged king of cacao.

Fittingly enough, Yamoussoukro was where I went to cover the war. Ivorians were stunned that their peaceable approach to life had collapsed into bloodshed. But looking back, that seemed the predictable chain of events.

From the beginning, Ivory Coast imported labor to make the miracle work. Like most of Africa, the country was carved artificially from a patchwork of historic ethnic homeland boundaries, with frontiers dividing some tribes in two. Baoules and Betes from the south were the dominant ethnic groups. In the north, Djoula and Fulani spilled over from Burkina Faso and Mali.

The new constitution granted enough rights to citizens to establish a ruling class. Tribal preferences and personal ties did the rest. Soon many young Ivorians delighted in a common boast: We don't like to work all that hard; we're an intellectual people.

Over the years, people traveled easily across borders and worked wherever they were needed. When it was time to harvest cacao or coffee or cotton, migrant laborers streamed in and then returned home. Workers from countries to the north, as well as to the west and east, settled down as permanent residents. An accurate census would most likely show Ivorian-born inhabitants to be substantially outnumbered by people with roots in Mali and Burkina Faso.

By the time Houphouët-Boigny died, Ivory Coast was less of a country than a giant labor exchange with a privileged class defined by nationality. Like Tito in Yugoslavia, the old man had dealt simply with ethnic tensions: He banned any outward expression of them. But everyone knew what they felt inside.

As long as money came in to cover presidential checks, the lid stayed on. Cacao beans, however, can buy only so much splendor. Despite promising oil exploration offshore, Ivory Coast had nothing much to sell except what it grew. There was coffee. Palm oil, pineapples, and tropical flowers added something. The country also chopped down and sold most of its irreplaceable stands of tropical hardwoods, leaving soil erosion in their stead.

For serious looting, Houphouët-Boigny relied on French aid. Among other arrangements, a time-honored ritual ended each fiscal year: Ivory Coast came up short; the Élysée Palace wrote a check. The president also tapped private businesses wishing to operate in his patch.

A successor, Henri Konan Bédié, struggled to carry on the Ivorian Miracle. But France, adapting itself to a broader Europe and a different world, was losing interest in its former colonies. Other foreign donors curtailed aid. Too much of the money was disappearing into Ivorian cabinet ministers' bank accounts while the country slipped steadily backward. Bédié was overthrown on Christmas Eve, 1999. General Robert Guei, the coup leader, organized a rigged election, which he managed to lose. Laurent Gbagbo, who won, set about trying to rebuild Ivory Coast in his own image. It was not a very impressive image.

Gbagbo blatantly favored his own Baoule tribe and other southerners, alienating tribes in the north. In September 2002, he cashiered an army unit that had been Guei's personal guard. This happened at a time when the wider world was dividing itself into religious camps. Although it was a secondary theme in Ivory Coast, outsiders stirring up trouble made much of an explosive fact: southerners were mostly Christian, if not animist; and northerners, by a large majority, were Muslim.

Just about anyone could have predicted what would happen next. Chinua Achebe captured the situation in the title of a novel he wrote forty years earlier in Nigeria, farther down the Chocolate Coast: *Things Fall Apart*.

*N*ot long after I returned from my visit with Léopold Ouegnin, the child slavery business came up again. An Ivorian delegation of dozens was the biggest single presence at the 2002 Paris Salon du Chocolat. In a speech billed as a press conference, the minister of agriculture made an impassioned plea.

"You must help us to counter this slander which endangers our very livelihood," he said. "If there is slavery in the Ivorian plantations, then you are looking at a former slave." As a child, he explained, he worked on his parents' plantation for no pay.

He also strayed into a puzzling discourse on lecithin in chocolate, which had no particular connection to Ivory Coast. But the minister said nothing about why Ouegnin killed himself with work and still came up short.

Ivory Coast had just implemented a new system of paying for raw cacao. Instead of having to accept an arbitrary price fixed by the state, growers could ask for rates based on the cocoa market in London. In theory, they would now benefit when international rates soared. In practice, they seemed worse off than ever. On the surface, it looked as though government officials were more interested in their own perks and prospects. The Paris salon was my chance to hear them out.

The agriculture minister was little help. His prepared speech referred often to Ivory Coast's push for quality but said nothing about how anything would improve. Afterward, he answered my questions with polite generality.

At the Ivory Coast exhibit area, I found willowy women serving melted chocolate on bananas. Men in frayed straw hats played lively music. Answers were harder to find.

Finally, I cornered a grower who had strong government connections. It was early in the day, and the stand was otherwise deserted. After a few friendly questions, he got up and announced: "You are monopolizing my time." In West Africa, this translates roughly to "Give me something if you want to talk to me."

The Ivorians were beginning to baffle me. Half the Abidjan cacao hierarchy had flown to France to explain their position. The minister had pleaded for international understanding and for help in putting down the rebels. World prices were at unparalleled heights, and Ivory Coast had a bumper crop. Chocolatiers in Europe and America were suddenly willing to pay high premiums for quality. So what was going on?

On the salon's last day, I was determined to find some explanation. I had joked around with the man in charge of a newly created government agency. His job was to see that growers got a good deal each season so that they would be eager to plant the next. I checked back every half hour, but he never showed up. Nor did any of the others. But what did I expect? It was a sunny Sunday in Paris.


*I*n 2003, I returned to Ivory Coast to track down some answers. By then the rebellion had spread. Along with the original insurgents who seized Bouaké and then took over the north, two separate groups had formed in the west. Both took wide areas of territory near the Liberian border.

France had sent twenty-five hundred troops to protect its citizens and keep what was left of its showcase ex-colony from collapsing. A rebel unit tested them at the outset and suffered thirty dead in the ensuing skirmish. All sides agreed to fly to Paris for peace talks.

This time I drove west to the grubby little port of San Pedro, through which 20 percent of the world's cacao is channeled each year. Houphouët-Boigny had built the port near a pristine stretch of lovely beach. A French couple run an attractive hotel on the water, but San Pedro is all business.

Trucks jolt down unpaved roads near the wharves, lurching over axle-breaking potholes. Halfhearted crews push containers around with forklifts. The wharf is big enough for two good-sized ships, but only one was in port, and no one seemed in a hurry to speed it on its way. The Ivorian army had set up positions in case rebels drove south. They exhibited no more zeal than the dockers.

The night I arrived, a kind local resident directed me to the Ivorian in charge of the Archer Daniels Midland processing operation. He was drinking beer with his pals. As I approached, he beamed as if a long-gone family member had walked back into his life. He had no idea who I was. That was simply African enthusiasm and good manners. When I announced my purpose, his smile lost several hundred watts. "I can say nothing about cacao, nothing," he said, polite but final.

Before going to San Pedro, I had phoned an executive of Cargill, who seemed pleased at the idea of a book on chocolate. He gave me a phone number for the plant manager in San Pedro. When I called, the manager, a Lebanese, cut off my first sentence. "I can say nothing about cacao, nothing," he said, nowhere near polite but decidedly final.

In San Pedro, I was at the Cargill gate before 7 a.m. When I dropped the manager's name, a guard let me inside to wait. The plant was simple enough, with a three-story tin-sided tower where workers processed cacao, separating cocoa butter from the beans and making powder from the remaining nibs. It was nothing to write home about. The manager arrived minutes later.

"I'm not going to lose my job for you," he said. This seemed a reasonable enough position, but I reminded him that his boss had sent me to him. "That is not my boss," he said. "You have to ask Mr. Winter."

The conversation did not improve. Finally he said, "If you want to learn about cacao, go into the bush and find someone who grows it." Then he popped the clutch and shot through the open gate.

That, of course, was the problem. I had found someone who grew cacao and, in far more gentle terms, he had explained that he was starving to death because of all the men in the middle who made money that never managed to reach the bush. The reality was more complex, I knew. But what was it?

The next step, I decided, would be the Bourse de Cacao et Café (BCC). In French, the word *bourse* suggests a commodities market. But this one does not work that way. Instead, according to economic reporters who cover it, it is an elaborate and mysterious organization designed to suck money from the cacao business.

My only course, I knew, was to track down Tape Doh, a small man in a never-absent silly black hat, who was president of the BCC. Normally, he is in Abidjan. But French officials had organized weeks of peace talks in Paris. Since this meant a free trip to France, nearly fifty Ivorians connected to the cacao business had gone along for the ride. Doh and his entourage were among them.

I returned to Paris and learned that a journalists' organization planned a press conference with Tape Doh and a coffee person. They would explain the rebellion's impact on agricultural exports. Since I had to be in London at the same time, I dispatched a researcher. She would ask questions, make a tape, and set up an interview. Doh arrived an hour and forty-five minutes late, with two muscular cronies, and then dropped off to sleep. Reporters learned far more than they wanted to know about coffee. But my researcher got me Doh's cell phone number.

After twenty-five tries, I reached Doh. We fixed a meeting for the next day at 10 a.m. His hotel was an hour away, and I started early. This was an important meeting. Hadn't the agriculture minister pleaded with reporters to help Ivory Coast get through its crisis?

Doh had gone out shortly before I arrived, so I waited. At 10:30, the woman at the desk looked over with a smile. "You're not alone," she said before launching into an amusing account of how Ivorian cacao people seemed to do their business. Just in case Doh had an urgent emergency, I left a card. She must have forgotten to give it to him.

*I* had missed Doh's non-press conference, in fact, because I was at the cocoa exchange in London. Or rather, I was calling on brokers. In New York, the exchange still uses open outcry, as at the Chicago commodities market, where grown men in funny-looking colored jackets scream their orders. London is computerized. Brokers at half a dozen companies buy and sell at their desks.

Cacao traders are a serious-minded bunch who all day long watch reality dance across their screens in hard numbers. Each year the London market buys and sells 26 million tons. In fact, the same 3 million or so actual tons are traded back and forth.

Brokers might enjoy a *chocolat fondant* at dinner, but this is business. They dismiss as "flavor cocoa" the good stuff for which a limited number of chocolatiers are ready to pay an above-market premium. They trade a commodity, like wheat or pork bellies. Nondescript as these traders may normally be, their business can make headlines.

In 2002, Anthony Ward of the trading firm Armajaro cornered 7 percent of the world market in cacao, correctly, and lucratively, predicting prices would soar. Prices hit an eighteen-year high late, near $2,500 a ton, when news from West Africa suggested a disappointing crop. Chocolate manufacturers had stayed out of the market when the prices doubled over 2001. But then they ran desperately short. Ward is now known as Chocolatefinger.

I sat down with one trader, a charming Frenchman of twenty-five years' experience, who cut rapidly to the heart of it. As he showed me how futures traded, his eyes constantly followed fast-changing figures down a dozen rows. "Look," he said at one point. "The spot price just jumped five dollars a ton."

He made a face when I asked about the Bourse de Cacao et Café and selected a diplomatic word for it: "Opaque." Like most of the Ivorian structure around it, he explained, its purpose was to feed off the system. The government provided farmers no subsidies or safety nets any more than it provided health care or pensions for factory workers.

Others in London, Abidjan, Paris, and Washington finally clarified the opacity. Ivory Coast's much-vaunted shift from an officially fixed price to open market rates came about because World Bank experts argued that it would be fairer to farmers. In practice, however, bloodsuckers in the middle simply found a different vulnerable spot on the neck.

At this point along the trail, I had begun to evolve Rosenblum's

First Law of Chocolate: The more someone refuses to talk about what he does, the more he is likely to be involved in a lousy product. Applying the converse of this law, I resolved to look for people who were happy to talk about what they did.

In the end, I finished my Ivory Coast research with a different Doh. After the Paris peace talks, which collapsed before the participants got home to Africa, the three rebel groups held a joint conference. I was interested in the leader of MPIGO—the popular Ivorian Movement of the Great West, which was in the heart of the cacao belt. To protect his family, he had chosen a nom de guerre: Sergeant Felix Doh.

Considering how heatedly he denied links to Liberia across the Cavally River, it seemed strange he had picked a name so evocative of Sergeant Samuel Doe, the mercurial young man who overthrew Liberia's president in 1980, plunging a peaceable country into murderous chaos.

The cacao crop was harvested and stored in warehouses, Sergeant Doh assured me. If successful negotiations dissolved the front lines, it could move quickly to ships at San Pedro. Farmers were eager to get back to business.

But things had already fallen apart. Paris newspapers carried front-page photos of women in tearful panic, cowering behind French troops who shielded them from rioters at the airport. Young Ivorians chanted at the departing French: "Go home and don't come back." Some would return, but Houphouët-Boigny's miracle was over.

Later, Nianzou Ano, a senior aide to President Gbagbo, confirmed for me Felix Doh's basic point: A huge amount of cacao was blocked in MPIGO territory. But Ano knew more about the business. Fighting had scared off small producers. Many had fled, and others were afraid to venture into their trees. The vital work of clearing and pruning was all but paralyzed. This portended future catastrophe.

Exactly as Ano had predicted, I saw months later, Ivory Coast's cacao production had begun to drop dramatically. Of the 1.3 million tons expected for the season ending in 2004, the total dropped below a million. In many areas, barely a tenth of what was expected showed up at the ports. And things were getting worse.

Irreparable damage had already been done, and Felix Doh's confidence seemed more like wishful thinking. Rebel administrators had priorities other than the complex business of storing and shipping cacao.

Meantime, "government-held territory" was not exactly under control. On the Cavally River, I had watched United Nations officials trying desperately to ferry Liberian refugees home after a decade of safety in Ivory Coast. Young Ivorians in fright wigs and Donald Duck masks, high on cannabis as well as newfound power, could torture or murder when the French were out of sight. If the situation was so bad that Liberians preferred their chances at home, peace was not likely to come any time soon.

Ivorian troops shot to death Jean Hélène, a reporter for Radio France International, in confused circumstances. Rebels killed two French soldiers. A peace agreement was once again falling apart.

I remembered when war shattered Sierra Leone, the diamond-studded country beyond Liberia along the West African coast. Suddenly Liberia, which has no diamonds, was a diamond exporter. It seemed as if Liberia, which produces almost no cacao, would appear mysteriously as an exporter of wayward beans. Then again, diamonds are forever. They can be shipped in a shirt pocket, no matter what mayhem rages around them. But as low-grade war settled in for a long stay in Ivory Coast, planters neglected their trees. Feeder roads were blocked, leaving harvested beans to spoil. Cacao, even Ivory Coast's mediocre cacao, is far less accommodating to turmoil.

When the 2004 season ended, London traders were caught off guard. Ghanaian planters, sensing a new opportunity to sell their best cacao, harvested a bumper crop. Exports rose from 497,000 tons to 595,000 tons in a year. Intrepid Lebanese trucked out most of Ivory Coast's cacao. The London price per ton dropped from a high of £1,503 in February 2003 to a low of £801 in March 2004.

But no one was betting heavily on the future.

In May, Rory Carroll of *The Guardian* reported on what he called the chocolate war around Broudoume, a microcosm of conflict across the cacao belt. Its causes were complex, but the result was clear: Indigenous Bete tribesmen attacked to take back plantations farmed by settlers from the north. Hundreds were killed, and thousands fled. Many of the Bete who moved in were inexperienced and unwilling to meet the trees' demanding needs. Almost immediately, yields dropped.

Meantime, in Abidjan, the Paris agreements fell apart. Opposition parties held what they called a peaceful demonstration on March 25. Government forces ended it by shooting at least sixty. French reporters said hundreds more were shot and hacked to death over the following days in revenge killings.

After a resounding United Nations condemnation, 6,250 U.N. troops headed to Ivory Coast to reinforce French forces, already swollen to nearly 4,500. Paris editorialists did not miss the significance of the date. It was ten years after genocide in Rwanda.

As for the system to compensate hard-pressed growers, any substantial reform seemed less than likely.

On April 16, 2004, Guy-André Kieffer, a French-Canadian freelance journalist who specialized in cacao, was kidnapped in Abidjan. He had just written yet another exposé on corruption in the cacao trade, this time about how government officials bought arms with export income meant for small-scale producers. In June, the Paris daily *Libération* devoted two pages to the missing Kieffer, referring to him in past tense.

"I'm getting sick of being a journalist," Kieffer had written a friend early in 2001. "I want to take some action to reform the cacao network so that small planters can finally make some profit." Later that year, the prime minister hired him to do just that. Only months later, after a ministerial shake-up, he was sacked.

Kieffer returned to journalism, using thinly veiled pseudonyms for his harsher attacks. He relied on good relations with Gbagbo for protection. Nonetheless, he sent his girlfriend home to Ghana for safety. Authorities threatened him with libel action. Finally, friends say, a wealthy Ivorian cacao czar offered him a substantial sum of money to find another topic. Kieffer turned it down.

## Chapter 7

## CLAUDIO DA PRÍNCIPE

When Claudio Corallo gets his abandoned cacao plantation back in shape—that is, after he reverses the ravages of nature, both human and mother, and accomplishes other assorted miracles in the jungle—he knows what coat of arms to put on the fine chocolate he plans to produce on his West African paradise island. "It will be an enormous cow pie, with flies buzzing around," he says. "What is more useful for anything that grows?"

A guffaw that punctuates his Florentine-flavored French suggests he is joking. Then again, Corallo is capable of just about anything. The point of his imagined logo is that the quality of chocolate depends not on any sleight of hand at the end stages, and even less on marketing, but rather on healthy trees that produce flavorful beans. He has not been to Hershey, Pennsylvania, but it is a safe bet that he would not like it very much.

Corallo is Crocodile Dundee, Gandhi-style, a slender man with amused eyes and short gray hair. When I met him at the Paris Salon du Chocolat, he was contentedly chewing on a half-smoked piece of soggy brown rope that turned out to be an Antico Toscano cigar. His self-effacing, gentle manner reveals a supreme serenity. Yet he lived for years growing coffee in the original heart of darkness, deeper in the Congolese jungle than even Conrad would go, facing down enough rebels and reptiles to terrify Tarzan.

When yet another war forced him to resettle, he chose São Tomé and Príncipe, the former Portuguese colony of two lovely islands in the armpit of Africa, just south of Nigeria. That was where African cacao was first planted, and Claudio resolved to restore its former glory.

"This smells like a wet horse, doesn't it?" he noted, striking a match to his cigar and adding notes of wet horse to the chocolate scents around him. By some miracle of the beatitude he projected, no one seemed to mind. He reached in the pocket of his red sports coat and produced a handful of roasted beans. "When cacao is good, you can eat it raw," he said. I peeled one and tried it. The crunchy dry texture took some getting used to, but he was right. It delivered an unadulterated hit of chocolaty flavor with an unmistakable hint of fresh olive oil.

Bits of Claudio's life came at me faster than I could absorb them. He had run a coffee plantation in the Bolivian highlands. He dug into the Tunisian desert doing something brave and strange. As we talked, he showed me a video of his version of the *African Queen,* built in Italy to link his remote Congo empire to Kinshasa, a thousand miles inland. Like the original, it could slip easily up narrow streams, under tangled growth. But Bogart's boat could not go from zero to thirty-eight knots in twenty seconds or cruise for twelve hundred miles without refueling.

We spoke in French, but Claudio also has perfect Spanish, Portuguese, and Lingala, the Congolese lingua franca. He never found a need for English.

I learned about Bettina, the beautiful daughter of a patrician Portuguese diplomat in Kinshasa who fell in love with him at fifteen. They married and went off into the jungle a day after her eighteenth birthday. Although Corallo grows coffee on São Tomé, he also has twenty thousand cacao trees at a century-old plantation on Príncipe, the smaller island to the north. He told me about the rich volcanic soils that nourish a superior cacao crop, and the innovative methods of processing the beans. It sounded like a happy counterpart to all of the mediocre cacao produced far away in Ivory Coast.

"You have to come down," he said finally. I went home and called my travel agent. A month later, he met me at São Tomé's little shed of an airport.

For a week, I watched Corallo blend science and art with simple humanity in the style of old-world geniuses who shared his Tuscan roots. His homemade fermentation boxes reminded me of the olive presses that Leonardo invented at Vinci. In fact, much of what he did recalled Leonardo. He brought a modern refiner from Spain and then reengineered it to his own demands. He deconstructed formulas no one had questioned for generations. Cow-turd label or not, Claudio da Príncipe seemed destined to make chocolate to remember.

*C*laudio left Florence for the Congo in 1974, at the age of twenty-three, as an eager young Italian aid worker with a degree in tropical agronomy. Before long, he realized the futility of aid projects that bring in unworkable outside ideas along with easy money that ends up in the wrong pockets. He tried being a coffee broker at one time, but he had no heart for the business. Then he decided to buy a plantation and produce his own coffee. Through force of will and against odds that would discourage any three men, he soon had a backlog of eager buyers in Italy.

A decent plantation is hard enough to establish when you don't have to sputter along for a thousand miles, dodging crocodiles and malarial mosquitoes, whenever you need to replace a busted widget. But Claudio had it worked out. He and Bettina spent up to two years at a time deep in their jungle, following the world outside with a short-wave radio antenna affixed to an eighteen-foot tower he lashed together in a weekend.

Claudio hunted meat for the table. Bettina learned another twenty ways to make pasta. "It got hard sometimes," he said. "Once I was in a little cabin fifty miles up a river from the main house and realized all I had to read was *One Hundred Years of Solitude*." That flashback brought a reflective cloud of wet-horse cigar smoke.

Bettina, locals said, was the first white woman who had ever lived in the region. For the births of two of their three children, she went to

Buenos Aires, where her father was the Portuguese ambassador. "I wrote her letters and gave them to a guy in a canoe, and they made their way to Kinshasa," Claudio said. "From there, they went into the post. Three months after I wrote them, they would appear in Argentina. None was ever lost. There is a respect for these things."

When his workers started to earn wages, he discovered they squandered them at a little settlement nearby, buying useless stuff from unscrupulous traders. So he instituted his own scrip: the soap standard. His monetary unit was a two-hundred-gram cake of Marseille soap, an item everybody understood.

Every day brought some new impossible challenge. When the head of the local riverboat mafia heard Claudio had planned to import his own craft, he tried to cut him off. Claudio finessed that problem with charm and diplomacy. A fanatic about anything that floats, he created so much excitement about his project that even his eventual riverboat competitors couldn't wait to see his boat in action.

One year, he produced 180,000 tons of coffee, but the world price plummeted. He lost $1.75 million. "If it had been my money, I could have shrugged it off," he said, "but all of it was borrowed." Somehow he made good on the loans.

"I took a loan for my boats of nine hundred thousand dollars from the African Development Bank, and I sent them into fits when I wanted to pay it back," he said. "They didn't know what to do. No one had ever done that before."

From the first days after Congolese independence in 1960, the former province of Kasai where Claudio grew coffee was plagued by rebellion and bandits. One day, he politely ran off his land a fearsome brigand known as Pire Kinois, who returned with a heavily armed gang.

"I spent the whole morning with an FAL jammed up my nose," he said. An FAL is a short, ugly semiautomatic assault rifle. But Claudio kept his cool. At one point, however, he was able to slip away for a moment to go into his house. "I had on shorts, and my legs were trembling so furiously that Bettina thought I was doing a mock jitterbug." By lunchtime, he and Pire Kinois were clinking beer glasses together.

*Kinois* means someone from Kinshasa, but Claudio still doesn't know if *Pire* is the local mispronunciation of *père*, "father," or if it means what it says in French: "The Worst."

Two separate times, marauding rebels overran his plantations. They took everything they could carry and left behind smoldering ruins. The first time, Claudio started again from scratch. The second time, he saw no sign that the rebels would melt away as they had in the past. His corner of the Congo seemed destined for endemic strife. He thought about Bettina and their three kids. The oldest, Ricciarda, was barely a teenager; already, she was as darkly beautiful as her mother. It was time to go.

Claudio recounts each of his tales with self-mocking humor, emphasizing his own terror and minimizing the danger he faced. The reality, however, is hard to miss. In early photos, he might be a Cinecittà matinee idol, with bushy chestnut hair, an Errol Flynn mustache, broad shoulders, and a dashing manner. Not that many years later, he is still a handsome man. But his close-cropped hair is steely gray. His features are drawn, and his weight is down after lengthy bouts of river blindness that nearly took his eyesight, dysentery, and several of the deadlier sorts of filarial diseases that decimate African communities. One morning, in a rare somber mood, he shook his head at the end of an anecdote. "You pay a price for this sort of life," he said.

His coffee plantation in Congo still haunts him. By the time he had to leave, he was boss of twenty-five hundred devoted workers and godfather to another four thousand of their family members. In his absence, the old crew keeps the trees healthy and produces a small crop that does not get to market. He is still owner, on paper, but it is still the tumultuous Congo. Not long before I met him, Claudio had managed to ship desperately needed supplies and a few luxuries to his workers. Rebels stole it all and, for good measure, beat up his foreman.

In those unusual down moments, Claudio allows himself a curse at the vicissitudes of life, but *"Madonna!"* is about as far as he will go. That, or *"Porca miseria!"* He ridicules churches and just about everything else about organized religion. But blasphemy is not in his nature.

When Claudio da Príncipe met me at the airport in São Tomé, he was guffawing happily, with a fresh Antico Toscano billowing a cheery cloud. He loved his cacao trees and was happy that someone had come to visit him. His tiny islands are another universe entirely from the Congo.

If São Tomé and Príncipe have plenty of malaria-bearing mosquitoes, bandits rarely hold guns to people's heads there. Neighbors might be secretly treacherous but they are friendly. There was a minor revolution in 1995, but it quickly fizzled. When coup leaders tried to gas up the army's only tankette, irate motorists made them wait in line at the pump like everyone else.

The Corallos live in simple splendor on the São Tomé waterside boulevard known as the Marginal. Their house is the one that is almost obscured by gorgeous bougainvillea in deep purple and brilliant crimson. Orchids spill from pots set into the monster-sized twisted stump of a fromager tree. The hedge is a vivid tangle of flowering vines with a name that even Claudio can't recall. Since he is the Italian honorary consul, a large flagpole looms by the house. But it is always bare, even on Italy's national day. He has no flag.

Each day, Claudio or Bettina, if not both, drive twenty minutes up a small mountain to Nova Moca, their coffee plantation. It is right next to a plantation called Monte Café, into which the African Development Bank and other donors pumped $14 million. The difference is that Nova Moca thrives while its neighbor is slowly sinking back into the jungle. A stately colonial mansion that was supposed to be a tourist hotel—part of the aid project—is sinking along with it. The $14 million can be found, mostly, in the European real estate of a crafty few.

Depending upon his mood, Monte Café sends Claudio into fits of laughter or bouts of despair. It is dramatic proof that any such tropical enterprise needs deliberation, commitment, and, above all, a guiding hand.

"It takes years to build a plantation," he said. "It cannot be forced or pushed too quickly, or there'll be an imbalance. And without balance, it is disaster. Each step must be taken carefully, with thought toward the next. Above all, you have to think of yourself as immortal."

Claudio, I saw immediately, was an accomplished agronomist, but his real strength is cultivating people. When an Italian volunteer aid agency sent him to a Bolivian village to work with coffee, he was a rare foreigner addressed as *compañero* rather than *gringo*. His Congolese workers stuck by him, no matter what. And in São Tomé and Príncipe, he is family to the people he helps.

At Nova Moca, I got a sense of how he did things. One by one, he visited each worker and listened to anything each had to say. "When they are good at their work, these people are very proud, respected in their communities," he said. "And without people like that, you're finished."

Every few minutes, he unfolded his trusty Opinel knife, retooled to his own specification, for some skillful operation. He pounced on patches of fungus invisible to the unpracticed eye. At a wild cinnamon tree, he stopped to carve us some tasty toothbrushes.

The plantation was jasmine-scented from the trees' robusta flowers. "The perfume was so strong in the Congo that it gave you a headache," Claudio said. "We had to close the windows at night."

We stopped at the collapsing remains of what had been a handsome two-story wood-frame colonial house. It was too termite-ridden to save. Instead, he was converting the barn, with a striking valley view, into the plantation house. "You have to live with your people," he said.

We stayed a few hours, but I was eager for the following morning. The rattling little plane that made up Air São Tomé and Príncipe's entire fleet would take us to the smaller island, where Claudio grew his cacao.

As we approached the island, Claudio eyed me carefully, and I couldn't figure out why. Then Príncipe suddenly appeared. I mur-

mured something like "Jesus!" and broke into a stupid grin. He burst out laughing. Everyone responds that way to the first glimpse of Príncipe, and Claudio loves to watch.

"Did you ever see the movie *Peter Pan?*" he asked. In Florentine French, that is *Pee-Ter Pahn.*

The whole island is colored in deeply saturated greens, from bright emerald to dark forest tones. Scarlet flowers highlight the tallest trees. Odd-shaped peaks and columns jut high above the jagged mountains. Waves roll over broad swaths of turquoise and lap onto beaches of brilliant white sand. In some places, the mountains drop dramatically to the sea. In others, they slope gently into forests of palms and bananas. I tried to think of someplace more beautiful. Maybe Moorea, possibly not. Even without Tinker Bell, Príncipe had my vote as paradise.

On São Tomé, the little capital is not exactly Lisbon—it has no traffic light, and film must be shipped to Europe for processing—but it is a bustling metropolis compared to the village of Santo Antonio on Príncipe. A small shop sells a few staples. One of the half-dozen churches is an Internet center. The colonial post office has airy verandas and a sloping tin roof. Piles of painstakingly collected junk lay forgotten at the house of a priest who left town. A couple of bars serve the few regulars who can afford a nasty local brew. A louver-sided hospital sits on the hill above the port office.

Two of Claudio's crew waited for us in his battered Toyota pickup. The windshield was so smashed up you couldn't see through it, but the sunroof was impeccable. We bounced up a sort of road to Terreiro Velho, the abandoned nineteenth-century plantation into which Claudio was steadily breathing new life.

The view was stunning beyond adjectives. From a low mountaintop perch, the land dropped away to a white sandy cove below, flanked by dramatic rock formations. Those bright red treetop flowers I saw from the air were far more beautiful up close. They were *Erythrina*, with massive smooth trunks that held towering leafy canopies above the jungle. Fromagers rose high from roots as gnarled as mangroves, with long pods hanging in eerie decoration. Mangoes, papayas, palms, and a dozen other trees fitted in among them.

This was paradise, all right, and there seemed to be zero chance that any Pire Kinois would disturb the peace. Civilization was always within sight, a far better state of affairs than in the depths of the Congo. But still, in a different sort of way, Claudio da Príncipe was pushing an even bigger stone up a steeper hill.

*C*offee is not easy to grow, but cacao is a killer. The first trees in Africa were planted in 1822, right next to Terreiro Velho, by Portuguese settlers who brought seedlings from Brazil. The variation, called *forastero amelonado* because of its melon-shaped pods, took to Príncipe. And cacao production relied on what can only be called slave labor.

African workers hacked away chunks of thick jungle to make room for the trees. Then they built elaborate estates of stone and timber for the colonial administrators, along with drying sheds and outbuildings. Plantations were linked by narrow-gauge railways so dried beans could be loaded into wagons and rolled down to port. At Terreiro Velho, rusty tracks still run across the cobblestones by the grand two-story house that Claudio will eventually have time to restore.

In 1900, São Tomé and Príncipe grew 13,900 tons of cacao. The figure rose to 36,500 tons in 1913 and hovered near 30,000 tons after World War I. Then it plummeted when English buyers led by the Cadbury family boycotted the islands because of what amounted to slavery. Figures crept up again. In 1973, just before Portugal granted independence to São Tomé and Príncipe, the output was 12,000 tons.

These days, annual production seldom barely surpasses three thousand tons. Portuguese planters fled along with their national flag. Plantation workers had had enough of slogging away for next to nothing. Unable to attract Western interest in their remote little island nation, the government aligned itself with Moscow. But central planning and state-run farms did not fit the culture. Disenchanted with the Soviet style, new leaders tried to reorganize cacao production so that small planters could work together to market their crop.

For better or worse, the old-style planters with a firm hand and a single-minded vision are gone for good. Nothing has yet replaced them.

"Here they've gone from colonialism to communism to cooperatives," Claudio said. "These are people with no spark of life in their eyes. We're not just talking about growing cacao but rather a whole new way to look at life. A cacao farmer needs a certain love for his crop, like a winemaker or an olive grower. That helps in anything, whether you're a farmer or a shoemaker or tailor."

Unlike in most former colonies, São Tomé and Príncipe's trees are still fairly pure versions of the first transplants. By accident of history and geography, the islands were spared an agricultural revolution that stressed high yield at the expense of taste and texture.

"In other places, people saw those immense rugby balls on the new hybrids and looked at yields per hectare, and they tore out their old trees," Claudio said. "But they forgot that cacao and coffee are plants just like any other. There's no magic. If I offer you trees that will produce ten or twenty times more, you'll tell me to get lost before I finish talking. You'd know instinctively that something too important would have to be traded away."

The future for his islands, he said, was quality rather than quantity. "Volcanic soil composition that you find only on Príncipe allows you to grow extremely good cacao. It has iron and laterite. We have to find a niche for our cacao, just as if it were wine or olives." But, he concluded, it would be a hell of a fight.

In the equatorial rain forest, even a single season of neglect can cripple a plantation. Undergrowth breeds fungal diseases and insects that destroy the pods, if not the trees themselves. Without regular pruning, production plummets. Trees grow too high. Tangled vines prevent workers from even approaching the trees, and the overhead canopy blocks out too much light.

"Look at this," he said, preferring as usual to show rather than tell. He plucked off a pod with a jagged hole on top. "This was a rat," he said. "Rats climb down the tree and eat from the top. Monkeys grab a pod and start from the bottom. When undergrowth is dense, you get both."

Príncipe is spared witches'-broom and some other virulent pests found elsewhere. But even in optimal conditions, planters calculate they lose 21 percent of their crop to disease and another 25 percent to pests.

Potential nightmares lurk in the back of every planter's mind. If witches'-broom struck Brazilian trees, might it find its way across an ocean grown narrow in a jet age? What about the monilia that devastated Costa Rica? Or black pod, enemy number one of the cacao world? Botany texts are thick with frightening casts of characters.

Thinking rationally, Claudio started with a small patch of trees by the water. He settled his family into an airy cabin on a dreamlike beach, and they set to work. Soon, local authorities implored him to take on Terreiro Velho, with trees scattered along vertical paths winding up to the plantation headquarters, a half hour's hike. Being Claudio, he agreed.

"Even before you start worrying about trees, you have to think of the human spirit of a plantation," Claudio told me. When I marveled aloud at what Terreiro Velho must have been like in the old days, he shuddered. "I could have never stood it then. All those people working so hard with long faces, with no stake in what they did. Just imagine what this place will be like with happy workers who feel like they belong here."

That human spirit, he added, must extend to distant surroundings. When he first settled on Príncipe, in the beachside cabin, it took half a day to walk to the town of San Antonio. The actual hike took only an hour. But along the way he stopped to chat with nearly everyone he came across. "You have to take the time," he said. "If you don't at first, you'll have to do it later, and it will be much harder."

As we drove around the island, it was clear he had done his spadework well.

"Oh, Claudio!" one man in a ragged shirt and spiffy hat yelled as we drove past. Claudio stopped and, after much backslapping, well-wishing, and exchange of gossip, we started up again.

"What did you think of that guy?" he asked.

"Seemed nice enough," I said, without much to go on.

"Biggest son of a bitch on the island," he replied, with one of his better guffaws. It seems the man had run one of the three self-help cooperatives Claudio organized for small cacao growers on Príncipe. The man took advantage of the position, but Claudio managed to bounce him out with such grace that the man bore no grudge.

A few miles down the road, Claudio spotted someone else, and his face beamed warmth. I was hoping he would ask my opinion so I could pronounce the guy a jerk, just for a laugh. At a glance, I could spot real human quality. I could also see biceps and a bulging chest.

Antonio Rochas had a small plot of cacao trees at the bottom of a steep ravine. At harvest time, he humped eighty pounds at a time on his back up to the road. "That's only because he fell sick and lost a lot of weight," Claudio said. "You should have seen what he could do when he was in top form."

One of Claudio's new projects was to bring a dozen donkeys to haul loads up and down the mountainsides. He had already found a sixty-year-old farmer who spoke perfect donkey to handle them. Trucks made no sense in a place without roads, and not many farmers could hump cacao like Antonio Rochas could.

Rochas was also a fisherman and a local entrepreneur with various irons in the fire. He apologized, saying that illness and other commitments had prevented him from picking up The Boat. As we drove into town, Claudio showed me The Boat, which is one of his *"porca miseria"* stories.

One day, it seems, a couple of fishermen mentioned they could perform wonders if only they had a decent boat. Plenty of fish schooled around out there. They just had to get to them. Claudio immediately found a boatbuilder in São Tomé. From his own pocket, he funded the project. He transported a sturdy yellow craft to San Antonio and deposited it for them on the beach. One year later, the boat sat where he left it, untouched.

Finally, he asked Rochas to take charge of the boat, at least to prevent it from rotting away out of the water. Eventually, Claudio's charity would find some purpose. At least he hoped it would.

In San Antonio, no one was yet using the broken industrial refrigerator he had bought to provide the town with a fish smoker. He pours his own money into good works, hiring people to repair the roads in front of their plots of land and funding classes for people eager for education. His gamble is that it will all pay off, with a motivated community committed to doing better. Also, Claudio da Príncipe, agnostic as he is, is likely to end up sainted.

With all of his friends and endless goodwill to man, his principal focus is still on cacao.

His house has no electricity. Each day starts at 5 a.m. with a freezing outdoor shower. A plastic pipe catches water running down from the mountaintop, except when someone in between needs a drink and whacks it with a machete. At sundown, Claudio straps a high-tech miner's light to his forehead and sits down to paperwork at his desk: a table with a pocket calculator, a plastic triangle, and a mug of pencils. Then he has his standard Príncipe meal of sardines or packaged soup.

In its glory days, the century-old house must have been magnificent. Many of the original blue Portuguese tiles have survived in the kitchen. Big breezy bedrooms upstairs had wide windows that looked over the splendor below. The bathroom, with its old monster tub chipped and coated in grime, was a write-off. Neighbors had long since stripped away anything useful, and the empty space left was used to store drums of smelly fuel.

But it was only a minor inconvenience to pad outside to a bathhouse made of woven-mat walls. Cold-water showers are refreshing in the tropics, after the initial shock. Shaving in the open air with a little mirror tacked to a tree has its rustic charm. I got used to the screwy roosters that could not tell time and started their morning racket at 4 a.m. Once ensconced, I would have been happy to rip up my return ticket and stay forever.

The real attraction was Claudio. Night after night, we sat for hours under a blaze of stars talking about life beyond the cacao trees. If Claudio lives a spartan life on Príncipe, and a cocoonlike family existence on São Tomé, he makes the most of every minute that comes his way.

"People in Europe have enough distractions that they can reach the end of their lives without even realizing that they have never lived," he said one night. A legion of friends around the world keeps him amused and up to date via e-mail. He doesn't feel he is missing much. His mother had just sent him a newspaper with a front-page article on Middle East peace talks and Christian-Muslim clashes in Turkey. It was dated December 12, the day she mailed it. But the article was from 1912, ninety years earlier.

While describing his daily struggle to achieve the dream at hand, he spun out previews of coming attractions. He wants to build a catamaran to ply between the two islands. The government runs occasional ferries, but three of them went down in one year. "We can't be tied to boats that sink with such impressive regularity."

Claudio never noticed chocolate while he was growing up in Italy. "For some reason, I didn't eat it as a kid," he said, "and when I grew up and really tasted it, I thought, *merda*, I've been missing this!" But he is picky about what he eats. A Mars bar he keeps for an emergency energy hit on the nearly bare shelf in his kitchen had gone untouched for months.

On another night, Ricciarda joined us. At sixteen, she already had plans. She wants to study law, perhaps in Portugal or France, and then come home to São Tomé and Príncipe. With her experience over the years, combined with a hard look at international business, she figures she will be well suited to carry on her father's work.

"I love this place and the life here," she said. She nodded with enthusiasm as Claudio talked about expanding into chocolate making. "Most people are comfortable with what they already know, so it will take time to change ideas. But it will happen."

In the meantime, there was Terreiro Velho to put back together. If all goes according to plan, the great house will find new glory, with soul along with electricity. That, of course, would have to wait.

"All of this is tobacco," he said, waving to a large patch of green-leaved plants he had cultivated. "If you want a cigar, give me a little bit of warning." Another guffaw. He had no intention of abandoning his Tuscan smokes. But one cacao pest enjoys a chaw of tobacco, which kills it.

Claudio's first priority was his drying shed, but first he had to undo decades of abandon. Unearthing the grounds was like rediscovering Angkor Wat. He and his kids were excited to find a single step emerge from a huge heap of dirt. By the time they finished, they had brought back a splendid double staircase with stone banisters decorated with carved rock sculptures. After tons more dirt were carted away, and encroaching trees uprooted, they found rock foundations massive enough to have anchored a Portuguese fort.

Local records reveal little about the original owners, and Claudio had been too busy to see what he might learn in Lisbon. "I asked some of the old guys around here what they remember," he said. "All any-one can tell me is there was a woman, probably the wife of the owner or the administrator, and she had a nasty temper and a mustache."

*F*inally, we reached the pièce de résistance, Claudio da Príncipe's fermentation and drying operation. For quality chocolate, these are the crucial first steps. A lot can go wrong further along the line, once beans are bagged and shipped. But the first precursors of flavor develop only days after pods are opened. Once this process starts, a master's hand is needed at every stage.

The shed, four thousand square feet, was built to last, covered by a galvanized and corrugated roof on a solid frame of rafters. In every corner, Claudio had made some personalized new variation on an old theme. His method was trial and error, taking nothing on faith, until he neared his idea of perfection.

In Claudio's view, the key to making good chocolate, far down the line, is a properly fermented bean. He believes that flavors must begin to develop at this first stage, right out of the pod. His nose follows the process carefully, from the early blast of sweet tropical fruit to the winelike alcoholic whiff. Only when the last subtle scent of acetic acid vanishes are the beans ready to be dried. Claudio ferments for two weeks, nearly twice as long as Léopold Ouegnin in Ivory Coast.

We inspected his latest idea for fermentation boxes. Carefully chosen planks of a hardwood called iroko were joined into large trapezoids, with two partitions inside. Each was designed so paddles could gently stir the mass. The idea was to keep out air and lock in moisture to give each of the beans even exposure to the heat of fermentation. Over time, the mucilage would disappear and leave chocolate-scented purplish beans ready for the drying process. The boxes were vitrified inside for easier cleaning and so that liquid would not permeate the wood.

Holes in the bottom of the boxes channeled juice from the mucilage into containers. Just about everyone else lets the sweet liquid drain away as so much waste. Claudio distills his into a cacao liqueur that blows your socks off but makes you smile with pleasure.

If all this took a lot of work, I could see distinct advantages over the more rustic method of wrapping the sticky contents of cacao pods in banana leaves and letting nature take its course.

"That might work for the first forty-eight hours," Claudio explained, "but you have the problem of thermal inertia. You have to aerate the cacao so the heat moves. That's why we take such trouble to keep beans from getting caught in the corners. The main thing is that with the sun alone, there is no consistency, no homogeneity. You can't direct it or control it."

After fermentation, Claudio designed several options. He built two vast expanses of flat clay tiles that serve as drying platforms. A fire of hot coals underneath is kept in carefully sealed compartments to prevent smoke from tainting the flavor of drying beans. Workers carefully shape the beans into long rows, using rake-like hoes, to ensure even temperatures.

But he also crafted his hot tub. This is a great round cylinder in which paddles gently tumble the beans as they dry over forced air.

Both of these processes achieve the same purpose as spreading beans out on a hard surface in the sun. In fact, cacao researchers at Montpellier, France, insist that well-managed sun-drying is best because of the chemical and physical ways that moisture exits the beans. But Claudio's method avoids the problems of freak precipitation, old oil stains, incontinent chickens, and the disruption of raking up and covering the cacao at the end of each day.

Claudio is not a great believer in reading manuals.

"I make a thousand different tests to find a cacao that I'd want to eat and have another, and then I go back and figure out what I did," he said. At every stage, he follows his intuition. When he decides on some new idea, he tries it out three different ways. Then he shapes it to practicality. "What's important is to keep it simple."

Early one morning, we took a hike to look at the trees. Claudio was in good spirits, as usual, but just thinking about the work he faced left me nearly paralyzed. Those twenty thousand cacao trees clamored for whatever attention he could spare when he was not worrying about coffee plants on the other island. He had trained thirty workers to do such routine jobs as removing suckers from the base of the trees eight times a year and whacking back encroaching brush. A few skilled hands did the annual hard pruning. It was the proprietor's job, however, to fret about the future.

I visited at the height of the season, but only a few shriveled pods hung from trunks and branches. Drought had left Príncipe gasping in thirst two years earlier. The following year, too much rain pounded down just as the flowers appeared. Had Claudio's trees been healthy and well-pruned, he might still have managed a decent enough crop. But, in the short time he had been at it, his Sisyphean stone was only getting started on its way uphill.

"Ah, look," Claudio said, brightening as we came to a small copse where workers had gotten a respectable start. "This is going to be okay." With his trusty folding Opinel knife, retooled to personal standards on a grinding wheel, he cut suckers, taking care to excise them cleanly at the base so the tree would quickly heal. Watching Claudio work, I suddenly began to understand the mysterious and persnickety cacao tree.

A smart planter shapes a young tree to grow from three main boughs that spread from a short trunk. Branches that extend from the three uprights find their happiest place between light and shade. These are cut back with regular pruning to concentrate the tree's force on producing healthy pods within easy reach. Branches are thinned and shaped so they do not compete with one another. Despite some formidable differences, I realized, Claudio tended his cacao trees the way he would tend olive trees in the hills of Tuscany.

"It's agriculture," Claudio said. "There is nothing mystical about cacao. It needs the right soil, the right growing conditions. It needs pruning and protection from bugs and diseases and parasites. Its roots have to be free to find nutrients. And then it grows."

That sounded convincing enough. But the whole enterprise also seemed to need a Claudio. The trickiest part of producing cacao is finding the right balances. Young trees, especially, need the shade of a jungle canopy. But they also need light and air. Predator bugs live in the tangled undergrowth that seems to appear overnight. Yet some brush is essential for the midges and other insects that pollinate the cacao.

The tree's curious botany equips it to produce pods in conditions under which most plants would give up the ghost. Its large deep-green leaves drop off near its base, forming a natural layer of insulation to trap moisture and create the thick rotted mulch that cacao trees love. A profusion of suckers ensures that new branches will grow toward light above, however thick the overhead canopy. The trouble is that the trees were designed for rats and monkeys, not chocolatiers. Misshapen, runty pods are good enough for rodents; all they have to do is distribute seeds.

Pruning is essential not only to shape a tree for easy picking but also to coax it to maximum production. Done well, it reduces competing branches so that more nutrients reach the most promising limbs. Fertilizer and pesticides might help, but both are expensive.

"All the trees around here are organic, although no one can afford to have them certified, because no one can afford the chemicals," Claudio said. He uses only copper sulfate—acceptable in organic farming—to reduce fungus. In any case, he said, skillful growers learn the best pest control is a healthy plantation with natural deterrents.

"Yes," he allowed at the end, "I suppose you have to know what you're doing."

The need for a healthy environment is one reason Claudio works so hard to encourage and educate his neighbors. Pests have a nasty habit of propagating in overgrown, neglected plantations and then visiting healthier ones nearby at dinnertime. Besides, if São Tomé is to produce notable cacao, it cannot be from Terreiro Velho alone. A lot of people have got to be convinced that all their hard work is worth their while.

Tending cacao trees is one thing. The obvious problem is what happens once the pods ripen. In Ivory Coast, small farmers solve this with a machete, some banana leaves, and a patch of highway tarmac. When beans seem to be the right color, they can be shoveled into jute sacks until the local Lebanese *traitant* sends a *pisteur* to collect them. But the end result is junk cacao.

Despite their tough-looking exteriors, cacao pods and the beans inside are as delicate as freshly picked olives. If a knife blade damages beans when the pod is cut, spoilage can spread quickly. As the beans dry, they must be kept away from any outside odor. When they are bagged and shipped, they are particularly vulnerable. Surely some cosmic justice allows the occasional whiff of Antico Toscano smoke, but otherwise the cacao gods are strict.

So, I asked Claudio, what do Príncipe growers do? He raised a finger, inviting patience. The next morning, he said, we would go to a *quebra*, a day of hard work, with some alcoholic rejoicing, when the crop comes in.

Early, as usual, we hopped into the Toyota and jounced our way to the Porta del Sol, which was built in 1999, one of three cooperative processing centers. It operates permanently during the harvest season, enabling farmers to bring whatever size load they have, whenever it is ready, and exchange it for cash on the spot. Some small producers extract the mucilage and beans at their own plots, saving themselves the effort of hauling husks that will only be tossed aside and burned. But most of them simply deliver sacks of ripe pods.

*Quebra* means "break." Instead of slicing open pods with a machete, endangering the beans inside, workers whack them with a wooden club. After a series of smart blows around the circumference, the pods break cleanly in two. Their contents are scooped out and placed atop a sloping wood plank. As the fresh beans in sticky goo slide down toward a plastic barrel, practiced eyes watch for imperfections. Any off-color bean or bean showing signs of germination is plucked out and dumped.

Afterward, the beans are left to ferment. Then they are spread out on a vast expanse of clay tiles, a larger version of Claudio's dryers at Terreiro Velho.

Claudio keeps track of every bean. Workers log each delivery, marking them down in the lined columns of a tattered school notebook. At a glance, he can see who produced what and how much was paid. Sitting at his spare table office, he showed me the latest reports. Rochas had hauled in more than a ton. Some less energetic neighbors brought a few pounds. It all counted.

The morning we visited Porta del Sol, Claudio was bummed. We were supposed to see a high-season *quebra* operating at full bore. These are held regularly, and farmers make a fiesta of it. Each brings in his load of pods or gooey beans, and the whole place rocks with activity. But this was São Tomé and Príncipe, where all schedules are only good intentions. The head of the cooperative had to go to the hospital; her youngest son came down with malaria. We saw only a limited version of the *quebra*, but it was clear enough.

Down a narrow path among fruiting cacao trees, Claudio showed me where he wants to build an overlook café for visitors. The view, as from Terreiro Velho, was breath-stopping. I could imagine busloads of beaming tourists sipping iced cocoa fresh from the source and buying chocolate bars, with Claudio's coat of arms or not.

The next time I saw Claudio, only months afterward, he was shopping for machinery and studying techniques he could reinvent. Claudio preferred the simplest approach. He experimented with the times and temperatures needed to roast different sorts of beans. But he shortened the usual long process of conching. If beans were good, he felt, too much manipulation produced chocolate he called *cadavere*, worked to a cadaverlike lifelessness.

After a few more months, trial and error had turned out some chocolate that he brought to friends in Tuscany. He used no vanilla. The powerful presence of cacao began with the scent alone. A taste revealed notes of tropical fruit with earthy undertones. It was wonderful.

By then, Italian chocolatiers had developed an interest in his singular beans. At a trade fair in Tuscany, he found his photograph displayed prominently in a newspaper over an obvious story: Local boy grows good chocolate.

This was one of those thousand-mile Confucian journeys that began with a single step. By the summer of 2004, Fortnum & Mason offered a line of new chocolate, wonderfully rough and full of rich, earthy flavor. Claudio da Príncipe had done it.

# Chapter 8

## VALRHONA VALHALLA

o hear the world's finest chocolatiers tell it, the Valrhona factory at Tain l'Hermitage in the heart of France is an earthly equivalent of heaven. The difference, many add, is that Saint Peter surely has a better attitude.

From the first moment I began to poke at the edges of chocolate, the name Valrhona seemed to take an outsized place in any conversation. Soon, I learned to nod sagely and listen. If you talk jewelry, you should at least pretend you know about Tiffany's. In fact, it is more than that. There are other top-end jewelers.

Valrhona makes about seven thousand tons of chocolate a year. This is one-hundredth of what the Swiss-based Barry Callebaut produces in factories once owned by Cacao Barry in France and Callebaut in Belgium. But, unlike its giant competitor, Valrhona produces only good chocolate. It is obsessive about quality in its limited range of products.

For industrial chocolate, giant companies like Hershey or Nestlé simply pour beans into one end of a factory and truck boxes of finished candy bars out the other. Some smaller-scale chocolatiers make their own base product from cacao they may buy at the source. But most people who work with chocolate, *fondeurs* or bakers, need a reliable wholesale supplier for their most crucial raw material. That is where Valrhona comes in. Valrhona also makes specialty chocolate bars and bonbons that are sold in retail stores.

François Pralus makes some exquisite chocolate base in Roanne, across the Rhône west of Lyon. The output is tiny, however, and it can lack consistency. Few others are even in the running. But for every chocolate pro who swears by Valrhona, there is another who swears at it.

Richard Donnelly, who produces fine ganaches and *pralinés* at his shop in Santa Cruz, California, spends five figures a year buying Valrhona base. Once he telephoned Valrhona's United States headquarters with a sensible technical question. "The guy told me that if I called myself a chocolatier, I would know the answer," Donnelly told me, as much amused as outraged at such a fine example of French arrogance. "And he hung up on me."

Valrhona denies this is a general attitude. At the company's booth at the Paris Salon du Chocolat, a senior executive began to explain to me their mannerly approach toward all comers. But his wandering eye picked out someone with whom he had more important business, and he turned away in midsentence.

Valrhona hides behind an aura of mystery. Its Web site dismisses history in a few words: An unnamed pastry chef in the Rhône Valley began the company, or its precursor, in 1924. It leaves the impression that the company is still run by a pastry chef's family, making no mention that Valrhona is, in fact, a subsidiary of Bongrain, a French food conglomerate that does $5 billion a year in business—and is far more involved in cheese than chocolate.

For a long time, Valrhona seemed to cultivate a deliberate policy of hauteur, a peculiarly French refinement on the general theory of snob appeal. Alan Porter of Britain's Chocolate Society worked four years to convince Valrhona executives that English palates were worthy of their product. Valrhona finally agreed to sell to Porter, explaining that they were willing to undertake what they called "a marketing experiment."

When Chloé was a mere independent chocolate consultant in Paris, she made an appointment to visit Valrhona. Her host neglected to pick her up at the train station, as arranged. Finding the factory impenetrable, she simply hiked up her skirt, scaled the wall, and tracked down the man she had come to see.

Years later, in her new role as Fortnum & Mason's confectionery buyer, she reshaped her department to feature Valrhona. She organized the store's annual chocolate dinner around the Valrhona specialties she liked best. Soon after, she made another appointment with Valhrona, this time as a customer eager to discuss new products. When she arrived in Tain, she found her meetings had been canceled—Valrhona's last-minute request for a reconfirmation failed to reach her on the road—and she had to storm the place a second time.

When the company decided to move into the American market, it played on this exclusivity. Many restaurateurs and bakers were reluctant to pay its prices, sometimes three times those of other chocolate base suppliers. But sales representatives targeted top chefs who wrote "Valrhona chocolate" on their menus, thus exciting the interest of American foodies. This, in a short time, built an almost mythical cachet.

Bernard Duclos, the company's North America representative, liked to say that Valrhona aimed to be the Mouton Rothschild of chocolate-dom. Perhaps he was addressing what he considered to be a gullible audience. But he seemed to me what the French would call a bit *gonflé*, that is, full of himself. A master winemaker not only manicures the same vines over generations but also assembles vintages that improve over decades. A chocolate maker, even Valrhona, buys beans, processes them, and stamps them with a sell-by date usually only months in the future.

Duclos made a point. Valrhona tasters had found that some single-variety beans actually do improve with a season of aging. Certain blends begin to approach the assemblage of wine. The analogy, however, is still a stretch.

With growing competition and a broader world market for high-quality chocolate, old attitudes began to change. Some of Valrhona's executives and representatives, on occasion, could be downright friendly.

Not entirely. David Lebovitz, a California pastry chef, a former star at Alice Waters's Chez Panisse in Berkeley who now writes books, is a chocolate expert of impeccable taste. He acknowledges that the Tain l'Hermitage masters make good chocolate, and he hates to speak ill of anyone. Nonetheless, he shudders at the mention of their name.

"I was amazed at how difficult they were to approach," he said, describing research he did in France for his own book on chocolate. This was in 2003, when Valrhona was on a charm offensive to counter threats from the giant Barry Callebaut and small Italian companies seeking to make inroads into its top-quality markets.

"Multiple attempts to contact Valhrona by phone and e-mail all went unanswered," Lebovitz said, "so I decided to talk to a representative in person at the Salon du Chocolat in Paris. He quickly sized me up and then rather haughtily dismissed me. I was stunned."

I was stunned, too. Lebovitz is an unusually nice guy, and he clearly knows his stuff.

"I really liked their chocolate, and I very much wanted to learn more about it since they were the pioneers in getting people to appreciate high-quality chocolate," Lebovitz continued. "I even wanted to enroll in classes at their factory, but for some reason they would not let me. Every chocolate company that I've ever been in touch with has been incredibly friendly and more than helpful. Valrhona does not seem to be interested in working with chefs and food writers, and it continues to puzzle me."

Later, I explained the case to the Valrhona executive in charge of contact with such professionals. I assumed there was some misunderstanding that he would be eager to put right. He had not heard of Lebovitz, he said, and he did not note down the name for any follow-up to put things right. If Saint Peter had barred the door, then fate had been written. The case was closed.

In the end, does it matter? Valrhona, by almost any measure, makes the best range of commercial-scale chocolate anywhere. Since the late 1990s, it has been available not only to professionals but also to anyone who finds the right specialty store and has the money to pay for it. Serious addicts can even track down what Valhrona calls its grands crus in three-kilo boxes of *fèves*—that means beans, but they are really small ovals of chocolate.

The hallowed original factory, stately with gabled, peaked roofs and brick walls meant to last, sits on a lovely stretch of the Rhône just above Valence. It is best approached by night, walking up an old barge-men's towpath under the heady scent of flowering trees. Long before you see it, your electrified olfactory senses tell you it is there. That rich aroma of dark chocolate lapping gently back and forth in vats behind the walls masks the riverbank bouquet of honeysuckle, jasmine, roses, or peach blossoms.

Success has brought an additional plant, much larger, at the edge of town. But the company's soul remains in the old quarters.

Getting permission to visit Valrhona is a little like applying for a North Korean visa. There is seldom an outright refusal, yet the visit does not take place unless someone decides it is in the company's interest.

For those who are deemed Valrhona-worthy, or who otherwise manage to weasel their way past the heavy steel gates, there is a pleas-ant surprise. The haughtiness of the public face is missing in the inner sanctum. Valrhona employs Frenchmen who, as God is my witness, all but whistle while they work. Among a full-time staff of four hundred, thirty-year veterans are common.

Confidences are not blithely divulged. Most employees would sooner eat a Mars bar than betray their family trust. Just in case, Val-rhona takes no chances. Sacks of beans are coded with numbers and left unlabeled. Only a few senior company officials can determine the country of origin, let alone the specific plantation.

"Too many people are trying to steal our secrets," said Guillaume Luquel, sales manager for northern Europe, who was tasked with showing me around. "We have to take every precaution we can."

I visited on a typical morning. Before entering the business end of the plant, I was dressed in a zip-up white gown and a gauze hat, and was given booties to put over my shoes. Not only my watch but also the turquoise bracelet that never leaves my right wrist went into a pocket. Valrhona wanted to take no chance that some baker in Brest might discover Navajo jewelry in a three-kilo cake of Venezuelan chocolate.

After preparation, briefing, and decontamination, Luquel pulled a cord to activate a giant red door. It rolled upward, and I followed him inside. The scene was straight out of any James Bond film you care to remember, toward the end when the good guys penetrate the bad guys' underground lab just as global destruction is about to occur. Men and women in white scurried about pushing wheeled carts. High-tech forklifts scooted past digital control panels that flashed displays in fire-engine red. Conveyor belts and chutes linked production chains.

But this was still old-world France. Salted among the fancy stainless-steel machinery, the odd relic with details in handsome polished wood performed some essential task in a reliable fashion dating back generations.

Luquel gave me a full tour, with generous explanation to my endless questions. But he never let me out of his sight. Some time later, when I asked for a men's room, he followed me upstairs to the door. Afterward, he gave me fresh gauze booties before we reentered the working areas.

At each stage, Luquel hovered close to make sure I did not write down the machine manufacturers' names. It was a pointless precaution. Valrhona relies on the usual suspects for crucial steps, the old-faithful German equipment I had seen often before.

Beans are roasted in G. W. Barth rotary pods, only 240 kilos at a time to ensure even distribution of heat. Roasting takes twenty-five to thirty minutes, and the temperature is kept near 100 degrees Centigrade (212 degrees Fahrenheit) to avoid any burned flavor. The grinder-huller is a lovely wood-sided French machine, an antique workhorse that no one could find if he wanted to copy Valrhona's process. Blowers whisk away the husks, and a rise in temperature melts what is left.

After the beans are roasted, hulled, and ground, the liquefied nibs go into giant Buhler five-roll millers. These refine the cacao into chocolate, blending in cocoa butter, sugar, and soy lecithin. By the time the chocolate moves on, it is broken down to particles of about fifteen microns, the optimum size for maximizing flavor.

From the miller, chocolate in solid chunks moves up conveyor belts to Bouermeister conches, where it is liquefied again. Paddles gently stir the chocolate for up to seventy-two hours, slowly releasing volatile molecules, from acetic acid to any number of other compounds that affect taste. Finally, the chocolate is tempered—heated, then cooled within a precise range—and it is ready to eat.

Valrhona is good not because of the machines themselves but rather because of the care exercised in how they are put to use. And that is only part of it.

To start with, the plant is designed on the French chefs' rigorous belief in forward motion and the separation of elements. In this general approach, each step follows the next in logical order. Raw materials move onward until they end up on a diner's plate. Disparate ingredients are handled with extreme care. No decent chef, for instance, would dream of cutting vegetables and fish with the same knife. All of this is efficient, but it also prevents any accidental tainting of flavors.

At Valrhona, each section is isolated so that temperature and air circulation can be strictly controlled. Access is limited to people who have a job to do. Overhead conduits like giant blimps filter and evacuate air to avoid contamination that might turn to mold. These improvements involved costly retrofits at the old plant. The new factory, opened in 2004, was designed with elaborate attention to airflow.

Off to one side, twenty specialists in a laboratory constantly test samples for quality and purity. Production chains include metal detectors just in case some visitor's turquoise bracelet manages to slip through the cracks.

Behind one enormous red door, signifying full quality alert, Valrhona makes its bonbons of ganache and *praliné*. For all the fancy equipment, the final touch is by human hand. I watched a small crew make *palets d'or*, both square and round, at the working end of a fifteen-meter-long wood-sided cooling tunnel. Each finished piece was topped with a waxed paper disk that stayed on for twenty-four hours, causing crystals in the chocolate to take on a rich gleaming sheen under the signature gold flecks.

Michel Chambert trundled a heavy metal cart past us, smiling to himself at some private thought. He laughed out loud when I told him French workers were not reputed to find such joy in their work. After thirty-one years, he was in charge of the *enrobeuses* that coated bonbons, and he had no plan to retire.

"It all comes down to the relationship people have to their jobs," he said. "People like it here, and we like each other. We're proud of what we make." I asked if he had a favorite Valrhona product, and he was stuck for an answer. "I eat this stuff all day long, grabbing a piece here and there. I like it all."

In an adjoining section, Marie-Noëlle Courtial sat by a conveyor belt that carried trays of freshly coated *pralinés*. With swift strokes of two flat forms embossed with different sets of patterns, she created complex geometric decorations on the gleaming chocolate. She had been on the job for thirty-two years and seemed to get a kick out of every fresh batch she sent down the line.

"Try one," she said, handing over a small square as if she were offering Adam a forbidden apple.

In the end, Valrhona bonbons might not receive the same personal attention as those made by France's best artisans, but I'd eat them anytime.


Valrhona is an odd duck for a corporate subsidiary. It was founded in 1924 by the father of Olivier Deloisy, who now owns La Chocolaterie de l'Opéra, a French company that sells products that are made to his specifications by Chocovic in the Catalonian mountains of Spain.

In 1984, Robert Linxe of La Maison du Chocolat mentioned Valrhona to his brother-in-law, Jean-Noël Bongrain. The small Rhône Valley chocolate maker was facing tough times. Perhaps it might be a good investment. Bongrain already had money in La Maison du Chocolat, which operated well without demanding his attention. He bought Valrhona as a wholly owned subsidiary.

These days, a group of sales managers and production experts run the company for Bongrain, making strategic decisions by joint consultation. They include both the people who create diehard loyalty from some professionals and those who make Valrhona an epithet among others.

In the early 1990s, Valrhona was still what the French call a *franco-français* company. There was business enough at home, and foreigners got its products only if they came to Tain l'Hermitage and banged hard enough on the door. Since 1995, however, annual sales have grown in the double digits. Permanent sales offices are scattered around the world, and business booms not only in the United States but also in Japan. Hardly anyone who loves quality chocolate, anywhere, fails to recognize that bright red thirty-degree triangle on Valrhona's label.

Bernard Duclos, Valrhona's man in North America, hopes for substantial growth, but he is wary. I mentioned to him what seemed to be a promising similarity. Until late in the 1990s, Americans paid little attention to olive oil, content to buy unexciting glop marketed by large companies with Italian names. Suddenly, sales of excellent small artisan brands soared as people discovered quality was worth the extra cost.

"It is different with chocolate," Duclos replied, and he is probably right. "When people started talking about good olive oil, Americans had little prior reference. It was something new for them, and they were essentially starting fresh. Everybody has a strong idea of what chocolate should be, based on what they have known all of their lives." That is, Hershey bars.

Valrhona is working hard at professional levels, betting that new tastes will filter downward to a wider public. Until 2002, the company ran a training center in a one-room schoolhouse near the plant. Now a gleaming new kitchen complex, with classrooms and laboratories, receives seven hundred chefs a year from around the world. They all pay, of course. Valrhona keeps a dozen full-time chefs and pâtissiers to demonstrate the art of chocolate, in Japan and Singapore as well as in the United States and Europe.

"The whole challenge now is for us to get bigger without losing our soul," Luquel told me as we finished the tour. That seemed a fair enough assessment. But the company's customers, even those who swallow hard before picking up the phone to place their orders, have a broader concern: They don't want Valrhona to lose its taste.

The Valrhona product range runs heavily to chips and chunks for big-time bakers. But its real pride is a collection of origin-specific chocolates. These come in bricks or three-kilo packages of *fèves* ("beans") for professionals. But they are also sold retail in bars wrapped in handsome labels.

Gran Couva, Valrhona says, was the first vintage domain chocolate on the market. That is like wine or olive oil from a single estate. Whether someone else was first does not really matter. The chocolate is terrific. It is made with 64 percent cacao, all *trinitario* grown at the Gran Couva plantation in Trinidad. Subtle notes of flowers build to a lingering sense of ripe jasmine.

But, like French vintners, Valrhona's master tasters lean toward blends made up of different beans with varying but complementary characteristics. Unlike vintners, they might choose their components from geographically distinct regions. Only seldom do they mix vintages—years—as cacao beans rarely get better with age. Playing on the similarities rather than the differences, they label their special blends with the winemakers' accolade, grand cru.

There is Manjari, a 64 percent blend of Madagascar cacao, which comes from strains of *criollo* and *trinitario* that found their way to the Indian Ocean centuries ago. Its slightly bitter bouquet has soft notes of berries and chokecherries, with a powerful burst of flavor early on and a long, rich finish. It stays near the top of Chloé's A-list, and it goes into the *palets d'or* of many fine chocolatiers.

Late in 2002, after two years of tasting and debating at Tain l'Hermitage, Valrhona released Araguani. This blends two Venezuelan terroirs with different soils and climates: the breeze-blown Caribbean coast and the steamy Andean foothills. With the advent of this new offering Manjari lovers suddenly found their loyalties divided.

Chloé was smitten. Up front, she found mixed aromas of grapes with a bit of chestnut and a faint, sweet bouquet of honey. A second phase smoothed into something more like toasted bread that developed slowly, without sweetness. And at the end, slight acidity lingered for a long time, tickling the tongue. "It is extremely balanced, and it goes on and on," she concluded. "I love it."

I love it, too. But my own favorite may be Caraïbe, from Venezuelan *trinitario*. It is 66 percent cacao, but the beans are sweet and fruity, with a trace of roasted almond and coffee.

Then again, maybe my favorite is Guanaja, which is named for the island off Honduras where Columbus tossed cacao beans to the bottom of a canoe—unaware that the discovery of chocolate literally lay at his feet. With 70 percent cacao, it is a powerful blend of *criollo* and *trinitario* from coastal regions of Venezuela. It, too, has nuances of ripe fruits and fresh flowers, but with an exceptional bitterness.

Jivara is the one milk chocolate of the set, powered by strong hints of caramel, with 40 percent cacao from South American plantations. There are others, and, Valrhona asserts, there will be more.

*F*or chocolate lovers, the Valrhona approach to public relations has turned out to be good news. In 1991, an affable Italian perfectionist named Alessio Tessieri visited the Tain l'Hermitage plant, along with his sister, Cecilia, and their mother. The family had a thriving business selling ingredients to Italian bakers. They wanted to handle Valrhona products and perhaps expand into making ganache and *pralinés* with Valrhona chocolate. It had taken them long months to arrange the appointment, and it did not start well.

"On the way in, we passed three Danes on their way out, with very long faces," Alessio told me. The man who received them explained, with a derisive laugh, how the previous visitors had thought Denmark was capable of appreciating fine French chocolate. Soon enough, it was clear that Valrhona thought the same thing about Italy, represented by a twenty-eight-year-old upstart and his twenty-five-year-old sister, in the company of their mother.

Alessio was furious. Looking back, he has calmed a bit. "Now I can understand Valrhona's business strategy, about not wanting to get into a small new market," he said, with a slightly embarrassed chuckle. "But I suppose I reacted more with pride than with reason."

Cecilia, however, still bristles as she recalls the meeting thirteen years later. "They told us that they did not think Italians were ready for their products, and they were not sure we could do them justice," she said. "Right then and there, it was war."

The family pooled all of its resources to start a company in the countryside east of Pisa. They called it Amedei, after Alessio and Cecilia's grandmother, whom both describe as a woman of ironbound honor who would not have taken a French slur lightly.

Soon enough, they made their point. By 2004, Amedei was turning out only a hundred tons a year, but specialty importers fought over it. American tastemakers discovered a range of excellent single-origin cacao, elegantly packaged. At ninety dollars a pound in some stores, it was perhaps the most expensive chocolate in America. "We are still looking for markets and slowly expanding," Alessio said, "but in size, we're really nothing. We're still at the level of poetry."

Enlightened visitors beat a path to Amedei's door. Instead of barred gates, they found a colorful welcoming façade. Guests toured the old-style granite refiners and settled into comfortable chairs in a paneled den to sample as much as they could handle.

From the beginning, Alessio went on the road to locate premium beans while Cecilia stayed home and learned what to do with them. Both excelled. Their beautifully boxed chocolates caught on fast. Almost everyone's favorites include the spicy Venezuelan Porcelana, made from *criollo* beans purchased at a source the Tessieris keep secret. I like their Madagascar chocolate, with notes of citrus ranging toward grapefruit and a crisp feel in the mouth that goes on and on. The Ecuador is earthier, with strong suggestions of black tobacco.

Although Alessio circled the equator for beans, he knew how to hit Valrhona where it hurt. He zeroed in on the tiny centuries-old Venezuelan coastal village of Chuao. The enclave, made up of descendants of freed African slaves, is reachable only by boat. Among the cacao cognoscenti, Chuao was referred to with the same reverence that wine lovers lavish on Romanée-Conti. But unlike Romanée-Conti, a tiny Burgundy vineyard that has had the same family ownership for centuries, Chuao is a collective of small planters who operate loosely as a group.

Chuao people are linked by a common heritage and led by elders who earn their respect. Each season, they amass their fermented beans and spread them out to dry in the sun on the village square by the old church. For most scientists who study the chemical reactions, this is the best drying method, provided it is done correctly. Moisture leaves the beans evenly, without changes brought on by extra heat.

For years, once the beans were dried and ready for the boat, Chuao growers sold the bulk of their crop to a single chocolate maker: Valrhona.

At first, the real story was an intriguing mystery. According to the Amedei camp, Alessio made his inroads by repeated visits and passionate lobbying. He spent months with Chuao producers to help them solve technical problems. He worried about their sick children. He bought baseball uniforms for the local team. And, most important, he agreed to pay a higher price for cacao. During 2002, according to this version of disputed history, Amedei locked up the Chuao supply—at least for the immediate future. That left Valrhona with only their stock from earlier years and beans acquired near enough to Chuao to carry the name.

Valrhona had a different story. As Luquel told it, Tessieri worked on a single malcontent in the group and convinced him to sell sixty sacks of beans. With this minimum input, Amedei had a legitimate certificate of origin and could not be attacked in court.

This was no simple mystery. To start with, there is a question over what constitutes Chuao cacao. Venezuelan labeling laws leave a wide margin for exporters to claim what they wish. Enforcement procedures have not been assiduous, what with a percolating revolution in Venezuela along with crippling general strikes.

The next valley over, Choroní, also produces an exceptionally good crop. Like Chuao, its trees still retain a great deal of their old *criollo* pedigree. And unlike Chuao, its more independent-minded producers are not bound by a cooperative tradition.

In all, actual production from in front of the Chuao village church might approach twenty tons of beans in a banner year; sometimes it is closer to seven tons. If you add up all the chocolate sold as Chuao by a dozen manufacturers, you find numbers exceeding fifty tons. This is like counting the people who claimed after the fact to have been members of the French Resistance during World War II. The number is impressive, but it is highly suspect.

An interesting part of the mystery was how different the two companies' similar Chuao beans came out as finished chocolate. As all chocolatiers insist, raw material is only part of the picture. To supplement my own nose, I asked Chloé to give both versions her full-bore treatment, complete with unsullied early-morning palate and quiet room free of background noise. Then she reported her verdict: "Don't make me choose."

In the Amedei, she sensed an immediate note of burnt caramel, but with a pleasantly consistent overall texture. An early hint of leather evolved into licorice and grapes. In the second stage—that is, the cruising speed after initial acceleration—she felt a slight acidity that enhanced the licorice, leading toward an end-of-mouth sensation of wild mushrooms.

"It is extremely intense and masculine, intense but exciting, with strong complexity and yet harmony," Chloé reported. "I can picture a young, beautiful man, full of fire, the kind that Pier Paolo Pasolini liked in his films."

The Valrhona, in contrast, came on sweet with an agreeable fatty sensation that suggested more cocoa butter. Though not as strong as

Amedei at first, it built quickly to a bouquet of dried plums and aromatic wood. She found it much more harmonious, mild, and balanced.

"This time," Chloé said, "I see another man, still masculine but without that same rebellious wild side. They are totally different. Put them both on my island."

There were other Chuao versions as well. François Pralus produced what he called a pure Chuao, although he was cagey about his source of beans. His label described it as "full of finesse, with notes of spices, soft tobacco, lightly smoked, a powerful nose, bitter with a lingering flavor." But he summed that all up in a single word that did not appear on the bright fuchsia label: "Leather." I had noted the same. It suggested nothing so strongly as a hard-ridden saddle.

But in mid-2004, there was no more choice to make. The Chuao producers' cooperative settled the issue with letters not only to Valrhona but also to Pralus and other European chocolate makers who used their name. Chuao cacao, they declared, went only to Amedei.

I visited the Tessieris soon after that registered letter reached its various destinations. When I mentioned the victory, Alessio tried hard not to smirk. His boyish round face was too expressive for him to pull it off.

Cecilia, who was focused on her own world in Amedei's small and immaculate production plant, did a better job of it. Her smirk was evident only when she spoke of blind-tasting panels that reported a marked preference for her Toscano blend, with 70 percent cacao content, over anything Valrhona had to offer.

"I just started working, learning every way I could," Cecilia said. "I thought if someone else can do it, why can't I? After working for hours in the lab, I started to like it, and I was proving a woman could do the work. Alessio is a man—he can go tromping around plantations. I'm happy here in the factory." A throaty chuckle suggested she was probably just as able as her brother to negotiate with cacao traders. But then, she also had a husband and two small sons besides all that chocolate.

Over time, Cecilia narrowed her range to a dozen types of chocolate. Her Toscano blends came in cacao content of 70 percent, 66 percent, and 63 percent, each different in composition and taste. Because more sugar went into the 63 percent blend, she found elements of bitter tannin to balance the sweetness. She designed her robust 70 percent to linger in the mouth, with no sharp peak, releasing sensations of fruits and flowers.

"This melts easily, and you can feel it as it reaches each of your sensory passages," she said of her prized 70 percent. I nodded in happy agreement, as each of my sensory passages checked in. "It is very elegant. For me, this is about the limit. People like to experiment with high percentages, but even 80 percent is too much for me. You need the sugar."

Cecilia made a dark Chuao exclusively from Alessio's treasured beans and another version with milk. The others in her range were from blends of South American, Caribbean, and Madagascar beans.

Besides pure chocolate, Cecilia developed a line of two dozen bonbons, some flavored with such Italian specialties as amaretto, grappa, *vin santo*, and *torrone*. But her treasure among them was a selection of six different Meditazione (Meditation) chocolates.

I zeroed in on Radici (Roots), a rhubarb-infused rectangle of dark *couverture*. With a goofy smile, I reached for a second. As it turned out, that was also one of Cecilia's favorites. "When I was a kid, I loved candies with rhubarb in them, and I had to satisfy myself," she explained.

Next I tried Scintelle (Sparks), an innocent-looking *palet d'or*. As advertised, it produced tiny flashes of a flavor it takes a moment to recognize. By the time I realized it was licorice—not anything I would have considered in chocolate—I had decided I liked it. A lot.

Then I suited up in gauze cap, paper robe, and booties for a tour of her domain. She uses the tried-and-true old Swiss and German equipment I had come to recognize, including round G. W. Barth roasters. Beans are ground to a fineness of twelve microns to ensure smooth texture. At the end, mechanical arms gently massage the finished chocolate for seventy-two hours in traditional conches. The simple little operation has one clear similarity to Valrhona: People seem to be very happy at their jobs.

"We're really proud of what we do here, and we want people to know about it," she said. "If anyone calls with a question or a problem, they get me directly on the phone. We want to be that kind of company."

Alessio is harder to find. While Cecilia makes chocolate, he is often gone, working on his cacao network. He has found suppliers in the Caribbean—on Grenada, Trinidad, and Jamaica—and in Madagascar. But he keeps going back to Venezuela, where, beyond Chuao, both Valrhona and Amedei have invested heavily.

"Venezuela clearly has the best potential," he said, "but it is a lot of work. Post-harvest management can be very, very bad, and can destroy top-quality beans. From the moment you crack open a pod, it all depends on management. There are mysterious factors at play, traditions to respect. In Chuao, only the women are allowed to dry the beans."

Alessio ensures that shipping containers are less than full to better control humidity. Beans are roasted as quickly as possible, although under proper conditions, cacao can be safely stored for a long time.

And then, of course, it is Venezuela. Strikes, banditry, and the vagaries of public administration all make an impact. Sometimes Colombian cacao of undetermined origin is smuggled across the border.

"For these reasons, we are planting our trees, to be freer, and we keep three agronomists working all the time to improve quality," Alessio said. He does not say where in Venezuela he has bought plantations. But his interest is clear. He spends much of his time in the rich forests south of Lake Maracaibo, where most of that priceless Porcelana originates.

To satisfy a much larger appetite for beans, Valrhona has also invested in Venezuelan plantations, as it has elsewhere along the equator. Valrhona works through a local affiliate known as Socaoven. Its director, a Venezuelan named Cai Rosenberg, operates in a climate of voracious middlemen and fierce competition.

During 2002, someone peppered Rosenberg's car with automatic gunfire. He was struck by half a dozen bullets, but by some miracle, none damaged a vital organ. His wife was also wounded. The assailant is still unknown, and the attack could have been for any number of reasons. But a point was clearly made. Even for the silk-tied Rhône Valley French bourgeoisie who market genteel sweetness, chocolate is serious business.

V alrhona is less worried about small competitors such as Amedei or Domori, farther up the Italian coast, than about the looming presence of Barry Callebaut.

Before assorted corporate takeovers and then a merger at the hands of a Swiss magnate named Klaus Jacob, Cacao Barry in France and Callebaut in Belgium made some very good chocolate. With sales approaching a million tons of product a year, Barry Callebaut AG turns out a great deal of mediocrity. Yet even with the new corporate structure, elements of the loosely linked company still make fine high-quality chocolate. Many Belgian craftsmen continue to swear by Callebaut products their grandfathers loved. A lot of Frenchmen still prefer something different from the Valrhona taste and style.

The Swiss-based company is in a position to get better if the market demands it. Jacob, balding and bespectacled with no direct heirs, clearly thinks about his legacy. In a sketch accompanying its international list of billionaires, *Forbes* said Jacob aspired to be a new Andrew Carnegie. He has given nearly a billion dollars to charitable causes in developing countries. And more is coming in. During 2004, the company's sales and profits were growing at double-digit annual rates. It made chocolate in thirty plants located in seventeen countries, with an annual turnover of about 3.6 billion Swiss francs.

At the obligatory lunch, which, in France, must follow a hard morning of chocolate tasting, Luquel was frank about Valrhona's fears. "They've got all the money they need, and we're their only target," he said. "When someone like that comes after you, it is wise to take note."

Few chocolate professionals expect Barry Callebaut to make a serious dent in Valrhona, even if the Swiss giant manages to curb its small rival's rate of growth. The best chocolatiers and pâtissiers think beyond price when they seek a specific taste. Barry Callebaut's huge advertising budget may influence the broader public, but it is hardly likely to sway professionals who know what they like.

In the end, fierce competition could turn out to be a happy blessing. So much the better if Barry Callebaut creates more fine chocolate on earth. And for those seeking a higher level, more charm among Valrhona's directors in Tain l'Hermitage should make it easier to get past the Pearly Gates.

•

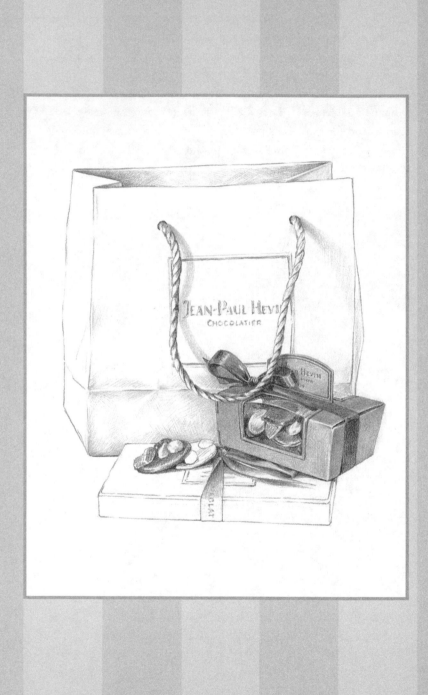

Chapter 9

# THE FRENCH MASTERS

ot far from Les Invalides in Paris, a jewelry store sits among neighborhood shops along the avenue de la Motte-Picquet. Its front is mostly a window that gleams like crystal. The rest is lacquered in rich dark brown, with a name lettered in purple: JEAN-PAUL HEVIN. Lovely baubles and elaborate creations nestle in velvet or in strawflower baskets or against origami backdrops. Intricate pieces are set into walls behind magnifying glass. None carry price tags, which saves confusion. Each item costs less than it would if it were really jewelry. But for chocolate, which it is, none of it is cheap.

If other *fondeurs* turn out even better-tasting ganaches and *pralinés,* no one does them more beautifully. Hévin wants his chocolate to excite taste buds, but there are four other senses to think about. It all matters, not only the first heady whiff and the subtle snap at each nibble but also the flashes of light reflected off the surface. When you have a product like his, you don't just stuff it in a bag.

Hévin's mastery goes far behind presentation. One time I found him at the Paris Salon du Chocolat behind a small vat of his latest specialty: a blend of dark chocolate with equal amounts of almond and hazelnut paste. He had created his own version of Europe's humble but beloved spread, Nutella. He dipped a plastic spoon into the mix and handed it to me. A blast of rich cacao, alive with nutty nuances, rocked me backward. As the creamy ooze melted on my tongue, subtle flavors settled in for a long stay. This was as close to Nutella as a Rolls-Royce was to Rollerblades.

When I asked Hévin how he did it, he raised an eyebrow and looked at me for a moment. Without a word, he made his answer crystal clear: You couldn't do this with a million years of practice. Why ask?

This was a typical Hévin response. "Chocolate amounts to art, but it is also a step-by-step workman's process in which everything has to come out right," he told me one morning. "You need the best possible ingredients, and you must take care with each of them. Without that, you might as well not bother." As this was hardly a new sentiment, I pushed for more specifics. Few came. It was as if I had asked Van Gogh why he chose cadmium and burnt orange to depict an olive grove. Artists often prefer not to caption their art.

Hévin packages himself with as much care as he puts into a *palet d'or*. When not in a white apron, he leans toward impeccably tailored collarless tunics in fashionable basic black. With close-cropped hair and a rough-cut handsome face, he would be a good fit in a Formula One race car. At the Salon du Chocolat, when selected artisans dress models in chocolate for a fashion parade, he routinely stops the show. One year he draped a willowy African woman in a racy bustier, a feather-motif miniskirt, and an elaborate navel-length necklace, all done in molded chocolate plumes, hearts, and disks.

Like so many others who specialize in chocolate, Hévin started out as a pastry chef and then followed his bliss. The art and innovation followed. He has half a dozen shops around Paris similar to the jewelry store near Les Invalides. According to his whim, there is often something new to try. One season, he offered the *"chocolat dynamique"* line, which uses ganache flavors such as ginger and kola nut, which are reputed to fire the libido. Other experiments, such as dark chocolate and Époisses cheese, are less likely to arouse the same ardor.

*I* much prefer a corner shop on the rue de l'Université, not far away, where Michel Chaudun makes chocolate that is not supposed to be confused with jewelry. He sticks with what he knows, such as his signature *chocolat aux éclats de fèves*. This is dark chocolate with crunchy bits of roasted cocoa beans; it is only slightly less addicting than morphine. His *mini-pavés*, cubes of ganache in gleaming *couverture*, are so delicate they seem liable to melt under a hard stare.

My own favorite chocolatier, anywhere, is Jacques Genin, who works almost unnoticed in a signless little lab in the seventeenth arrondissement. But when I asked him if he had a favorite, he named Chaudun.

"What a master," Jacques said. "He just does his work and doesn't make any noise about it. Notice that he never says a bad word about another chocolatier. A real pro." In Jacques's view, the years that Chaudun spent at La Maison du Chocolat during the 1980s were what gave the place its initial greatness.

Chaudun is a modest man of small stature, almost birdlike, with a flushed red face and, on most days, an easy smile. He is at his kettles by dawn. He is also found behind the counter on Saturday afternoons, packaging bonbons one by one for kids who have saved up their allowance. Chaudun sometimes seems embarrassed at the sums he rings up. But when so much depends upon superior ingredients handled skillfully in an intricate series of steps, a product gets expensive.

During 2004, prices fell in the range of fifty dollars a pound for top-level chocolatiers with shops of their own. For candy, that is a lot. For a recreational drug, that seems pretty cheap.

A *fondeur,* Chaudun selects a range of base chocolate from the catalogues of Valrhona and Barry Callebaut. It has taken him years to learn exactly what happens with each when he adds his own sleights of hand to a new formula. Do not bother asking him to reveal specifics.

His tiny shop is an enlightening window on the world of real chocolate. Its small front room jams solid at holidays when the pickiest of French bons vivants make their rounds. Shoppers pause outside to contemplate artful displays: sacks of beans set against old-world maps or sculptures of chocolate fantasies. Inside, they wait in line by the display counter, inebriated with aromas from the kitchen in back. Few seem eager to move on to their next stop.

Quiet periods are even better, when the shop is often empty, and Chaudun has time to rhapsodize.

"My whole world is here," he told me, with a sweep of the hand that took in no more than two cramped rooms and an alcove office. "I don't need to go out and explore jungles, or go to big conferences, or spend my time on television. I make chocolate."

But when I mentioned my plans to follow the chocolate trail, Chaudun's eyes flashed a spark of what could only be wanderlust. I got to the part about going to Mexican rain forests to seek out the origins of chocolate, and he nodded with enthusiasm. This was no surprise. No one who devotes a life to chocolate can be indifferent to those wise old gods who chose cacao for their sacraments.

Chaudun started as a pastry apprentice at fourteen and then studied in Switzerland. In 1980, he joined La Maison du Chocolat, pioneering a style of innovation and quality that made the Parisian specialty house the gold standard of cacaodom. After six years, he left as *chef chocolatier* in bitter discord with La Maison's hierarchy. To this day, he refuses to discuss the details, and his biography makes no mention of his old nemesis. In 1986, Chaudun opened his own shop and never looked back.

These days he worries that a new sort of world economy endangers dyed-in-the-wool craftsmen who struggle to survive. Still, his campaigning is confined to essays and press releases kept in a drawer, written in pencil with the same deft strokes he uses for flourishes on his chocolates.

His angst centers on two little words which, for all his gentle demeanor, can ignite him to fury: vegetable fat. Real chocolate is made of three ingredients: cocoa solids, cocoa butter, and sugar. A touch of soy lecithin, often used as an emulsifier, is hardly perceptible. But cocoa butter is valuable, sought after by cosmetics makers.

Industrial manufacturers have found a way to cheat on Van Houten's discovery, that crucial stage when separated cocoa butter is blended back into the chocolate liquor. Many are eager to replace as much of the cocoa butter as they can with other fats, such as palm kernel oil. The cocoa butter they save ends up on sunbathers in Saint-Tropez or on women's faces in fancy cosmetics. Substitute oils can add a cloying, fatty texture to finished chocolate.

Unlike most fine chocolatiers, Chaudun believes that few consumers can tell the difference if a manufacturer sneaks in a substitute. Still, he is adamant. For him, it is an article of faith.

"There is only one right way to make pure, honest chocolate," he says. "You cannot cut corners." And if mass-market confectioners insist on cutting corners, he adds, it is a travesty to allow them to compete with the real thing at prices the purists cannot match.

Chaudun was referring to a bitter decade-long controversy across Europe. In 2003, France finally lost the battle led by Britain, among other member states of the European Union. The French government insisted that diluted products be labeled something else besides chocolate. One wit came up with "*cocholat.*" *Cochon* means "pig." Chaudun would have been happy with, say, "disgusting garbage." In the end, the EU ruled that up to 5 percent of chocolate could be a substitute fat.

Scientists have tests to determine whether something besides cocoa butter has been added to the mix, but they have no way to determine the amount. As a result, pure chocolate advocates accuse some manufacturers of adding up to 10 percent of cheaper fat.

Jacques Genin had warned me about Chaudun's fabled moods: "He's an unusual guy, all right. When he feels like talking about chocolate, he will go on for hours with a tenderness and expertise you can't imagine. And some days, old friends can't get a nod of hello out of him."

On my first visit, I caught Chaudun in fine form. "Here, I'll show you," he said, flinging back a swinging door so we could enter his kitchen. For the next few minutes, I kept peering behind refrigerators and stoves in a vain search for the rest of the kitchen-laboratory.

Except for a long-belted *enrobeuse* for coating bonbons, it might have been any ambitious housewife's personal realm. Mixers turned in one corner. Sacks, cans, and bundles were stowed in another. Action centered on a sturdy iron range, where copper pots of flavored creams slowly turned themselves to ganache.

I was surprised by one aspect of the operation: All three helpers crammed into the small space were Japanese. In the new world of chocolate, even artisan small-timers push outward. But while others send finished products abroad, Chaudun dispatches acolytes. The Japanese study his magic and take it home to a Tokyo shop that bears his name.

Later, in his alcove office, Chaudun pulled from a drawer a flimsy fax-machine copy of his reflections.

In response to a self-posed question typed on one page—"Michel Chaudun, why have you chosen chocolate?"—he had written:

> Chocolate has always brought me great pleasure, being a gourmet and a gourmand, and I have always loved it . . . Chocolate is marvelous; it brings a smile to the lips, it makes eyes shine, and it flutters the eyelids . . . I think above all it is a drug, nicely seductive, which marks the sweet hours of our existence. Bitter as the pain it consoles, but sweeter than the love it inspires.

As Jacques had said, Chaudun avoids unkind words for his specific competitors. But he offered a sweeping generality about the business as a whole.

"They'll just lie to you," he said when I mentioned that I was about to visit Valrhona. "They all lie." Everyone's most tightly held secret, he said, was the source of the basic ingredient. "Chocolate makers either won't say anything about where they get their best beans, or if they do, they'll tell you something to throw you off the track." And *fondeurs* are just as reticent about their favorite types of finished chocolate.

I made a parting stab at learning more about Chaudun's A-list. He only chuckled. "I could tell you," he said, "but I'd have to lie to you."

A little truth would have been welcome. But the important thing was that bag of *chocolats aux éclats de fèves* I carried out the door. Half were gone by the time I reached my car.

*F*or connoisseurs around the world, the reference point remains La Maison du Chocolat. Robert Linxe started the company in 1977. He is still there, in the immediate background. Since 1987, it has been owned discreetly by Bongrain, the huge French food conglomerate that also owns Valrhona. The arrangement manages to prove that big is not necessarily a drawback to fine artisan chocolate making as long as someone is watching all the time, and no one is cutting corners.

La Maison has two shops in Manhattan, one in a nineteenth-century building on Madison Avenue and another in Rockefeller Center. By 2004, there was a shop in London on Piccadilly and a second one planned in the fanciest part of Tokyo. Five are scattered around Paris. Each piece is made and sent vacuum-packed at a few degrees above freezing to far-flung outlets. But the headquarters remains in a tiny old-world shop on the rue du Faubourg Saint-Honoré, halfway between the fabled tables of Taillevent and the flower market at the Place des Ternes.

Luscious-looking wares crowd every shelf at La Maison, but any visitor's eye is drawn to a thirty-two-piece sampler in a simple box. Inside the open cover, printed script sets forth Linxe's philosophy: "Tasting is all an art: the art of looking; the art of tasting; the art of taking one's time." Translating that remark, I reflected on its cultural nuance. *Tasting* was not repeated in the original. In the first instance, Linxe had said *la dégustation,* which really means "the taking advantage of what God and two thousand years of civilization have allowed to land on your tongue." Whether that is mere snooty French superiority is no argument I'd want to have at mealtimes.

Up a spiral staircase, behind a cluttered little linoleum-covered desk in a spare paper-strewn loft, I found the patriarch. Linxe, in semi-retirement at seventy-four, had lost none of the zeal that propelled him into chocolate a half century earlier. With sparse gray hair, horn-rimmed glasses, and delicate features, he was a quiet, slender man in a black cashmere blazer. Hardly pretentious, he wore a plastic ballpoint around his neck on a brown shoelace. But when he detected nearby interest in his chocolate, he puffed up and swooped in like a balding eagle late for lunch.

I often record interviews, but for this one, the tape was all but unusable. It was punctuated with the scraping of chairs, excited sighs and gasps, furious ruffling of papers in old files against the background of a bustling chocolate business down those open spiral stairs.

Minutes into our conversation, Linxe was darting about the small room for visual aids. At one point, he seized what looked like a small stone double bed.

"Do you know what this is?" he asked.

"Sure," I replied. "That's Chloé's metate."

Linxe stopped for a moment, gaping like a trout out of water. By coincidence, Chloé had mentioned that she had given Linxe as a gift her miniature Mexican grinding stone. The world of good chocolate is a small one.

When I asked about his early training at the now-defunct COBA academy in Basel, Switzerland, Linxe soared past me to clutch a tattered schoolboy's notebook from an overstuffed shelf.

"Look at these," he said, thumbing through the pages. "All of this work, all these calculations, formulas, recipes." It was, in fact, an amazing document. Every page of the thick notebook, from 1953, was covered in his tiny calligraphy. Molecular diagrams followed elaborate lists of the price of ingredients. Each hand-etched sentence was its own work of art. Linxe had submitted it for his final exam.

"Here, read this," he told me, pointing to a note written by Jules Perliat, director of the legendary academy for chocolatiers which has since closed its doors: "This workbook does honor to its author. He follows the right course of our profession. We are certain that he will succeed in it."

No one can dispute that prophecy. While waiting for my appointment, I had sampled a few stalwarts of La Maison du Chocolat. One was a *palet d'or* that was no thicker than an After Eight mint, a wafer-thin layer of dark ganache in an *enrobage* that snapped loudly at each bite. Later, Linxe handed me two pieces that made him proud. The Andalousie was dark *enrobage* over ganache flavored delicately with yellow shavings of fresh lemon peel. The Rigoletto (he loves opera) was filled with an unusual blend of ganache and *praliné*, rich in almond and luxuriant on the tongue.

Then I tried his signature Bacchus. The chocolate itself, evolved over the years, is now a Valrhona Venezuela mix. But it is only the pleasant backdrop to the starring ganache, which is flavored with Smyrna raisins from Turkey, steeped in hot water to a puffy white and then flambéed in a pan with old Caribbean rum. When flames burn from red to a low blue, just as the last alcohol vanishes, a lid is clamped on. The grapes are left to macerate for fifteen days. By the time they are turned into ganache in finely enrobed oblong bonbons, only enough peel is left for a hint of tasty texture. Rum-raisin was never like this.

When Linxe came back from training in Switzerland, he labored in chocolate making in other people's employ at a time when few Frenchmen appreciated real quality chocolate. France consumed mostly mediocre products made from Ivory Coast cacao. Switzerland and Belgium were still Europe's pacesetters. An admirer convinced him that he was not made to work for someone else. And, fortuitously, he married a wealthy woman.

Linxe's first shop on the rue Wagram, la Marquise de Presle, was an uphill struggle. "For seven years, I worked like a slave under a heavy deficit, always in the red," he said. "I never got home before one a.m., making everything fresh for the next morning. If not for a father-in-law who believed in me and lent money, I wouldn't have survived."

That was during the 1960s, when France's undisputed king of chocolate was the late "Papy" Bernachon, in Lyon. As Linxe recalls it, a leading food writer raved about his Bacchus in 1968, comparing him to the Lyonnais legend. But Paris was preoccupied with riots in the streets, and few people hurried to his door.

Linxe opened La Maison du Chocolat in 1977. He hardly succeeded on his own. Chaudun spent six years at his stoves in the early years before bad blood boiled over. And there were others. But after a quarter century of consistent quality, La Maison is the chocolate standard. If its products may not have the soaring notes of genius that I sometimes found with Jacques Genin, they maintain an absolute quality, wherever they are sold.

Linxe's illustrated book, among the best of a library of tomes by chocolatiers, makes clear he suffers from no false modesty. He does not explain how to be a master, he says, because that is not something one learns. His main shop is opposite the Salle Pleyel, a center of fine music, he notes. And he makes his own kind of music.

"If one ranks me among the experts in chocolate, it is not only because I work with it and I explore without letup a noble and demanding product," he writes,

> but also because I can still feel its latent resources, its still hidden treasures, like a jeweler with precious metals, a cabinetmaker with rare woods, or a parfumier with dabs of scent. We creative artists are fortunate to have in our hands each day an exceptional material . . . Do not take this as provocation. It is simply a way of saying that chocolate does not always let itself happen. It does not give itself easily to those who do not know it.

Chocolate, he adds, is not a matter of changing fashion. ("This year, chocolate will be worn very dark and extra-dry," he adds in a mocking aside.) It follows an irreversible evolution.

> I have chosen for a very long time to rehabilitate "real" chocolate. This has distance, and it brings together power, aroma, length in the mouth. It is a question of balance, of harmony. This might seem abstract for an apparent *friandise* as banal as chocolate, but it is like a great wine, in which connoisseurs can appreciate structure, power, roundness, and texture.

And Linxe is not one to measure his words in conversation. "I believe you have to say the good but also the bad," he told me. This was when I slipped in a question about Chaudun. "Oh, he's fine for making fancy little designs out of chocolate," Linxe said. "But as a real craftsman, I don't think so."

To make memorable chocolate, he said, you need above all the palate to recognize it. You need the imagination to create but also the technical skill to repeat any miracle that happens to occur in the process. And then you must have the concentration to stay there at your pots, hour after hour, year after year.

But then who, I asked, did he think made good chocolate in France, or anywhere else?

"It's all good, but . . ." he began, clearly not meaning it. "Look, I'll show you," he said, grabbing a scrap of paper and a pencil. He sketched a sort of Eiffel Tower and drew three lines across it. "Here, you have people who make good chocolate," he said, wiggling pen marks across the lowest line. Moving to the second line, he continued, "And here, you have very good chocolate." Then he pointed to the apex. "Up here is the super extra chocolate which defies description."

I pressed harder: Who was up in that rarefied air?

Linxe's small smile widened to a beatific grin. "Me," he said. "I don't really see any others."


*I*n fact, ranking chocolatiers is an impossible job anywhere, let alone in France, where reputations can rise and fall like skirt hems according to fashion. The Club de Croqueurs de Chocolat publishes an annual guide, with ratings, but it can be arbitrary. Chaudun, who resists providing a roomful of free samples for club dinners, was dropped to a second-rank category. And some of the great French artisans are specialists.

Henri Le Roux, in the lovely little Brittany port of Quiberon, enlivens his chocolate with what is likely the world's best salted-butter caramel. Joël Durand, in the fashionable Provence town of Saint-Rémy, scents his ganache with such local flavors as rosemary and lavenders.

In Normandy, Michel Cluizel is a mix between artisan and industrialist. His small plant produces chocolate from beans he carefully selects at plantations on three continents. Cluizel uses no soy lecithin, which purists appreciate. And more important to most of us, he makes some wonderful chocolate.

In France, one does not merely eat chocolate, or bake with it. At his three-star belle époque restaurant near the Louvre, Le Grand Véfour, Guy Martin offers lamb chops with chocolate-coffee sauce.

Martin starts with a lamb stock made from bones, carrots, onions, parsley, a bay leaf, and thyme. To the reduced stock, he adds a shot of espresso and melted dark chocolate. Then he whisks in butter, salt, and ground fennel seeds. The lamb is browned and basted with blueberry preserves and Dijon mustard. It is then baked for five minutes at 400 degrees F. To serve, he sauces a plate and tosses on peeled and seeded white grape halves. And then, because he is Guy Martin, he sprinkles the edges with fennel seeds and ground coffee.

I did not test this recipe any more than I tried to duplicate Martina's mole in Mexico. Some magic is best left to the magicians.

*T*he French are fairly new to their role as chocolate masters. Until the early 1970s, trade agreements kept France tied to its former African possessions. For decades, bitter Ivory Coast robusta coffee was the price Paris paid for its colonial policy. It was the same with low-quality Ivorian *forastero* cacao. Belgians made better chocolate, and no one argued about it. When other markets opened, however, the picture began to change.

Now, with a great world chocolate awakening, fancy *fondeurs* are only a part of it. Along with Valrhona, smaller artisans make their own specialties from beans they find on their equatorial forays.

One of them is Chloé's favorite chocolate maker. She keeps a broad range for varying moods and times of day. But when I pinned her down, she did not hesitate a moment: "Late at night when it is just me and my chocolate, and I go for what I really love, it is Pralus."

*F*rançois Pralus makes his own chocolate from beans he knows personally. Compared to the million tons produced each year at Barry Callebaut, he is not exactly a major player. But his crisply delicious *couverture* is likely to be the last thing a diner tastes before getting up from any number of France's fanciest Michelin-starred tables.

Pralus is what the French call *"un original."* It is meant, mostly, as a compliment. With his surfer tan, iron-gray crew cut, morning-at-the-gym build, and a hail-fellow laugh that stops traffic, he is not one to blend unnoticed into any background. But he is old-world French. He grew up in Roanne, in the comfortable Rhône River heartland near Lyon, where eating well is a serious civic obligation.

From Roanne's train station, the nearest spot for nourishment is Troisgros, the ancestral temple of fine French cuisine, now run by Michel Troisgros. As a lifelong friend of Pralus, he makes rich use of the local chocolate. But so do Pierre Gagnaire, Guy Martin, Guy Savoy, and others who demand quality twinned with class.

I met Pralus at the Salon du Chocolat. In fact, I could not have missed him if I tried. His outsize booth was packed with attractive wares and jammed with eager buyers. From the opening bell to the last weary hour, every day of the show, he was there to shake hands or slap backs as the occasion demanded.

In a culture where culinary stars can tend toward obsessive shyness or unattractive arrogance, Pralus is a refreshing rarity. Like Linxe, he makes something he is proud of, and he is ready to tell the world about it, one person at a time.

The heart of Pralus's empire is the same little shop in downtown Roanne that his father opened after World War II. Old pictures recall the tone of earlier days: purveyors of serious sweets in relaxed attitudes. Much of the atmosphere remains the same. Regulars line up early for their old favorites. Pralus himself is often there, exchanging gossip and asking after grandchildren. But things are not exactly the same. A restless innovator, he carries his personal touch far beyond the Rhône Valley.

He still makes the Praluline, his father's grand triumph, a large round brioche studded with chunks of pink candied almonds. Pralulines stay fresh for only a few days, but he couriers them to addicts at the ends of the earth.

He has opened shops around France and is exploring ways to expand beyond. For a touch of class, Pralus abandoned the classic cardboard *ballotin*. Instead, even small assortments of chocolates are packed in polished inlaid boxes handcrafted from tropical woods in Madagascar.

But the major change is the large shed across town where Pralus roasts beans and, with a ragtag assemblage of machinery, makes his own chocolate. He set up his small plant a decade ago and took on the established masters.

"I got tired of calling up Valrhona and saying that I want so many kilos of this and so many kilos of that," he explained. "I knew it would be a lot of extra work. My father told me I was an idiot. Friends thought I should be locked up. But I wanted to control quality from the very first steps and find ways of doing things better."

Lloveras, the Catalan purveyor of chocolate-making machinery, provided him with a prototype of what would turn out to be a grand success: the Universal. This all-in-one machine takes winnowed beans and converts them, step by step in the same rotating drum, into conched chocolate ready to be tempered. Purists argue that the result amounts to the difference between machine-washed and hand-washed laundry. Nothing is ever without its partisans in the chocolate business.

Pralus has circled the equator in search of beans. In the end, he chose a dozen suppliers from South America, Africa, and Asia. With a perfectionist's obsession and an air-travel card, he is always looking for something new.

In Pralus's little empire, you begin to understand why simply stating a preference for dark chocolate over milk chocolate is no more selective than choosing red wine over white. Reds go from Pétrus to unlabeled *pinard*, with a great deal in between. Neither high price nor fancy packaging is a reliable guide.

The popular practice of declaring the country of origin is no more helpful. "France" on a wine label may offer promise, but some French wines are barely suitable for dousing a kitchen fire. "Venezuela" on chocolate might mean selected beans from prized plantations or some nasty stuff from elsewhere in a large country.

Early in the 1990s, long before it got to be a fad, Pralus decided to act as a sort of chocolate sommelier. He chose beans of carefully selected origins and labeled them for customers who knew the difference. These days, he offers his assorted selections in ten 50-gram squares, his Pyramide. Each square is wrapped in a distinctive bright color, and all of them are bundled together with raffia strips.

His favorite is Madagascar, packaged in a lively lemon-green. Its label suggests "a fresh nose lightly mentholated and fruity, acidic and long on the tongue." After a few trips to the exotic island off southern Africa, he decided to buy his own plantation.

I liked his Colombian chocolate, which he describes accurately: "powerful nose, well-balanced flavors, coffee, buttermilk caramel, a slightly astringent final note." And I loved the Ghana, in rich purple paper; its long-lasting flavor is peppered with spicy peaks and only a hint of vanilla. The Trinidad is redolent of smoky dried herbs and blond tobacco. The Ecuador hints of figs and candied citrus, rich on the tongue.

It was fun trying to identify the flavor notes that were printed in handwriting-like script on those colorful wrappers. But in the end, chocolate is not wine. Or even olive oil. Some tastes linger longer, but volatile flavor elements race through a brief life span. Each bean, and each batch, can surprise you.

Those flimsy paper wrappings do little to lock in flavor. If you like Pralus, I learned, eat it fast or at least store it far from the garlic and pipe tobacco.

Pralus's factory reflects his style. A hundred things seem to be happening at once, crammed into a tight space according to some unseen order. If picturesque, it has its drawbacks. Chloé nailed one problem at a glance. Every so often, the ganache developed a sort of moldy yeast. If this poses no threat to health and is usually undetectable to us amateurs, it is nothing a fancy confectioner wants to put on a plate. The culprits were microorganisms floating around in underfiltered warm air. When Chloé chided him, Pralus laughed off what he called UFOs in his chocolate. But he quickly addressed the phenomenon.

Pralus took me to the meandering house he built at the edge of Roanne. The view, dramatic and yet peaceful, stretched halfway to Lyon. He had hung a few of his canvases: abstract women he paints by smearing a brush with melted chocolate. The door was a massive wood block carved with a São Tomé cacao-growing motif.

I had brought a fresh notebook, but Pralus's message is simple enough to scribble on the back of an envelope. He is passionate about chocolate and, as with his other passions, he pushes to the limits. He makes what he likes and lets details take care of themselves. And a well-trained staff follows his orders, even when he is there only in spirit.

He can throw himself into an experimental recipe, creating some masterful new creation, and then forget how he did it because he took no notes. He charges off in one direction and then, caught by some pressing reality, veers off in another. Pralus, I quickly saw, is not one for tedious repetition.

It was Pralus who introduced me to Claudio da Príncipe. In some ways, their adventuresome souls are perfectly matched. The two spent a happy week in São Tomé brewing cacao white lightning and cooking up grand ideas. One of the colorful plaques in Pralus's raffia-tied collection is labeled GRAND CRU CLAUDIO CORALLO.

But Claudio's relaxed exterior masks a scientist's soul. He gets an idea and worries it to death, keeping after it until it comes out right. And then he does it again. Pralus, for better or worse, follows his whim. Then his attention is attracted elsewhere, and he is off in another direction.

I should have known when I made the appointment. Just before Christmas, most chocolate people are too busy to stop and tie their shoes. When I first rang up Roanne, I apologized for the timing but explained that I wanted to see him in operation during the holiday crush.

No problem, Pralus replied. Just say when. But I should be certain to call first, he added. He might be away for a while getting his pilot's license.

# Chapter 10

# BELGIUM: HOBBIT CHOCOLATE

Christmas routinely settles over Belgium with a decided shortage of peace on earth. At NATO headquarters, generals fret over terrorism and distant rumbles of war. At the European Union, ministers squabble on, usually about money. But in the heart of the capital, you can sit in the midst of old-world splendor and eavesdrop as the Brussels bourgeoisie, comfortable as Hobbits, discusses the best place to buy their holiday chocolate.

Brussels's showpiece is the Grand-Place, perhaps the most thrilling patch of cityscape left in Europe. The four-hundred-year-old guild halls that flank it are grandiose and kitsch at the same time, as if craftsmen who hung the ornate iron balustrades from the pointy stone towers had drunk too much lunchtime beer. Elaborate façades soar up to multicolored slate roofs. Leaded glass decorates each building, like paintings in a gallery. City Hall, the centerpiece, is a carved stone fantasy, with balconies dominating a vast cobblestone square below. It is plainly the seat of a people who like their pleasures and mean to stay put.

At street level, there is no mistaking the overriding theme. Shop windows are awash in chocolate, under all the big names that the outside world knows so well: Leonidas, Godiva, Neuhaus. Souvenir joints offer weird novelties in waxy chocolate, stamped with words that let tourists bring home obvious tokens of where they have been.

But serious Belgian chocolate buyers head for a newer place, the Grand-Sablon. Arriving early, I moved into a corner café table to soak in the ambiance.

In a world of fast food and junky shops, the Grand-Sablon is a throwback to a different age. Sometimes it gets a bit hectic, such as when President Bill Clinton appeared at the Restaurant Saint-Martin for his morning doughnut. But more often, it is a calm refuge for people who like things the way they used to be.

On the dark-paneled walls of the Grand Mayeur, photos of Clark Gable and David Niven are lost among portraits of Flemish screen idols who seem to pre-date the talkies. Men in frayed wool suits and outrageous mustaches plume clouds of pipe smoke. Chic women spoon butter and homemade jam onto thick slices of toast. A busty waitress in black fires back amused retorts at remarks by male customers that could cost them jail time in certain lawyer-laced societies.

The man next to me that morning, in a camel-hair sweater and half-glasses, sucked deeply at his cigarette as he digested his newspaper. He was the perfect old-world Belgian, the sort who dines amply, in no particular hurry, on large cuts of meat in cream sauce. A middle-aged couple visiting from elsewhere in Belgium must have had the same impression. Sitting down beside him, they sought his counsel on where to buy good chocolate.

After a moment, I butted into the conversation. You do that sort of thing in Brussels, especially over morning coffee in old-wood havens like the Grand Mayeur.

Jean-Louis Thier, a retired antiques dealer, loved his chocolate and was no snob about it. He remained fond of Côte d'Or, a family operation that was long ago acquired by Kraft and now takes up substantial supermarket shelf space. He mentioned Neuhaus, which began as a small shop in 1857. Neuhaus revolutionized the business with its *ballotin*, an attractive domed cardboard box to replace the cones of paper that artisans once used. But Neuhaus had grown to be a corporate-style worldwide purveyor of chocolate. Thier also touted Leonidas, another globe-girdling big player.

This was my first random sample of a local expert, and I was already beginning to wonder.

"Belgian chocolate is by far the best, no comparison to that stuff in France," Thier told me. "Frenchmen come here and buy chocolate by the kilo."

I asked him why.

"Because it's made with pure butter," he replied. "In France, they all use margarine."

This threw me at first. Chocolate is usually made with cocoa butter. The worst stuff is cut with different sorts of vegetable oil. Cream goes into blends for ganache. Butter is used only for certain fillings.

As the conversation continued, I realized what Thier meant. Belgian chocolate was better because it was Belgian. This was a mere article of faith.

I remembered that Fancy Food Show party in New York, when a string of Belgian strangers berated me because they had heard I thought France made better chocolate. Travel abroad soon reveals the folly of simplistic cultural generalities. But most nations have their defining characteristics, for better or worse. In the particular case of Belgium, the subject of chocolate is touchy ground. Living in the shadow of France, the butt of endless French gibes, Belgians often suffer in silence. On matters of chocolate, they draw their line in the sand.

French tastes centered on cacao. Thier was talking less about chocolate than the stuff that it encased—the finished creamy, sugary, boozy, nutty fillings identified with the delights that were finally placed on a shelf.

By then, it was 10 a.m., opening time on the Grand-Sablon. I thanked my first Belgian witness and went out to see for myself.

*I* knew where I wanted to go. Face-to-face across the broad square, far apart yet within glowering distance, were two of the world's grand chocolatiers. Paul Wittamer, the traditionalist, made not only the rich bonbons that Belgians call *pralines,* but also a range of otherworldly cakes and pastries in the shop his grandfather opened in 1910. And Pierre Marcolini, a flamboyant empire builder, sold his delicate pralines and single-varietal chocolate bars in a stylish showroom he opened after spending a year with Wittamer. It is wise not to mention one to the other.

Paul Wittamer was where I had hoped to find him, at work in his kitchens a few days before a Belgian Christmas. He was pacing at some speed, his eyes scanning the room while he talked into a cell phone. By the time he broke free to nod a welcome, guilt had overcome me. I'd stay only a moment, I said, and then come back at a better time. He wouldn't hear of it. Chocolate was his life, and he was eager to talk.

Wittamer, tall, graying, and gaunt with a self-effacing air of shyness, addressed his subject in serious terms. This was not poetry but rather a highly precise set of formulas, temperatures, and procedures. Yes, he allowed, a certain alchemy came into play. Imagination was a large part of it. As with most things, in the kitchen or elsewhere, skill depended on understanding the nature of each ingredient. But, he said, chocolate was different.

Almost everything else offers some leeway. A half minute too long in the water still leaves most pasta al dente. It takes some time before crème brûlée is more than a figure of speech. But a careless drop of water in molten chocolate can be fatal. Each degree, each tick of the timer, has its importance.

"There comes a point where you just have to feel it," Wittamer said. "It's something you learn with experience, if you work at it and have the sense for it." Here again was that sense of nuance that marked the best practitioners. Anyone could speak a straightforward language, such as Spanish, by learning vocabulary, pronunciation, and grammar. But one spoke Mandarin Chinese only after mastering the four tones that differentiate one seemingly similar word from another.

At one point, I mentioned that Marcolini was planning to process cacao and make his own chocolate from scratch. Wittamer's gentlemanly mien twisted to a scowl. That, he said, was a gimmick. Marcolini might make a small amount for show, but what was the point when specialists produced fine raw material? Why waste the time competing for beans in a cutthroat global market? "We don't make chocolate," he concluded. "We create with it."

Until the mid-1960s, the Wittamers made only pastry and ice cream. Paul's grandfather, Henri, opened the shop in 1910 and stuck to baking good bread. He died in 1945, just as the Belgians emerged from a long war and struggled to survive on ration cards. His son, another Henri, decided to make something fancier. He and his wife, Yvonne, turned out cakes and pastries distinctive enough to put the Grand-Sablon on Belgium's culinary map.

In the 1960s, an antiques market opened nearby and dealers moved in to set up shops, bringing fresh crowds to the old store. Henri had his hands full baking the old favorites for a loyal clientele; he saw no reason to change. But Paul (that is his second name; he is actually Henri III) wanted to make chocolates. He studied at the prestigious and now defunct COBA academy in Basel, Switzerland. Then he worked alongside Robert Linxe at La Maison du Chocolat in Paris. When he came back home, he was equally adept at Belgian pralines and classic almond *pralinés*—no relation—with the accent over the *e*.

Henri III still bakes a mean chocolate gâteau. His Black Forest cake, with its clouds of chocolate mousse, is among the world's wonders. Four years after the fact, he put on display a photograph he had treasured in private. Pope Paul VI beamed at him with pleasure, the after-effect of a *torte printempière* that Wittamer had been flown to Rome to prepare for the pontiff's dessert.

When King Albert II was about to take a wife in 1999, he sampled twenty different Wittamer cakes before settling on a chocolate creation to slice at the dinner.

But a separate section of the Wittamer shop several doors down from the main bakery does its own brisk trade. I had explored it while waiting for my appointment with the boss. The store itself is a creation. A large fuchsia *W* is painted on the awning over a blue sky and fluffy clouds. (After Marcolini hired Delvaux, the leather designer, to fashion his packaging, Wittamer's sister, Myriam, commissioned her own trendy display consultants.)

For Easter, Myriam teamed the high-profile hat maker Elvis Pompilio with her in-house secret weapon, a cheery chocolate artist from Manchester named Michael Lewis Anderson. Pompilio produced two trademark designs: a veiled pillbox and a velvet riding hat. Anderson copied them in chocolate. At Christmas, Anderson needed no outside inspiration. He sculpted a Nativity scene, complete with fleecy lambs and hay in the manger and a background of old Bethlehem carved stone architecture.

Anderson, who is also Wittamer's public persona and all-around alter ego, was waiting for me amid the chocolate. One after the other, he plucked pralines from the shelves.

"You can't miss this one," he said, handing me a chocolate champagne cork filled with Grand Marnier–flavored fresh cream and topped with dark *couverture*. Next was a pyramid coated in crushed red raspberry. I skipped the horse's head with hazelnut inside, but found myself sampling infusions of Earl Grey tea, ginger, lemon, and several others before I could get Anderson to stop. This was a man who loved his work.

In each of the samples, chocolate played a secondary role to the other stronger flavors. Sugar muscled forward with each bite. But I ended with the standard: a luscious *palet d'or* of plain ganache with WITTAMER stamped all over it in gold. It was worthy of the name.

Anderson had a different approach to chocolate art than did Patrick Roger in Sceaux. Rather than taking molten *couverture* off the line, he used a special modeling chocolate. When I asked if it was edible, he snapped off a wise man's big toe and handed it to me. You could eat it, all right, but then again you could also eat modeling clay.

Later, I sat down with Wittamer to discuss grand themes. "Whatever people like in their chocolate," he said, "the only constant thing that matters is quality. Tastes vary, like in everything." He dismissed polemic over Belgian versus French chocolates as pointless chauvinism from both sides. This was simply a matter of differing styles.

"Belgium is in a crossroads position with certain influences from all directions," he explained. "Besides Belgians, we sell also to the Dutch, the French, the Swiss, and we combine facets of all these tastes. Belgian chocolate is made most often with molds, which means the coating is thicker. Because of this harder outside shell, we can use softer centers, with more fresh cream and greater variety of fillings than the French. Our pralines are larger than theirs. They use a thinner *couverture.*"

That made perfect sense. Frenchmen prefer their mussels with a little garlic and parsley, steamed simply as *moules marinières.* Belgians like theirs fried or doused in cream. France eats endives in salads or braised with ham. In Belgium, France's take-it-or-leave-it endive is the revered *chicon,* a national obsession that can star by itself at dinnertime.

Chocolate, to French gourmets, is the final touch of elegance at the end of a good meal, or a minor treat to be savored occasionally. Belgians like their chocolates with substance, the sort of sizable sweet blobs of comfort that J.R.R. Tolkien might place in Bilbo Baggins's warm parlor.

But what about Switzerland? When I started on the chocolate trail, I expected that to be my holy grail. My impression was that much of the world shared that view. But the more I investigated, the more I found that chocolatiers and connoisseurs turned up their noses at Swiss chocolate. Wittamer was one of them.

A few Swiss artisans made exceptional bonbons, Wittamer allowed, especially in Basel. But mostly, he said, the Swiss all buy the same base ingredients from the same suppliers. "It all tastes alike, everywhere," Wittamer said. "Mostly, it's a problem of labor costs. Making chocolate takes a lot of intensive work and time. Wages there are too high."

When I asked about mass-market chocolate, he was generous. For most consumers, price counts. And handmade chocolates are expensive. Although a lot of industrial confection is inedible junk, he said, some brands offer excellent quality at a fraction of what high-end chocolatiers have to charge.

"In the end, each person has his own idea about what constitutes good chocolate," Wittamer said, echoing his earlier thought. It was a point I had heard often before. "We train a lot of people from Tokyo here, but when they get home they make their own adjustments. It's only natural. The Japanese have their own tastes and flavors."

We had moved to Wittamer's cozy restaurant above the bakery. As we pawed over pictures of the early years, his niece, Leslie, brought a cup of foaming hot chocolate. She also set down a plate of assorted petits fours and tidbits that I wolfed down so fast I neglected to make notes.

"We do a lot of chocolates with alcohol because people want them," Wittamer said. "I like to experiment with unusual things and find new flavors. But after a while it just gets to be silly." I mentioned Jean-Paul Hévin's white chocolate with cheese. "You come to a point where you forget what you're supposed to be doing. The idea, in the end, is only to create wonderful chocolates."

Wittamer estimated his annual production at twenty-seven tons. That is a lot for a small shop, about the same level as François Pralus in Roanne. And it was nearly Christmas. The guilt finally got to me, and I insisted that he go back to work. He handed me back over to Michael Lewis Anderson, who led me off for a look at the inner sanctum.

We maneuvered through a few doors and hallways until we emerged into a vast, long room that exuded every rich aroma a chocolate lover holds holy. Although Wittamer's two shops on the Grand-Sablon were separated by other businesses, he had acquired all the space behind.

Out front, where long lines of customers waited patiently for their turn, it looked like an ordinary busy day. Except for Michael's decorations, not much suggested the frenzied run-up to a Belgian Christmas. But, I discovered, it was all happening out back.

The kitchen was jammed with machinery I had come to know. *Enrobeuses* sprayed a curtain of *couverture* over ganache centers, and conveyor belts carried finished pralines through twenty-foot-long cooling chambers. At the end, women stenciled gold-leaf markings on each of the moving chocolates. In a far corner, others boxed, bundled, and stacked.

A man of generous mustache and all-suffering eyes synchronized movements like an orchestra conductor. Periodically, he moved to a great tub of cream that turned slowly as he blended in chocolate bricks and assorted flavor infusions. He reminded me of Martina making mole under the volcano. Nothing seemed to be measured, but by sheer force of experience, he had it down to the gram.

Michael and I moved like bullfighters to avoid laden carts trundling past. Workers' smocks were smeared thickly in brown. It looked as though we had walked in on a chocolate food fight. As women scurried to keep up with pralines rolling down the lines, all I could think of was that classic *I Love Lucy* episode where Lucille Ball ends up entangled in a conveyor belt, stuffing her mouth with runaway chocolates.

*P*ierre Marcolini, a sometimes charming if hard-driven entrepreneur, looks at the staid artisan chocolate world somewhat as Attila the Hun viewed ancient Rome. There is much to conquer. Late in 2002, he bought machinery to roast beans and make some of his chocolate from scratch. He opened shops in London, Paris, and Tokyo, along with his half-dozen Belgian outlets and one in Malmö, Sweden. He had imperial plans reaching from New York to Moscow.

Marcolini's chocolate factory near Brussels Airport is another world entirely from the stately old Grand-Sablon. Visitors enter a spacious lobby, with the latest products on artful display. The man himself is part of the show. Not overly worried about formality, he might appear at a fancy occasion in rumpled corduroys. But, for him, PIERRE MARCOLINI on chocolate is sacred. His logo is a shaded line drawing of a cacao pod, in rich chocolate brown, over his name in bold sans-serif letters.

Along with his pralines and *pralinés*, he offers such specialties as a set of single-varietal chocolate bars packaged in heavy embossed cardboard and protected with a clear plastic liner.

Unlike many chocolatiers who work in cramped quarters zealously protected from prying eyes, his factory is made to be seen. Gleaming new machines are spaced far apart on tiled floors in rooms separated by glass walls. He buys the best equipment he can find, sometimes seeking inspiration by visiting competitors and taking surreptitious notes. Work surfaces are stainless steel. Everyone wears hospital white, down to protective gauze booties. Part of it is for hygiene. But probably more, it is how the Belgian empire builder likes to do things.

As we toured the plant together, Marcolini led me out the back door. By no accident, he was within sight of Brussels's airport from where he could rush his fresh products around the world.

"Here is the best part," he said, with a broad grin, gesturing to an empty field of purple and yellow wildflowers stretching off in the other direction away from the airport, large enough to accommodate Hershey, Pennsylvania. "Look at all that room to expand."

Wittamer gave the impression that he would be happy to live out his days listening to cream bubble in his own small realm. Marcolini seemed determined to leave a broad trail of chocolate from the Grand-Sablon to Ginza.

Though a dyed-in-the-wool Belgian and proud of it, Marcolini beamed in pleasure when I repeated Pierre Hermé's assessment of his work: "*Ah oui*. He makes French chocolate in Belgium."

I first met Marcolini at the Salon du Chocolat in Paris. It did not go well. I stopped at his booth with a friend in tow, a Hollywood producer who declared a deep love for chocolate. When I announced my purpose, Marcolini gestured to his full line on display and invited us to take our pick. As I admired the gleaming rows and searched for a signature dark *palet d'or*, my friend snatched up a piece of white chocolate. This was no more than cocoa butter, devoid of real chocolate. Marcolini's smile tightened, and he found some urgent business elsewhere.

Later in Brussels, however, with an enthusiastic introduction from Chloé, he welcomed me as a family member. I spent the day at his factory and decided that in some ways Shakespearean ambition is not so bad. He would make a perfectly acceptable Julius Caesar. One merely had to be careful not to mention any place he might be tempted to conquer.

Sometime later, I saw that was no idle thought. Chloé mentioned to him that she had visited a plantation in Mexico that still grew nearly pure *criollo*. She told him she had gone with an American friend who wanted to start making chocolate with the rare beans. Her friend soon learned that Marcolini had swooped in and bought up the next five years' crop.

As most of his colleagues did, Marcolini started young. "I always took two desserts as a kid," he said. "I saw that was going to cost me in the future, so I figured I'd better make some choices for myself. When I started working with sugar, I realized how many things you can do with it. I learned the important thing is to keep in mind how human tastes relate to it, to proportions and nuances."

He is not shy about the title he won in France: "World Champion

Pâtissier, 1995." It was emblazoned on the awning of his Grand-Sablon shop.

These days, handsome with chestnut hair and a beefy frame that suggests a life of second desserts, Marcolini still approaches chocolate like an eager kid. He is obsessed by ideas and innovations. The day I visited, he was enthralled with a new toy, a neatly calibrated guillotine that allowed him to slice open rows of cacao beans to sample the quality of any batch that came his way.

A more elaborate toy was set up by his high-tech desk: a satellite sensing system that uses spy chips embedded in sacks of beans. With it, he monitors each shipment from his equatorial suppliers. The chips send up regular readings, which a computer tracks on graphs. "With this thing," he said, "I can tell any time a transporter lets the temperature rise anywhere along the route."

Marcolini's wife, Nicoletta, had more traditional tastes. Her half of the office was lined with chocolate molds, beautiful objets d'art from generations past for making intricate molded animals and holiday motifs.

As Wittamer had said, Marcolini made only a small amount of chocolate from beans, despite his sales pitches suggesting the contrary. But Marcolini espoused François Pralus's point of view. Why depend on someone else? If things went according to plan, he could locate reliable producers and buy beans that he knew personally. Whether or not the economic numbers made sense, he said, he saw it as a philosophical decision.

"With chocolate, what's important is the quality of the basic ingredient," Marcolini told me. If a crop is superior, he will buy it before harvest. "I'm ready to pay a good price for beans, and that's my advantage." The cacao business is like that. In Trinidad, he visited a plantation that had been locked up by Valrhona. "The guy had twenty tons all ready to go to France. He winked at me and said, 'Of course, if you give me more, it's yours.'"

In the meantime, Marcolini shops around carefully for his *couverture*. He buys from Valrhona and the Chocolaterie de l'Opéra in Paris. And others as well. Each product he makes requires a different texture and taste, and he knows what he wants.

It is not just the chocolate. In one corner of his warehouse, sacks of almonds were stacked carefully waiting to be crushed. "Those are from Spain," he said. "They cost me a fortune, but they're the best." His hazelnuts, equally choice, come from northern Italy. Taste is important but so is uniformity of size for mixing.

Vanilla beans from Madagascar, long, moist, and purple, were stored with elaborate care. Choice Spanish oranges were laid out, ready to be candied. Chinese jasmine tea, fresh ginger, and all the rest of his ingredients were prepped for final blending.

With a theatrical flourish, Marcolini showed me his new operations room. A cylindrical roaster, after twenty minutes at 160 degrees, spilled out richly scented *nacional* beans from Ecuador to be hulled and crushed to nibs. Cacao, cocoa butter, and sugar were heated and mixed into chocolate liquor. Finally, the finished blend spent days in a conche.

In the end, Marcolini said, a good chocolatier must think beyond borders. Preferences may vary from culture to culture, he explained, but taste is universal.

"Look at classical music, which touches people profoundly, whether they are in Japan, the United States, or in Argentina," he said. "When something is really good, everyone likes it. With chocolate, we all have to improve, to raise the level, to make people understand how wonderful this product can be. That is my goal."

In 2003, Belgian promoters launched Chocoa, their own version of the successful French Salon du Chocolat. It was a noble effort, but there was little about it to comfort Belgian chocolate chauvinists. Only a trickle of visitors braved the raindrops to come to the industrial fairgrounds near Brussels. Most were professionals who found few surprises.

Marcolini showed up, reluctantly if dutifully, but only to help judge chocolate creations by promising young artisans. Wittamer was not there.

Tradition was represented by Mary, a jewel of a shop that has done business on Brussels's rue Royale for a century and a half. George W.

Bush dropped by when he came to town. But even with that culinary endorsement, few people in the salon's sparse crowd stopped to sample its sugary and fussy chocolates.

Some assured me that Belgium faced no challenge. At the end of one row, I found Christian Vanderkerken of Chocolaterie Manon, whose pralines and conversation had been memorable when we last met. With a dramatic mustache and piercing eyes, he delivered strongly held views. The French were late-blooming parvenus whose momentary glory would not last. "Until recently, they hardly made any chocolate worth thinking about," he told me. "Now they have made it a fad, and everyone there thinks he is a genius. There is still no comparison to what we make here."

According to the Belgian Foreign Trade Board, there is scant room for improvement in Belgium's chocolate industry. Its special report on chocolate, "The Star of the Palate," proclaims: "Each and every chocolate maker (there are currently around 500 producers of handmade and factory-made chocolate in the Kingdom) unquestionably offers a perfect, masterly product."

Unquestionably?

Some wonderful stuff emerges from many of those producers, and Belgium certainly takes its chocolate seriously. I had no quibble with one conclusion of the report: "Two percent of the population admit to never eating chocolate, a fact which is highly unlikely to undermine the reputation of the national black gold or to threaten the chocolate makers present in the market."

But was it *all* so good? What mysterious extranational source was infiltrating cheap tourist shops with dull brown Silly Putty proudly labeled "Belgian chocolate"? In a world of border-spanning companies that fuse old names and make sweeping generalized boasts with no basis for credibility, what is Belgian chocolate?

Côte d'Or, for instance, did Belgium proud from its founding in 1883 until it hit the big time. "The company's breakthrough in foreign markets is due largely to its remarkable and eye-catching participation in the Brussels Universal Exposition in 1958," the Belgian Trade Board's report said.

The secret of the global success . . . lies in its selection of top quality cocoa beans, imported from Central America and Africa. Ever since it was first established, Côte d'Or has always selected the finest beans, giving its chocolate its inimitable powerful taste, since they make up more than 50 percent of the cocoa mixture.

Today, the Côte d'Or brand is the market leader in Belgium. Many of its products are still terrific. But given intense competition for a limited supply of "the finest beans" and artisan chocolatiers' willingness to pay extra, is Côte d'Or still so successful with its raw material? And, finally, is Côte d'Or really Belgian if it is owned by Kraft Foods?

For generations, the cornerstone of Belgian chocolate was Callebaut. Chocolatiers relied on its consistent *couverture* of a style they knew and loved. In 1998, Callebaut merged with Cacao Barry in France, under the industrial umbrella of Klaus Jacob. Some elements of Callebaut still function the old way in Belgium, as Valrhona does under Bongrain in France. But it is unsettling for any chocolate chauvinist who calls the new corporate headquarters of the historic Belgian institution. It is in Switzerland.

When I toured the Grand-Sablon, it was hard to miss the big Leonidas sign. There are, in fact, seventeen hundred of those signs on shops across Belgium and the rest of Europe, as well as another three hundred elsewhere in the world. At the San Francisco Fancy Food Show, I took a hard look.

As I had been told, the chocolate is sweet and fatty. Chunky pralines lack the finish that suggests fine chocolate. The no-nonsense packaging is hardly romantic. An odd-looking Spartan warrior on the logo is a bit daunting. But there is something lovable about Leonidas.

The company dates back to 1913, and its roots are actually in the United States. A Greek-Cypriot American confectioner named Leonidas Kestekidis started making chocolate about the same time as Milton Hershey. At the Brussels World Fair of 1910, he fell in love with a comely Belgian lady. After an exposition in Ghent three years later, Leonidas the Greek moved his act to Belgium.

While Neuhaus developed its fancy *ballotin*, Leonidas devised a half-open counter to sell pralines directly to passersby. His thrust was democracy in chocolate. He found ways to produce well, but cheaply, and he kept his prices as low as he could. In 1970, the company was listed on the Belgian stock exchange, but later generations of Leonidas's extended family still played a role.

Today, Leonidas remains Belgian. Its products are made in an old plant not far from Brussels, and they are flown at low temperatures to its farthest-flung outlets.

"Our philosophy is still that you shouldn't have to be rich to enjoy really good chocolate," Kurt Kroothoep said as he plied me with samples. A Belgian based in California, he represents Leonidas in North America.

The pralines were too sweet. Creamy fillings overwhelmed the unremarkable chocolate around them. But by then I had become an execrable cacao snob. This was real Belgian chocolate, fairly priced, and plenty of people liked it.

As Kroothoep explained it, most of the pralines were meant to be eaten within forty-nine days, and they were labeled as such. Subtracting transportation, that was six weeks. This meant that some preservatives had to be added, and using the freshest dairy cream was out of the question. But the product was perfectly respectable, even rigorous for a company that had to worry about a slim-margin bottom line.

Before leaving the Leonidas display in San Francisco, I gripped Kroothoep by the right shoulder and gave him the old eyeball test. If he had another job and was free to tell the truth, I asked, what would be his favorite chocolate in the world? He met my trusty lie-detector gaze and replied with a slight flush of embarrassment: "Really? Leonidas." I think he meant it.

At that Fancy Food Show in 2004, I finally met the people behind the other name associated across the world with fine Belgian chocolate: Godiva. That is a different story altogether.

# Chapter 11

# THE EMPRESS IS ALL CLOTHES

ierre Marcolini tells a great story about Godiva Choco-latier. It seems that an amiable Belgian named Joseph Draps loved his family-made product, and he handed out samples wherever he went. On a plane to New York in the 1960s, he passed a box of pralines to an American seated next to him. "Ah," the stranger exulted, "I know these; they are my wife's favorites." He urged Draps to visit him at the Waldorf-Astoria. When Draps did, the American asked how much the business was worth. And, on hearing the figure, he wrote a check for twice as much.

Of course, like so many great stories, it isn't quite true. Draps's niece, Jo, who runs a chocolate museum in Brussels, laughed when I checked it with her. "It does make pretty good history, doesn't it?" she told me. Joseph Draps is dead, she said, but for an accurate version, she suggested I call her father, Pierre. Though long since retired, Pierre was a partner in Godiva with his brothers back in the 1960s.

"Well," he said when I repeated the story to him, "not exactly." In fact, he remembered the American, a Mr. Murphy, who walked into the shop on the Grand-Place. Instead of the usual five hundred grams of chocolate that most customers requested, he wanted to buy the whole place. The brothers were stunned at the idea. The business had been in the family since their father started it in 1929 and named it after the legendary naked lady of Coventry. But they came up with a figure. The man accepted.

What is true in both accounts is that the American buyer was Bev Murphy, then head of the Campbell Soup Company. At first his company bought one-third of the business and obtained exclusive export rights. In 1974, Campbell's ate the whole thing. For three decades, Godiva Chocolatier has been no more Belgian than those red-and-white cans of chicken noodle soup that inhabit nearly every kitchen cabinet in America.

Despite its more than two hundred boutiques in major American cities and at least a thousand more outlets in U.S. department or specialty stores, not to speak of the rest of the world, Godiva is not easy to get to know. My first calls were directed to an advertising agency, which in turn referred me to press releases on Godiva's Web site. This is hardly an acceptable way for reporters to gather information. But, for starters, the canned history made for an interesting read.

"It's not surprising that Godiva Chocolatier, Inc., one of the creators of the world's most elegant handcrafted chocolates, originated in Brussels," it said. "For generations, Belgium has had a tradition of perfectionism, from its Rubens paintings and Gothic architecture to products made of intricate lace, glittering crystal and its fabulous cuisine."

Joseph Draps, who sold his chocolate piece by piece, lives on in official Godiva lore: "He had a remarkable eye for detail . . . and he perfected a unique formula of rich chocolate with unparalleled smoothness." It would take me a long time to find a live voice to explain how even the remarkable eye and steady hand of the long-dead Draps could keep track of all that chocolate.

In fact, my initial one-way communication with a Web site raised more questions than it answered. "Godiva," it said, "was first to create the concept of premium chocolate." I knew plenty of pedigreed chocolate makers who would argue with that. The master chocolatier Thierry Muret was quoted as saying Godiva's hallmark was freshness; inferior chocolates had a longer shelf life. But then why were so many Godiva products marked with sell-by dates that were more than six months in the future?

The site also offered a refreshing flash of reality: "Our growing popularity is due to our innovative approaches in manufacturing, advertising and packaging."

Godiva displays are, by and large, beautiful. At each outlet, bonbons nestle against golden glitter, skillfully arranged to fire the senses. For each season and every holiday, something clever catches the eye. Salespeople are almost always friendly and eager to help.

The problem is that so much of this tempting chocolate tasted to me as if someone dumped a lot of sugar into melted candle wax. A greasy feel blunts the few flavor notes that emerge from the chocolate. Too often, powerful ingredients overwhelm the chocolate entirely. I sometimes sensed a metallic tinge. That, of course, was just me. The many professionals I consulted were usually less charitable. Chloé tried it, unidentified, and reported hints of an overfilled ashtray.

But Godiva has its enthusiastic fans; plenty of people say they love the stuff. I needed to know more about this mysterious luxury label.


*A*n official brushoff proclaims: "Since Godiva Chocolatier, Inc., is a wholly owned subsidiary, we do not publish a separate financial statement, and do not discuss total sales, advertising costs or financial performance."

But the Campbell Soup Company is owned by stockholders. A Securities and Exchange Commission filing late in 2003 said Godiva was thriving less than its image suggested. Sales had increased at airport duty-free shops and in the Asia-Pacific region, but same-store sales in America were lower than in 2002.

In Campbell's annual report, Douglas R. Conant, a smiling CEO in shirtsleeves, observed, "Godiva continues to be one of the most recognized luxury brands in the world today. However, its growth continued to be affected by softness in consumer spending for luxury goods."

I tried every number on the site but was offered only creative ways to buy chocolate. Minor persistence turned up a corporate number in New York. When I explained my purpose, the operator gave me the company's advertising agency. I called back to insist on a press department, or at least a company spokesperson. I got the public relations company that handles Godiva on contract.

The account executive was pleasant but cautious. No, she said immediately, it would not be possible to visit Godiva's American plant in Pennsylvania. When I asked to see a company officer in New York, she suggested a telephone interview. For good measure, I mentioned that even Valrhona had let me through its hermetically sealed doors— surely that would cut some ice. She would get back to me. Right.

At the San Francisco Fancy Food Show in 2004, I left my card at the Godiva booth. Not long after, I got a call from Eugene Dunkin, chief executive officer of Godiva in North America and former head of European operations. He was about to conduct a meeting with his staff, he said, but he would be happy to make some time for an interview.

I met Dunkin at a mezzanine conference room at the Marriott, a few blocks from the hubbub of the show. He was a pleasant surprise. He seemed like an awfully nice guy, shaved and powdered to boardroom standards but easygoing and friendly.

"We go for the glorious gasp," Dunkin said, referring to that moment when a consumer, pushed toward sensory orgasm by all that golden glitter, sinks teeth into what lies beneath. "We put a lot of stock in the *ahhh* factor."

At every stage, he linked past to present. He spoke of Draps as though the long-deceased old man were still sipping schnapps in the next room. He talked with pride about the rickety four-story old factory they still used in Brussels. "You ride up the old elevator, thinking it won't make it," he said, "and then you get to the aroma of roasted hazelnuts. You could bottle the air and sell it."

Dunkin said less about the impenetrable American plant in Reading, Pennsylvania, which starts with liquid chocolate base to save time and money. I asked him if there were major formula differences between the plants in Belgium and the United States.

"The simple answer is yes," he said. "It was more complicated when we set up because Americans didn't understand dark chocolate." More recently, he said, American tastes have evolved not only in chocolate but also in coffee, wines, and clothing. "There's been a real elevation in taste. Along the way, changes were made, and our plants are engineered to deliver the same experience."

Repeatedly, Dunkin referred to "premium chocolate," and he praised Campbell Soup for pioneering this premium chocolate in North America. On its Web site, Godiva proclaims itself the world leader in premium chocolate.

At one point, I asked Dunkin to define the phrase. What, precisely, was "premium chocolate"?

He paused a moment to think and then replied, "I suppose you would say price point." By that definition, if Hershey's quintupled its price, that familiar old brown bar would be the world's greatest chocolate.

Dunkin chuckled and demurred when I pressed for details about the company. After some fencing, he allowed that its turnover was well into the hundreds of millions of dollars. He was equally vague about beans. Godiva does not make its own chocolate. It buys its basic ingredient from Callebaut, and it is apparently not shy about using cacao from Ivory Coast or anyplace else where the price is right. "Of course," Dunkin said, "we keep our formulas locked away in a little black box."

Campbell, he said, has been a boon to the company. "To their credit, they have always been supportive. They recognize that we are an indulgence brand, not a supermarket brand. Although Campbell executives want to get involved, strategically they are very hands-off. And very generous."

Godiva saw what Dunkin called monster growth in the United States during the 1990s while it lagged behind in Europe. After 2000, it filled such black spots on the map as Singapore and Bulgaria. From Hong Kong, it was launched across the Pacific Rim.

The more I pressed Dunkin for details about what was in Godiva chocolate, the more he stressed the aura around it. Regularly, Godiva's market researchers put together samplings of shoppers to test their reactions to products; executives lurk behind one-way glass and watch.

"You should see the intensity of emotions," Dunkin told me, describing one such session. "The thrill accumulates, the anticipation . . . it's not too far from sex."

He had just developed a special line, "G," an even fancier package than normal, which would retail for $110 a pound at only a handful of stores. That is, twice the price of chocolate sold at La Maison du Chocolat in Paris. The idea is to hire top designers and artists to make things beautiful.

"Look, we're a multi-hundred-million-dollar business," Dunkin said. "We give them the latitude to create magic."

Even the regular stuff is designed to evoke that *ahhhhhh*. "It is no accident that our packaging is so rich-looking and our displays are so attractive," Dunkin said. "We hire the best consultants and designers. Even the experience of opening our boxes is important. We pay a lot of money for those hand-tied bows. This is all about pleasure, the glorious gasp. Across America, we are the gold standard, equivalent to Tiffany's little blue box." As we talked, new people streamed into the room, sat down, and glanced over to where we sat. The consummate host, Dunkin steered me outside while graciously responding to any question I put to him.

The problem with the interview was that while he responded, he was not really answering. Our conversation kept veering back toward the box and not the chocolate. This was the first man I had met on the chocolate trail who seemed not to care beans about the actual basic ingredient. Or maybe he was just being cagey in a very polite way. In any case, I thanked him, and he went back in to run his meeting.

Dunkin had concluded on a note of happy optimism: "There will be growth in chocolate at the premium end. And we own the marketplace."

*B*ack in Paris, I made another visit with Dunkin's words in mind. Had I been too harsh in my judgments? Godiva's flagship shop—a classy corner store with broad appetizing windows—is barely a minute's stroll from the Ritz. Inside, the salespeople were so warm and welcoming that I had to remind myself I was in France.

A woman behind the counter answered each of my questions with enthusiasm but a thin grasp of chocolate making. When she offered samples, I asked for a *palet d'or*. She produced a well-made square with little taste to it. It was nearly as hard as *praliné*, but without any almonds. Just in case it did have some real cream in it, I was relieved to see it still had another four months of shelf life.

Clearly, Godiva marketers had been following trends. She handed me something marked 85 percent cacao content, a hot new item, but no one had given her clues as to the origin of the beans. It was suspiciously sweet for 85 percent.

Finally, guilt forced me to retreat. I was taking up her time and wasting samples offered in good spirit. To ease my mind, I bought a plain bar of dark chocolate. I did not, however, eat enough to report on the taste. With thanks to the woman, I left her to collect seventy-two euros a kilo from all those other people waiting their turn.

All things considered, one has to hand it to Godiva. Whatever the directors in New York may know about chocolate, they certainly understand human nature. Draps's old cachet is now worldwide. And even if it is meaningless and based on hype, it far outstrips its weight in gold. On my visit to Hershey, Pennsylvania, I asked a woman who had grown up in the area if she had tasted fine European chocolate. "Oh, yes," she said. "I've had Godiva."

So what if that shelf life the company's chief chocolatier had vaunted was twice that of lowly Leonidas?

Godiva has seized unoccupied high ground in an America eager for something more than Hershey and Mars. In parts of Asia, Africa, and South America where the rich—newly or otherwise—want to splurge on the gold standard, the world leader in "premium chocolate" is ready to oblige.

Other large companies sell bonbons in fancy boxes for special occasions. But Godiva strategists have discovered the secret: They made their chocolate prettier than most and expensive enough to be exclusive.

As each holiday approaches, cleverly wrapped gift packages appear in gold-bedecked windows. They exert a strong pull. A huge percentage of sales are for gifts, and it is hard to resist their physical appeal.

Full disclosure requires me to admit my own weakness. In New York, eager to thank a hotel receptionist for her usual kindness, I pondered the possibilities. Just then, I passed the Godiva shop on Lexington. The sales staff inside was friendly, and Halloween boxes with orange and black accents were classy yet amusing. I succumbed. My gift was a hit, greeted with happy squeals from the whole front desk. People love the idea of luxury, and that's what Godiva puts in a box.

*Chapter 12*

# In the Land of Rose and Vile Creams

*J*enny Cork, the departing chocolate buyer at Fortnum & Mason, took a tentative nibble at a bonbon she plucked from the box I placed on her desk. She grimaced and pitched the thing into a nearby wastebasket with all the force of Michael Jordan slamming a dunk. I was hardly offended; the whole box followed. I didn't notice whether she tasted a rose or a violet cream, but one was as bad as the other. And England loves them both with a blind passion.

"It is a very English taste," she allowed, noting that her own selection at least had a more delicate chocolate *couverture* with flavors inside that evoked an English garden rather than some kid's chemistry lab. She was even fond of violet creams from Audrey's Chocolates in Brighton. But mine, too, had come from a high-end little chocolate shop around the corner, with a faithful clientele dating back generations. It had, in fact, a royal warrant to attest that it was a regular supplier to Her Majesty the Queen.

In culinary matters, Britain labors uphill under a burdensome reputation. All those generations of serving things called bubble and squeak or mushy peas have blurred the reality of a brave new approach to mealtime. With only a little discernment, the pickiest of foodies can

find toothsome innovation just about anywhere in the United Kingdom. When it comes to chocolate, however, it still takes some search-
ing. Great Britain, the nation that was the first in the world to eat
chocolate back in 1674, today goes for some pretty vile stuff.

Jenny Cork worked hard to balance out the rose and violet creams
on Fortnum & Mason shelves. She spent years on a job that had her on
a constant prowl across Europe in search of something good. In her
basement corner, she went through sample after sample of local offerings, and she tossed 95 percent of them in her trusty garbage pail. But
she was hopeful that better times were coming to Britain.

"Criteria have changed a lot in fourteen years," she said. "The
British were very different then, the tastes weren't sophisticated enough.
You didn't hear about quality chocolate at all. Now people are pre-
pared to try something new, to spend the money for real chocolate.
That has enabled us to have Valrhona and Marcolini."

Still, Jenny acknowledged, domestic artisan chocolatiers were a
very rare breed. Even fancy little shops relied heavily on a few large
companies with an unremarkable output. The broad British taste runs
to commercial candy bars she dismisses as "candle wax in some sort of
dark stuff."

As time went on, I found some excellent English-made chocolate.
Eventually, La Maison du Chocolat and Pierre Marcolini each
opened up stores in response to a growing demand for quality. But my
initial chocolate tour of London went quickly.

I stopped first at Charbonnel et Walker, which opened for business
in a small shop on Bond Street in 1875 and has been in Mayfair ever
since. In handsome surroundings, it offers chocolates with the telltale
uniformity that suggests passage through automated machines. Its royal
warrant hung on the wall, not far from the late Queen Mum's favorite
chocolate mints. Though waxy and oversweet, they were strong enough
to excite an aged palate. Several other disappointments followed.

A larger picture grew clear to me at Selfridge's, the mammoth stone
temple to British consumption. As might be expected, it was fully

stocked. Display cases offered the usual suspects from the Continent. Red and black Valrhona logos filled one long case, with a sales attendant hovering behind. The best of Britain was there, in stacks and piles. Bendick's, having given up its shop in Mayfair, was selling its chocolate-covered ginger in a discreet corner.

But the focus was on novelty rather than taste. Odd-shaped chocolate animals and cacao-accented paraphernalia, such as cricket bats, evoked little of the love bean's distinct charm. And at the center of it all, ringing the island of cash registers, were rows upon rows of industrial junk chocolate. Nearly every package had the legally stipulated admission—in tiny letters on the back of the wrapper—that it contained vegetable fats. This was Michel Chaudun's worst nightmare.

A century ago, the Cadburys and the Frys, Quakers with a long view, were pioneers in bringing decent chocolate to the masses in small and colorful packages. But now, defenders of the faith assert, Britain is trying to kill chocolate.

In the mid-1990s, British industry supported a Continent-wide assassination attempt. Against howls of protest from France and Belgium, it succeeded. Pushed by big manufacturers, the European Union ruled that as of August 2003, up to 5 percent of chocolate could contain cheaper vegetable fats. Such substitutes as palm or mango-kernel oil cost five to ten times less than cocoa butter, and more cocoa butter could be sold to eager cosmetics makers.

This was the crisis chocolatiers had evoked in France. Although Britain allowed manufacturers to cut cocoa butter ahead of schedule, EU norm 2000/36/EG was formalized in April of 2003. Real war was still sputtering along in Iraq, but the influential French daily *Le Monde* gave most of a page to the decisive running battle of Europe's chocolate war.

"This could lead to a massacre of chocolate," Isabelle Guenée, secretary general of the French Confederation of Chocolatiers and Confiseurs, told *Le Monde*. "Today, it is five percent, but nothing guarantees that won't increase later. Anyway, no current method allows any control of this percentage. If an industrialist seeking profit uses seven percent or ten percent, there is no way to know."

The fight over substitutions dates back to the 1970s, when Britain, along with Ireland and Denmark, sought to enter the European Economic Community. One of its conditions, adopted in 1973, was that the members, six at the time, sanctify the practice of replacing some cocoa butter with vegetable fat in chocolate.

During 2001, Italy and Spain were ordered by the European Court of Justice to comply with the 1973 regulation. Both countries insisted on requiring labels to say "chocolate derivatives." But by then, a begrudging compromise had already been reached to be put in place during 2003. The EEC had become the fifteen-member European Union, which would later expand to include twenty-five states, from Portugal to Poland. Franz Fischler, EU commissioner for agriculture and food issues, noted that the old rule in force did not specify what substitute oils could be used or in what quantity. The new law continues to allow 5 percent substitution, but it is limited to six oils known as cocoa butter equivalents (CBEs): palm oil, karate, illipe, sal, kokum, and mango-kernel oil.

Even in France, some people agreed with Fischler.

"This is much ado about nothing," declared Sylvain Margou, secretary general of the French Chambre Syndicale Nationale des Chocolatiers, a trade group that links producers of all sizes. "Industrialists and artisans won't modify their recipes at the risk of losing customers."

But Christian Constant, a Paris *fondeur,* draped his doorway in black. And if most French and Belgian artisans hollered bloody murder, so did British holdouts who believed in the nobility of cacao. Soon e-mails flew back and forth among them. A planned London chocolate week ought to be canceled, they argued, because not enough producers could present "real chocolate" without lying about it.

In the Tarn, the chocolatier Yves Thuriès sculpted a hundred-pound bust of French interior minister Nicolas Sarkozy in real chocolate. He brought it to the ministry in Paris as a reflection of what

French *fondeurs* thought of the EU ruling on substituting vegetable fat. "This is imitation chocolate, surimi chocolate," Thuriès told reporters. "The EU should have imposed that label or at least required manufacturers to mention the vegetable fat. Instead, it is us who have to justify ourselves by declaring that we use pure cacao without any adulterations."

The new borderless European Union is having another sort of impact on old-world chocolate. Take Terry's, formerly of York.

In 1886, Joseph Terry turned his father's thriving confectionery business toward chocolate. After World War I, his sons joined the business. Terry's of York was soon beloved for its Chocolate Orange and All Gold chocolate. The Terrys made a point of finding quality beans; they bought a Venezuelan plantation to ensure a supply. The old plant, with its brick clock tower, was a symbol of British spirit. During World War II, it made aircraft propellers instead of chocolate. Many of its workers went to fight.

The catering giant, Forte, bought Terry's in 1963, followed by Colgate-Palmolive. United Biscuits acquired the company in 1975. And Kraft General Foods took over in 1993, folding the group in with Jacobs Suchard to create Terry's Suchard. And in 2004, Kraft announced it was closing operations in York, parceling out production to Sweden, Belgium, Slovakia, and Poland.

The problem, the Kraft executive Jonathan Horrell told me, was that the 1920s plant was too cumbersome for modern manufacturing. Instead of building a new one, Kraft decided to use existing capacity in Sweden and Belgium. Some production would go to Bratislava, in Slovakia. And the famed Chocolate Orange would be made in Poland, where wages were far lower than in Western Europe. "We came to the sad conclusion that business was no longer viable in York," Horrell said. The 316 workers would be paid off well.

In London, *The Guardian* wrote a stiff editorial, which concluded: "Without being wildly xenophobic, British chocolate tastes better to the British palate too."

Most likely. In any case, Terry's of Warsaw lacks that old ring.

*B*ut a little bit of looking produces fine chocolate, British-made and the other kind.

"We're about chocolate, not chocolates," Alan Porter said in the small London shop he runs for The Chocolate Society. In English English, that says it all. The plural noun covers the whole subject: candy bars, bonbons, paper-wrapped oddities, molded gimmicks, the works. In the singular, *chocolate* refers to what Porter describes in self-mocking overstatement as "the magnificence of what fine dark chocolate is all about."

The Chocolate Society was founded in 1989, and it picked up five thousand members over the next decade. Unlike the Club de Croqueurs de Chocolat in Paris, it is a loose-knit organization that does not take itself too seriously.

"We're not trying to do anything worldwide," Porter said. "We're just a friendly little society. If we asked our members to come to meetings, they wouldn't. We try to, and it does not happen." The society also tried setting up demonstrations and tastings as a change of pace at business conventions. That ended up costing too much money. In Britain, proselytizing in the church of chocolate takes a missionary's zeal.

Porter is not exactly a dark-robed Jesuit, but he is undaunted. His halo of silver curls is almost electric with energy. As often as not, a cellular phone is pressed to one ear. He has that uniquely English capacity to look businesslike and sober while flashing wry humor with a ruffling of eyebrows. Colorful spectacle frames and a lively tie suggest a preference for flair over formality. And he loves to talk chocolate.

"The picture has changed drastically in recent years," he said. "You can go into ordinary neighborhood delicatessens all over England and find decent dark chocolate. People are starting to understand."

Porter built a business of importing Valrhona products. He put up with four years of Gallic hauteur before the French company decided to experiment, as Valrhona executives put it, in England. Porter was their lab rat.

These days, Britain imports tons of Valrhona chocolate each year, from professional blocks and chips to the full range of retail chocolate bars. But like Jenny Cork, Porter sees the quality market as a tiny slice of the whole. If real chocolate is to move beyond deli shelves, it will be a struggle.

"It's still very small," he said. "The majority of food is bought in supermarkets. We don't have pâtisseries. The little shops are disappearing as fast as pubs. It's supermarkets, supermarkets, supermarkets. Our small shopkeepers don't understand the idea of focusing on a product and developing a clientele for it."

Porter started out working as a farmer at the age of eighteen but quickly veered into fine food. He trained as a chef and, working his way along through pastry, ended up in chocolate. He had found his bliss and appeared ready to carry on the noble battle.

Chantal Coady is another of Britain's small band of believers, an original pioneer of The Chocolate Society. She opened her London shop, Rococo, in 1983. Since then she has written a chocolate buyer's guide and a chocolate cookbook. She also senses a turn toward quality, but like Porter, she cannot quantify it. Eventually, she believes, converts will reach a critical mass.

When Chantal first opened her shop, she relied on a hard core of regulars. "Now people are becoming more aware of the whole issue of chocolate," she said. "Tastes are changing from white to dark." Customers listen as she patiently explains nuances, borrowing from the vocabulary of wine. She draws from a prodigious knowledge acquired over years of visiting equatorial plantations and the test kitchens of chocolate alchemists.

From the repeat business, and the occasional out-and-out junkie, Chantal knows she is making new connections. After we spoke, she introduced me to Richard von Geusau, a South African who had read her first book and beat a path to her door. Fired with zeal, he had set up a thriving chocolate business in Cape Town.

"It's just amazing how fast people learn to appreciate good chocolate once they're exposed to it," he said, ticking off the restaurants and fancy food shops in Cape Province that now clamor for his products.

"We find this all the time," Chantal added. When it comes to good chocolate, converts tend not to backslide. Still, she has to stock rose and violet creams. "That's what people want most."

My favorite *fondeur* in Britain is Gerry Coleman, a young Irish disciple of Marcolini. He trained in Brussels and then opened L'Artisan du Chocolat near Sloane Square. Meticulous and single-minded, Coleman works long hours with his Belgian wife, Anne-Françoise, at their immaculate lab in Kent.

A handsome little folder explains Coleman's purpose: "To create the highest quality couture chocolate products in Great Britain and one of the best worldwide." It also tells the English what they should do with his chocolate: Store it between 14 and 17 degrees Centigrade (about 57 and 63 degrees F), but let it warm a few degrees before eating; start with blended-bean ganache before single-bean specialties, and keep to one geographic region at a time. For infused ganaches, start with subtle and work toward strong. The idea is to appreciate nuances in acidity, bitterness, and mouthfeel.

Most of all, Coleman all but ordered, eat the chocolate within two to three weeks. The sooner the better.

"A superb chocolate is recognized by its strength, its length in the mouth, its balance of taste sensations and interesting textures," the leaflet explained.

Gerry and Anne-Françoise deliver what they promise at their shop. A *palet d'or* of Madagascar-type *criollo* has all the red-fruit muscle of a good wine. Infused ganaches of Earl Grey tea or lavender honey offer a light, fresh taste. There are a lot more choices, including one called Tobacco, by request only, which was suggested by the chef Heston Blumenthal of the Fat Duck. As Gerry puts it: "First the pipe tobacco flavors of caramel, coffee, and vanilla; then a tickle on the throat and a buzz of the tobacco released."

Gerry's L'Artisan du Chocolat soon built a loyal clientele, not only among the neighborhood Sloane Rangers but also with chocophiles who follow their noses halfway across Britain. It does a bustling business with restaurants and hotels. Gordon Ramsey, a fabled English chef, buys it in bulk.

Marcolini himself opened a shop in London, and La Maison du Chocolat came over from Paris and rented spacious quarters just across Piccadilly from Fortnum & Mason. Crowds were not breaking down either of their doors. But Robert Linxe is upbeat about the London venture. Day after day, La Maison remains an empty house, its fresh ganaches and *pralinés* quietly edging toward sell-by dates in gleaming glass cases. But sales figures show someone is buying that fancy French chocolate.

It is not only the shops. When the Moroccan restaurateur Mourad Mazouz decided to open his imaginative Sketch in London, he enlisted Pierre Gagnaire, my own favorite among France's three-star chefs. And a main feature of the place, below the main dining room, was a café that specialized in fine chocolate pastries.

In the end, I decided, Britain would be the chocolate bellwether. That is, the success of the world's cacao revolution could be gauged by the pace at which Britons switch from chocolates to chocolate. This might take generations, but I, for one, am not placing any bets on that. If *magret de canard* can bump lamb with mint jelly off the restaurant menus, can fine chocolate be far behind?

On that first visit to Selfridge's, I found Rita Antoniou next to the Bendick's Chocolates where she had been, in one way or another, for most of her seventy-plus years. She joined the company when she was twenty. "Now they just keep me around like the furniture," she said. She had, however, just pounced on me as a likely new customer with all the enthusiasm of a kid trying hard to land her first job.

Rita loved Bendick's products, and she nearly wept as she described how high rents had forced the company to give up its shop in Mayfair. Still, she said, customers found their way to Selfridge's to stock up on the bittermints that their grandparents loved. Rita glowed with pride when I mentioned I knew that one of the members of the royal household was a Jack Russell terrier named Bendick.

"People like the chocolates they grew up with," she said, "and that's what they stay with." Plenty of people had told me the same thing at different times in different places. When I tried a favorite of the Bendick line, sweet ginger encased in a flavorless hard chocolate, it seemed clear that some cultural lines were not meant to be crossed. I'd prefer a Hershey's Kiss any day. But evidence was much stronger that tastes can, and do, change.

I decided to try an experiment. I bought a bar of Michel Cluizel's Premier Cru d'Hacienda and broke off a chunk for Rita. This was the hard stuff, 66 percent dark chocolate from Venezuela, with no mints or ginger, no rose or violet. Rita tasted it carefully and then smiled. "You know," she said, "when you finish it, you've still got a sensation on the palate. I quite like this. I think I could go stronger."

In early 2003, when Jenny Cork moved upstairs to Fortnum & Mason's cookware department, Chloé moved in. Not exactly. Timid-looking as she is, Chloé is a Franco-Teutonic bombshell. She persuaded the staid management to find her an upstairs window that let in real daylight, rather than the basement cubicle assigned to Confectionery. Then, looking out at Great Britain, she set about attempting to change the national taste in chocolate.

She had the company's support. That fine old temple of English comestibles had a clear idea in mind when it passed up so many other candidates for the job. Fortnum & Mason decided it was good business to promote the idea that loving good chocolate was different from being addicted to sugar. And Chloé was on the case.

For a while, her e-mails to me reflected optimism. At her tastings, she beamed with satisfaction when people who had grown up on kippers, baked beans, and Cadbury's Daily Milk bars zeroed in on the dark chocolate creations of her Continental heroes. Early on, she reported: "I just finished my first conference, thirty-five stockbrokers . . . when after Valrhonas and plain ganaches they came to the violet cream, they said 'it tastes like soap.' I was the happiest frog in the room!"

She visited out-of-the-way Italian producers. Soon she struck a deal with Valrhona to import directly from Tain l'Hermitage. She made room for Cluizel and Marcolini, carefully instructing her staff on how to present new tastes to old customers.

And then Chloé began to worry. For one thing, new chocolate fads were doing less to educate palates than to confuse things even more.

"One day, a woman came in and demanded *criollo*," Chloé told me. "She was so desperate that she was shaking and could hardly talk." The woman, as the story emerged, owned a London antiques shop that had nearly gone broke when her mother fell sick several years earlier. Her boyfriend's father, a very rich American, had written a check that saved her business. She was ready to die for the man. And he was in London, now, just ending a six-week visit.

"The father had just read somewhere that *criollo* chocolate was the best, and she had to get him some," Chloé said. "He'd read that it cost so much per gram—she had some number written down—and that's what she wanted. She wouldn't listen to my staff, so they called me. I sat her down for fifteen minutes and explained that no one really made pure *criollo* chocolate. She got more desperate. I showed her my CV and some clippings to prove that I was supposed to be expert. She wasn't swayed."

Finally, Chloé went in the back to check packaging for the word *criollo*. Although chocolate makers threw the term around in conversation, truth in packaging forced most to keep it off their boxes. After a while, Chloé found an Amedei sampler with some high *criollo* content chocolate.

"The woman grabbed it, but she was still wavering," Chloé said. "To convince her, I charged a price that was three times higher than the real one. And she left happy."

When she started the job, Chloé took a hard look at Fortnum & Mason's untouchable major suppliers. In examining their recipes, she said, she discovered that even Britain's top-range manufacturers often do not use cream or milk. They mix substitute fats with water and inferior chocolate, often with chemical preservatives, to boost shelf life.

"I talked to companies and tried to persuade them at least to use a better quality of chocolate base," Chloé said. "Barry Callebaut makes a wide range, and if they insisted on going there, they could spend a little more and get something better. But it turned out that demand for quality was so low in England that Barry Callebaut stopped marketing its more expensive chocolate. If you're a young chocolatier just starting out, testing the samples on offer, you won't even get to taste good chocolate."

Chloé was starting to steam. "Look, I have nothing against fudge or rose and violet creams as long as you regard them as candy," she said. "But real chocolate demands to be fresh. Fortnum and Mason won't consider stocking products with less than six months' shelf life because that's what customers are used to. Maybe if they replaced those wooden counters with refrigerators, people would start to understand."

Champagne truffles put Chloé over the top. They are one of Britain's best-loved chocolate delicacies; when I mentioned them she had to pause a moment to catch her breath. In France or Belgium, Champagne truffles last no more than a few weeks before the cream inside starts to turn. "Here you can keep them for nine months," she wrote me. "To give you an idea: the Champagne truffle, bestseller by far. Composition: long-life milk or plain chocolate, vegetable fat, sugar, white rum, sorbic acid, marc de Champagne (1.85%). The vegetable fat is partially hydrogenated [and] consists of rapeseed, palm, soya, and coconut. Bon appétit."

At one point, store executives put together a sampler they wanted to call Chloé's Choice. She wanted to slip a note in each one saying, "I wouldn't touch this stuff." But, more than anything specific, it was a function of why the Frenchman's slur for the English is "*les rosbifs.*" Food, she believes, is not their thing.

"They're not learning," Chloé concluded. "You can see it in the sales figures. Lindor is one of the most popular items. It's good, but you can't taste a cocoa bean in it. When people do eat dark chocolate, they buy Green and Black, a Fair Trade brand. The idea is noble, but it isn't good chocolate. This is not taste, it's politics."

———

*I*n the end, Chloé decided to give up her dream job. After a year at Fortnum & Mason, she abandoned her optimism and made plans to try to work on Americans instead.

"This country is not ready to understand six weeks' shelf life. The elite who wants something good usually buys their chocolate abroad. Maybe that might change, but I'm not waiting. Whatever happens in the United States will take at least ten years to reach the United Kingdom. It's just because they don't have a clue what food means. *Punto.*"

That was a bit sweeping, considering what now comes out of the best kitchens in London and the hinterlands beyond. But as far as chocolate is concerned, a train ride through the Channel tunnel still seems to be the best bet.

# Chapter 13

## SWITZERLAND, AND BEYOND

*I*n Geneva, I had what seemed like a fine idea. I wanted to find the best of those artisan Swiss chocolatiers everyone talked about but could never identify, so I went to see Pasquale De Cesare. He was retiring after forty years as the resourceful concierge of the Geneva InterContinental hotel. He had never steered me wrong.

Without a moment's reflection, Pasquale wrote down a name and an address. "This man," he assured me with a confident smile, "is the best you'll find." To double-check, I sought advice from his nighttime colleague, who had spent three decades at the job. His response was the same. And just for good measure, I tried the first cabbie I could find who had not grown up in North Africa.

The address, once fashionable, was deep in the peep-show district. I had reached the owner by telephone at his lab, and he offered to meet me at the shop. He showed up as promised, moving slowly on a cane. He was ninety. His sons helped out, but he put in a full day's work.

I desperately wanted to like this kind old man's chocolate. He talked about it soulfully, recounting the long years he had spent in the business since the end of World War II. When I asked to try his favorite, he produced what he called his "summer special." It was a lumpy truffle with a curious cloying feel on the palate. With pride, he explained how he used vegetable fat so the chocolate did not melt during warm months. The *couverture* was from one of those big Swiss industrial plants Wittamer had spoken about. It was not worth writing home about.

After some more pleasant conversation, I left with profuse thanks. On the way out, I paused to talk to a young couple from New York. They were both exulting in the presence of so much Swiss chocolate.

"Chocolate doesn't get any better," the man had told the woman. I horned in to ask why he thought so. "It's Swiss," he said. "Everyone knows they make the best." The woman nodded. I asked them if they had sampled anything from France. Neither knew the French made chocolate.

Good artisan Swiss chocolatiers exist, even if they are now hard to find. They still make some sweet milk chocolate from contented cows munching herbs and high grass in Alpine meadows. That image, however, is part of a reality that died long ago. Fortunately for Switzerland, most of us have yet to catch on.

Eventually, in the mountains near Zurich, I found Max Felchlin AG, which turned out to be one of my favorite chocolate factories anywhere. But it was not easy.


*T*he Swiss pay a high price for their economic and political independence, as well as the social safety net that protects them from cradle to crypt. If Heidi still lugged overflowing milk pails in the shadow of the Matterhorn, her employer would be saddled with payroll taxes and a massive load of paperwork. Handmade chocolate requires costly pairs of hired hands.

Switzerland still leads the charts in chocolate consumption. According to statistics compiled in 2000 by Belgian researchers and distributed by the American Chocolate Manufacturers Association, the Swiss consumed 22.36 pounds per capita, followed by the Austrians at 20.13, the Irish at 19.47, and the Germans at 18.04. The British, Norwegians, and Danes fell in the range of 17 pounds. Belgians came further behind, at 13.16, followed by Australians and then Swedes.

Americans' per capita chocolate consumption was 11.64, just over half the Swiss figure. The French came just behind, at 11.38. Italians averaged only 6.13 pounds.

Such comparative figures require a bit of scrutiny. To begin with, researchers tally "chocolate confections" and not the main ingredient itself. Also, while the Swiss buy a lot of their singular style of chocolate, many purchases are by foreign visitors dazzled by an old reputation that refuses to wither away. But there is more to it than that. In these globalized times, it is hard to know what's in a number.

Barry Callebaut is headquartered in Switzerland, owned by the Swiss industrialist Klaus Jacob. But most of its chocolate is made elsewhere. Kraft Foods also shows up on the chart, with brands that originate in Switzerland.

Nestlé's catalogue of European chocolate offers such Italian hallmarks as Perugina and those dark chocolate hazelnut kisses, Baci. And, of course, After Eight mints. Although Nestlé is Swiss, its production is heavily farmed out to European Union countries where wages are lower and trade barriers have all but disappeared.

Long before the European Union adopted the euro as its common currency and expanded to twenty-five member nations in 2004, Switzerland was finding itself out in the cold.

In 1995, Nestlé launched a new chocolate bar with great fanfare but then had to manufacture it in Spain and Greece. The following year, Dario Kuster, director of the Swiss chocolate makers' association, Chocosuisse, told *The Washington Post*: "Step by step, Swiss chocolate production is dislocated outside Switzerland." Subsequent events have proven him right.

It is hard enough to track chocolate production still located within the country. While Switzerland has let some light into its once opaque banking secrecy, Swiss chocolate is still a murky subject. It is not illegal for manufacturers and artisan chocolatiers to divulge secrets. However, little is as it seems.

oday, wonderful chocolate is sold in Zurich and its environs at Confiserie Sprüngli. This sounds as if it is part of the large international group Chocoladefabriken Lindt & Sprüngli. And it once was. Soon after David Sprüngli opened his first confectionery shop in 1836, he went into the confectionery business with Rodolphe Lindt. But, heading separate ways, the families split in 1892. Sprüngli's sons wanted a retail business, where Zurich society could while away pleasant afternoons. The Lindts, inventors and industrialists, went big-time. Now Lindt & Sprüngli is a publicly traded chocolate empire based in Bern. To make things confusing, no one has since decided to change the old name.

"I suppose we just never felt the need," Tomas Prenosil, Sprüngli's thirty-eight-year-old chief executive officer, told me. Though originally a Czech, he left Prague after the tumultuous spring of 1968, and his brother married a Sprüngli daughter. "Maybe we'll get around to it one of these days." But there seemed to be no particular hurry. Confiserie Sprüngli buys most of its liquid chocolate base from Lindt & Sprüngli.

No one who looks closely is likely to confuse the two companies. Sprüngli has only seventeen shops, including an outlet at Zurich Airport, but none of them are far enough away for cream to lose freshness in the back of a truck. Geneva, for instance, at four hours on the freeway, is too long a ride. Only the family is involved in decisions. "When we sit down for a board meeting, there are only five of us," Prenosil said.

Company headquarters are up the stairs above a stately, squat Zuricher-style building on Paradeplatz. Across the courtyard, a lovingly tended museum contains century-old ledgers, original molds, and some of the early hardware the Lindts and Sprünglis used to pioneer chocolate making. But the action is at street level, where shoppers cram into the ornate *confiserie*. Counters display everything from gravity-defying, mouthwatering chocolate cakes to sliced cold cuts for sandwiches. It is still the sort of place David Sprüngli must have imagined.

Before I left, Prenosil wrapped up a luscious-looking dark lump dusted with cocoa powder. It was, he said, the fresh-cream *truffe du jour,* and he insisted that it be eaten before the day's end. Talk about needless advice.

*L*indt & Sprüngli's products are easier to find. For instance, it maintains a spacious shop on Fifth Avenue in New York, across from Tiffany's and next to all the fancy European luxury-brand outlets. The company's founding date, 1845, is featured prominently, and repeatedly, all across the colorful showroom. Historical displays recall Rodolphe Lindt, whose invention of the conche freed chocolate from its grainy texture and less attractive flavor elements.

As in most such high-end Fifth Avenue shops, the staff is pleasant and eager to help. "These are delicious," I heard one woman tell a customer, offering a sugary pink and white concoction from a large cacao-less display. When I explained my purpose, the woman asked if I would like to taste a new specialty bar of 85 percent chocolate. I said I did. She broke off a piece of the same Lindt chocolate in familiar packages offered in supermarkets from the Bronx to the backstreets of Kyoto. It was perfectly good, with no excitement to it.

For me, Lindt can be one of best price-per-pound items in anybody's supermarket. It is clean and consistent. A new milk chocolate *praliné* bar Lindt brought out in 2003 is better than some artisan attempts in fancy small shops. But it is mass-market chocolate, with all the limitations of bigness. Its range for innovation is limited. Its raw materials must come in bulk. Its product must taste roughly the same year after year, although cacao, like grapes and olives, does not grow that way.

I asked the saleswoman if she had something more particular to the shop, perhaps a signature piece that was only chocolate without filling. She shook her head and replied, "I don't think we have anything like that." Poking around on my own, I found a plate of small flat rectangles next to a card reading, "Lindt's Signature Chocolate."

It was good sweet chocolate, the kind hoteliers put on pillows all over Switzerland. No particular taste pushed ahead of any other. Not much lingered on the tongue. I would recommend it to any milk chocolate fiend in need of a dose. But it hardly bore the dignity of 160 years. And Lindt & Sprüngli seemed like a curious fit as a Fifth Avenue specialty shop.

The old Swiss company was doing well. In 2003, despite a drop in tourism because of the Iraq war and the deadly SARS virus, the company reported sales of 1.8 billion Swiss francs. That is more than a billion dollars, a 7.8 percent increase over 2002.

Clearly, it suits tastes in the United States. During 2004, *Cook's Illustrated* magazine organized a blind tasting for seventy-five American food editors at its Boston headquarters. The editors ranked ten dark chocolates. The fabled French grand cru entries were skunked. Valrhona's Manjari ranked only sixth, followed by its Guanaja. Scharffen Berger's Semisweet came first, but Lindt's Excellence was third. That would be a decent-enough showing for industrial chocolate. But the second-place chocolate was Ghirardelli Bittersweet. That old landmark San Francisco company is owned by Lindt & Sprüngli.

Just as with giant banks that used to be private clubs or industrial watchmakers who were once corner jewelry shops, Swiss confectioners have moved to a different plane. The goal is no longer handmade innovation but rather a reliable final product of absolute consistency, with skillful quality control over all ingredients. The Swiss can certainly handle that.

*B*ut then there is Max Felchlin AG in the lakeside town of Schwyz. By the time I got there, toward the end of my research, I had given up the idea of picking chocolate for a desert island. I would need a refrigerated freighter floating offshore. But, if pressed to the wall, it would be hard to give up Felchlin's Maracaibo.

The little factory produces about twenty-five hundred tons a year, including a Grand Cru line made with select South American and African beans. But it steadfastly sticks to its founder's policy of focusing on wholesale supply to professionals who make finished products under their own name. Sprüngli, for example.

When I visited Tomas Prenosil, he told me he used a lot of Felchlin chocolate, heaping praise on its taste and quality. It is the only non-Lindt base he uses. Later, Mary Scarvalone, the artist whose drawings enliven these chapters, asked a friend passing through Zurich Airport to pick up some examples of Sprüngli products made with Felchlin chocolate. The clerk was miffed. Sprüngli, she declared, used only Sprüngli chocolate.

Even today, Max Felchlin AG seems like a miniature Milton Hershey vision set in genteel surroundings. Max Josef Felchlin set up shop in 1908 as an importer of honey. Soon after, he began making chocolate. The founder's official portrait looks modeled for a hundred-franc note: ruddy and determined with a furrowed brow, a modest mustache, and perfectly clipped iron-gray hair. All in all, he seemed the personification of received ideas about old Switzerland. He is remembered as a good man who took care of workers, a man of culture who collected paintings and sculpture that give his old family complex—now company headquarters—the air of a landscaped art museum.

Felchlin proclaimed his watchwords, from Goethe, in an inscription over the stately entryway: "Der Geist, aus dem wir Handeln, ist das Höchste." Supreme is the spirit from which we act.

The last family member, Suzanne Felchlin, died in 2004 at the age of eighty. But the old man had thought ahead. He set up a foundation of trusted friends from Schwyz to be the majority owner. And Christian Aschwanden, chief executive officer since 1992, safeguards the old philosophy: to make the best chocolate possible for chefs, bakers, pâtissiers, and confectioners.

"Our role is to support these people who maintain their own high standards," Aschwanden explained, in his elegant dark-wood office overlooking handsome gardens. "We don't want to hide ourselves. We are here to tell people what we do. But we want to support top-notch chefs and others who work with chocolate. And we do not want to compete with our customers."

This enforced humility has no visible impact on Sepp Schoenbachler, a pear-shaped, balding Felchlin manager with a serious mien whose eyes nonetheless gleam whenever he says the word *chocolate*. When I first called and mentioned my intended trip, and he replied, "No wor-

ries," I knew I was in good hands. He was the perfect composite, a
meticulous Swiss engineer with enough adventure in him to go hang
out in Australia and bring back a bride.

Sepp joined the company in 1999 after a varied career in food technology. Like Cecilia Tessieri at Amedei, he came at chocolate peripher-
ally and learned about it by spending days on end working through
mistakes. His colleague goes off scouting for superior beans. His job is
to get the most out of them.

Soon after Sepp's initial experiments, Felchlin dropped a bomb on
the tidy community of Swiss industrial chocolatiers. Sepp followed orders to make the best chocolate possible; he soon learned the value of
single-origin beans. He found that superior cacao could be pushed to
new limits of roasting and milling, producing exciting new flavors.
Each type of cacao reacted differently, requiring altered nuances of
time and temperature. This was nothing new to French pioneers already working in this direction. But in Switzerland, it was revolution.

When Felchlin began to label the origin of cacao in its fine specialty
products, big industrial companies howled in protest.

"They were furious, and several threatened to sue us for breaking
the sacred Swiss tradition of secrecy," Sepp said, with a chuckle. "They
called us traitors and demanded to know how we could do such a
thing." But the only secret the big companies were protecting, he
added, was that they were using cheaper bulk beans. After a while, the
large companies decided that joining the new trend was far more useful
than fighting it.

Felchlin's adventure into quality, like Amedei's war with Valrhona
and other such developments in the United States as well as in Europe,
signaled a sea change for cacao growers around the equator. While the
overwhelming demand was still for containers of nameless beans traded
on the London and New York exchanges, a new market was fast developing for "flavor beans" of known parentage.

Big companies such as Lindt & Sprüngli soon got into the act. It
was no longer enough for buyers to beat the bushes for the handful of
producers who grew fine cacao under optimum conditions. Old plantations would have to be revived, and new ones established. Countries

such as Vietnam and Indonesia, which had only dabbled in cacao, saw fresh opportunity. The impact on price would not be clear for years. But one eventual result seemed likely: Chocolate makers who looked for better cacao would find it.

Sepp's most crucial early lesson was that even the best cacao is no more than raw material. It does not guarantee good chocolate any more than 18-karat gold assures beautiful jewelry without skilled hands to work it. Gold, in fact, can be melted down for another try.

"It is so easy to ruin cacao, or to waste it," Sepp said, recounting the experiments that brought him to that conclusion. He had spent months on end experimenting with roasting times, heat levels, grind adjustments, and speeds. Steam heat has a different effect than hot water. As molten chocolate cools, the temperature curve is crucial.

"Every bean has its own characteristics which reveal themselves in a rainbow, and you have to work to bring out each color," he said. "The big companies use such huge amounts that they must emphasize production, not quality. They can only run the beans through and castrate them."

As Sepp talked, his stolid Swiss side faded, and yet more Aussie pervaded his fluent English.

"You have to know whether the bean produces hard or soft cocoa butter," he said. "Everything matters. Certain beans may look like nothing special, but if you understand them and can work with them, maybe there is a good surprise. It's like an old house. Some people can say it's ugly and walk away. But if you take out some walls, put in a window, suddenly it is beautiful."

For a while, Sepp veered back into technology. He was lyrical again. "In good cacao, there are maybe seven hundred different elements that have to do with flavor," he said. "You have to move slowly, carefully, to try to discover as many as you can. If you go too fast, you simply trample all the flowers."

As we spoke, we headed into the barnlike heart of the factory, sparkling clean as most chocolate plants are everywhere. Sepp talked and waved his arms as we moved from stage to stage.

As usual, beans begin the process with cleaning, in a great rattling and clouds of dust. That is where the old nails and bullet cartridges drop off the line. But Felchlin then steams them to kill bacteria, sterilizing them hundreds of times more thoroughly than Swiss food laws stipulate. From there, they go the ball-shaped Barth roasters, the crushers, and the winnowers. The *mélangeurs* blend the ground nibs with cocoa butter, sugar, and maybe milk powder, working the mixture until it is pasty chocolate. After that, trusty Buhler five-roll millers refine it to a smooth molten mix.

I had seen a lot of variations of this before, and Sepp had a destination in mind. He flung aside some plastic curtains and announced, "These are my babies."

When he first took the job, Sepp fell in love with Felchlin's museum-worthy longitudinal conches. Each was the same sort of crude apparatus—the *Langschieber,* or "long shover"—that Rodolphe Lindt had developed. Four of them stood in a row, working away, long troughs with massive oblong arms pushing paddles back and forth in the chocolate. Jules Verne might have imagined them as prototype robots. Each machine handled 200 kilos, only 440 pounds, at a time.

Felchlin also used more modern conches, but Sepp chose these for the good stuff, massaging his best chocolate for seventy-two hours at temperatures and speeds he watched with zeal.

As I had come to learn, every chocolate master has his personal obsession. With Claudio Corallo in São Tomé, it is roasting. He believes that if beans are good enough, too much conching works them to death. But he likes his chocolate real, full of strong flavor and slightly gritty. With Sepp, it is getting a conche to remove just the right nasty volatile components without losing the good ones.

"Everyone told me these old machines could not handle chocolate with greater than fifty-five percent cacao," he said. "For three days, I slept next to these things." When he produced a smooth and flavorful Madagascar chocolate at 64 percent, he had a factory full of believers.

Then he began to push other limits and try new things. He made two batches of chocolate for Japanese buyers using the same beans and same refining process. Because he made minor changes at the end, one batch had a completely different taste from the other.

As experiments into new levels of quality began to show results, directors made a strategic decision. It was likely what Max Josef Felchlin would have done.

"There is no way we can do the same things as Lindt and survive," Sepp explained. "We did not want to do what big companies did. Instead, we decided to go back to our roots. We want to focus on what is really good."

The one obvious direction was the dark side. Enough companies catered to the Swiss penchant for sweet milk chocolate. Felchlin still made their run-of-the-mill ingredients for bakers and pâtissiers. But it also introduced its small Grand Cru line. And the star of it, for me, is that rich and lively Maracaibo.

As the name suggests, the beans come from south of Venezuela's Lake Maracaibo, in the region where Amedei gets its Porcelana. This is an early cradle of *criollo*, and much of the old strains remain. Felchlin classes its Maracaibo as bittersweet, at 65 percent cacao content. Tasting it again and again, I found little to dispute the company's own description: "The well-balanced combination of coffee and plum aroma enhances the distinct cocoa flavor. The traditional gentle processing method unfolds the aromas of orange blossom and cinnamon which convey . . . a festive character, enhanced with a light sweet raisin bouquet leading to a long final sensation."

Such descriptions by chocolate makers are of varied utility. Some are no more than wishful thinking and poetry. Others reflect thoughtful deliberation by panels of skilled specialists who commune with their taste buds and olfactory senses. If you pay attention, and sample a chocolate before your morning coffee and cigarette, it is amazing how many of these notes make themselves plain. And even if they don't, good chocolate is worth the effort.

Felchlin makes this easier with a clever reference tool in the form of a wheel, developed with Swiss university researchers. It has an inner circle of seven categories: vegetable, flowery, fruity, roasted, nutty, spicy, and miscellaneous. Each has a further breakdown. "Miscellaneous," for instance, takes in tobacco, butter, cream/milk, bread, honey, and beeswax. Fruity might be apricot preserves, currant preserves, red berries, orange, dried fruit, dried plums, dried bananas, and wild berries.

The idea is to start with chocolate with low cacao content and work upward. Your first clues come with a deep sniff, and by breaking off a bit to feel the texture. Rubbing the chocolate between your thumb and forefinger warms it, releasing volatile aroma components. With the first bite, you notice the snap. As the chocolate melts on your tongue, layers of flavors develop. Hold your breath a moment and exhale through the nose. This all takes some practice, and it is not high science. But it is wonderful.

In my last meeting with Aschwanden, it seemed as if Sepp's enthusiasm had scored a point. Perhaps, he said, Felchlin might package a line of chocolate bars available directly to the public. But only, he added, through confectionery shops.

If Switzerland was the early heartland of chocolate, today's variations have gone a long way beyond their origins. Excellent chocolate might be found almost anywhere. So might weird novelties. The kosher bars and bonbons offered by Chocolaterie Damyel in Sarcelles, near Paris, are straightforward enough. But what about the Ukrainian candy company in Kiev that offers finger-sized sticks of congealed pork fat in dark chocolate?

And then there is that intriguing Russian chocolate I kept seeing at every turn. From the fancy food shows in America to that little gathering outside of Brussels, I noticed a small booth offering bars marked "Product of Russia." Its logo was imposing: an elegant cursive *K* on a rich burgundy field, under a regal crown, over the woodcut name on a cocoa-brown panel that might have graced the bow of a nineteenth-century ship: A. Korkunov.

Discreet letters at the top promised "High Quality, Refined Taste," and thirty-point script characters proclaimed what was inside: "Dark Chocolate." Curiosity overcame me, and I read the literature stacked up at the booth.

After the Soviet Union imploded, a young military officer named Andrei Korkunov, with thirty dollars in his pocket, turned hustler in the new anything-goes Russia. He tried his hand at just about everything. Blue jeans paid off no better than did pig iron. One day, a cash-strapped Czech wheeler-dealer paid him for a shipment of computers with three containers of chocolate.

"It was better than nothing," he recalled for the *Moscow Times* in 2001, when he was thirty-eight. When his mystery chocolate was snapped up overnight by cacao-starved Russians, he thought big. He designed an old-style coat of arms reminiscent of czarist days. And in 1999, he launched A. Korkunov Chocolatier.

"Many think Korkunov is a bearded old man," he told the Russian newspaper. A portrait showed him as a well-fed young mogul in a dark tie, with a stern businessman gaze. "People think I'm a descendant of some historic nobleman." By then, two years into the business, many Russians were already calling him the Chocolate King.

Because they were used to tolerating Soviet-made chocolate that might be confused with soap, Russians wolfed down Korkunov's offerings. He bought Italian machinery, hired Italian bonbon makers he found in Moscow, and acquired beans from somewhere. When a collapsed ruble put imported chocolate beyond anyone's reach, he spurred production.

By 2004, Korkunov had built a second plant that was one and a half times as big as his original quarters. He set up an American beachhead in Englewood, New Jersey, selling across much of the United States. He did not look far for his English-language sales pitch: "From Russia with Love."

From a few thousand tons a year, Korkunov increased production to more than six thousand tons, with a turnover of $45 million, and big plans to keep going. His Italian-style bonbons are heavy on hazelnuts and praline filling. One, of course, is named Criollo. The 72 percent bar has a quirky taste that Korkunov boasted was addictive. Once you try it, he told the *Moscow Times,* you will never want anything else.

I tried it, and I wanted something else. It had a metallic taste and a synthetic feel, with a gummy texture and an astringency that pushed aside other nuances. But it certainly looked like it might be good.

# Chapter 14

## WHERE'S THE NUTELLA?

uring 2002, as terrorism stalked the planet, police in the Italian town of Pordenone tracked a mysterious man people called *il unabomber.* At first, suspicion settled on a thirty-five-year-old student, but a search of his home near Treviso turned up nothing. Tension grew among an anxious public. The terrorist had struck where it hurt: He had booby-trapped a jar of Nutella.

For uninitiated travelers, that ubiquitous jar of dusty brown hazelnut-flavored chocolate spread is just another item on the hotel breakfast buffet table. This is fine with the locals, of course, because then they can have all the more Nutella to eat.

As several dozen disparate European nations try to form a more perfect union, they fight an uphill battle. Statesmen decided a new currency, the euro, would hold them tightly together. When it was launched at midnight on December 31, 2001, however, it faced an uncertain future. Britons kept their pound sterling. Scandinavians were unconvinced. And there were all those central and eastern Europeans yet to join. At a distance, the answer was obvious. Europe should have chosen a common symbol more universally loved than money. Nutella, for instance.

For the tragically unenlightened, Nutella is chocolaty glop that comes in glass jars or plastic tubs. It is meant to be spread on bread, but more often than not, it is licked straight off the knife.

"The worst-kept secret in Europe is where mothers hide the Nutella from their kids," Cecile Allegra said, laughing aloud as she pictured her own mother trying nobly but in vain to secret away the family-size jar. High up, down at floor level behind forgotten canned goods, in the bedroom closet with the old shoes, it didn't really matter. About the most Signora Allegra could hope for was two days before one of her brood sniffed it out.

Cecile, a Paris-based foreign correspondent, grew up in Rome before moving to France for school. Her memories are of Italian-style Nutella, which is heavier on the hazelnuts and lighter on sugar than is the French variation. Another of those ill-kept secrets is that the president of Ferrero, the Italian company that owns Nutella and licenses it around the world, also prefers the French formula.

Chloé is an unapologetic Nutella nut. One Christmas holiday, her brother, Tristan, visited her while she was on a United Nations assignment to Haiti. The trip was a last-minute decision, and she found she had nothing to eat in the house. Both lived happily for a week on her reserve stock of Nutella. On the last day, they made a film: "Fatal Attraction."

For a backdrop, Chloé stacked jars of Nutella on an ironing board. And then, one at a time, they recalled their Nutella moments.

One tragedy was the Great Nutella Squander. Growing up in Mexico City, Chloé and Tristan lived for the economy-size tub that sat on their breakfast table, replenished only sporadically when someone managed to make the trip from Europe. Some stuffy Paris friends visited her parents and, as asked, brought a jar with them. They had no idea what it was or what it meant. Chloé's mother put it on the table. Good hostess that she was, she urged her friends to try some. With no enthusiasm or appreciation, both spooned great heaps onto their toast, seriously depleting the fresh supply. Chloé watched with horror she has yet to forget.

But nothing approaches the Great Airport Incident. Once Chloé's mother returned from Paris to Mexico City with the usual huge jar, and she was stopped at customs. An inspector refused to let it through. At first, she thought of the usual Mexican solution: a small gift. But the man was serious; food was forbidden. Suddenly, Madame Doutre-Roussel had an inspiration. This was not food, she said. It was cosmetics. To make the point, she smeared Nutella generously across her cheeks and forehead. It worked.

Chloé and Tristan watched the scene from behind thick glass, unable to hear what was going on. All they could see was that their mother had lost her mind. Worse, she was wasting the family's precious Nutella. And all they could do was leap up and down, flinging themselves against the glass wall in helpless frustration.

Years later, a grown-up Chloé visited a Nutella plant and watched steel paddles mixing chocolate, ground nuts, and sugar in a giant vat. A friend who went with her watched with concern. Chloé seemed dangerously close to a swan dive.

The Nutella formula was invented out of necessity after World War II. Italy was short of chocolate, but it had plenty of hazelnuts and other non-chocolate fillers. Pietro Ferrero, an enterprising pastry maker who later built up a food empire, mixed toasted hazelnuts with cocoa powder, cocoa butter, and vegetable oil to make what he called *pasta gianduja*. In February 1946, he sold 660 pounds of the stuff. Soon after, he was in hot pursuit of more hazelnut growers.

In 1949, Ferrero came up with a more spreadable version of Supercrema Gianduja. Pretty soon, Italian food stores had a special counter for a Nutella schmear. Kids paid a few lire to have their slice of bread topped in the stuff. The new name was adopted in 1964, and Nutella oozed across Europe and beyond.

Today, the mix has changed. A thirteen-ounce jar of Nutella contains fifty hazelnuts, a cup and a half of skim milk, enough cocoa to make it brown, and a lot of sugar. Worldwide sales of Nutella amount to two million quintals a year, Ferrero reports. That is half a billion pounds of Nutella. The core market is Western Europe, but Nutella is just about everywhere.

For a while, I collected stories from friends and contacts by simply saying the word *Nutella* and seeing what came of it.

As expected, I got a rise out of Nico Jenkins, the son of my food-loving friend Nancy Harmon Jenkins and her ex-husband, Loren Jenkins, a foreign correspondent who came in from the cold. Nico grew up in Italy. Like his famous-chef sister, Sara, he loves to eat well. As a former maître d' at Le Cirque 2000, he knows how to go about it.

Nico and two friends once sailed a small boat across the Atlantic, headed for America. They thought they had carefully rationed their Nutella supply to make the trip. But the level dropped precipitously. Then on the night watch, the lonely man at the helm cracked under the strain. When Nico and the other guy found the jar licked clean, they nearly keelhauled the culprit.

Boris Vlasic, one of the finest and funniest journalists in Croatia, was thrilled with the breakup of Yugoslavia in 1992. "We could stop being dangerous smugglers," he said. "We had to make secret runs over the Yugoslav border for Nutella and jeans," he said, adding that he could have done without the jeans. "Nutella is not food; it's a medicine, a drug, a cure for anything. If you have any kind of problem, you just need Nutella. My wife gets mad at me when I buy two jars at the store, but when it is on sale, it is your sacred duty to buy it."

Boris is married to Snjezana Vukic, my level-headed Associated Press colleague. She rolls her eyes when her husband and Nutella appear in the same sentence. But she gave me his cell phone number. Weeks later, as she was about to give birth to their first child, I happened to reach him on his way to the hospital. At one point, I mentioned that Nutella was made with different recipes in each country. I could hear Boris stiffen.

"I'm living in darkness," he said. "It's not fair. Look, call Snjezana and tell her I've gone around the world to buy Nutella. She knows me. She'll understand."

In a globalized world, American kids have mastered the European trick of smearing the insides of a glass Nutella jar to disguise unauthorized raids. As any kid knows, this is no mean feat. If the cosmetics job is too thinly done, you are busted. But if done too well, your mother will not add a new jar to her shopping list.

My friend Franny Sullivan discovered Nutella as a young teacher in the Dominican Republic after graduating from Duke. She and her roommates survived mainly on peanut butter and jelly sandwiches. Then someone discovered Nutella.

"We had to ration ourselves to one jar a week," she said. "I'd get a jar and eat it for two days, and then they would hide it for a while. I did the same for them." When I asked what the attraction was, she gave me one of those "duh" looks. "It's chocolate. Spreadable chocolate."

Back in Greenwich Village, Franny's local grocer kept a steady supply. Except, of course, during 2003, when an unexpected run emptied his shelves. It seems that Los Angeles Lakers star Kobe Bryant had become a Nutella nut when his father played basketball in Italy. Ferrero hired him to appear on its jars in America. When he was charged with rape, he was taken off the label. But the Kobe Bryant jars that remained in circulation sold like, um, Nutella.

The Kobe Bryant scandal hardly dented Nutella's image in America. Nor is Nutella as unknown as I thought. A Google search produced 325,000 references. A company Web site devoted to it offers ideas on such things as Nutella hot dog (a regular bun, with a banana as the hot dog and Nutella as the mustard), Nutella pumpkin pie, s'mores, and a tortilla rollup with raisins and chopped nuts.

Italy remains the Nutella homeland. In Bologna and Genoa, a *Nutellaria* offers a dozen ways to indulge, including Nutella pizza, focaccia, cornflakes, and tacos. Gigi Padovani, born in the Nutella capital, Alba, wrote a whole book about it, entitled—what else? It ends with observations from well-known Italians, including this remark by the writer Luciano Ligabue: "I have three or four certainties in life, and Nutella is one of them."

Even such culinary chauvinists as the French have succumbed. Nutella France sells 80 million jars of the stuff a year. And, for me, nothing comes close to the Paris-street-corner specialty: a warm crêpe slathered in Nutella.

When I visited Claudio Corallo in São Tomé, I found a jar of Nutella occupying a place of honor in his kitchen. His well-disciplined kids were above midnight raids. But just with the normal breakfast hits, the level dropped at a dizzying rate. Before I left, Claudio handed me a prized volume from his library. It was a small booklet, cleverly written in non-Italian by Riccardo Cassini, entitled *Nutella Nutellae, Racconti Poliglotti*. It began with the Creation, in far-fetched Italianate English. ("Na cifra," repeated often, is Italian slang for "in great abundance.")

> Once upon a time, many many, ma'na cifra of many years ago, at the beginning of the initiation of the mond, there was the caos. One day, God (God is the nome d'art of Dio), God, who was disoccupated, had a folgorant idea and so God created the Nutell. And God saw that the Nutell was good, very good, very very good, good na cifra.
>
> The mangiation of God was long, he manged one million of barattols of Nutell sfrutting the fact that God has not a Mamm that strills if you sbaf too much Nutell . . . And after this mangiation, God invented the Water Closed Run, the cors in the cabinet, and some Nutell's derivates like the red bubbons, the panz, the cellulit . . .

And so on. After putting Nutella on earth, God invented Adamo ed Eva. He placed them in a Paradise: "You have gratis restaurants, cinemas, theaters, all the Paradise is yours: air conditioned, autom riscaldament, moquette, parquet, tresset, bidet, omelette, eccet eccet . . . There's just one thing, remember, in tutt the Paradise just one thing absolutely prohibited." God showed Adamo ed Eva the Nutella tree and declared it forbidden "because I want all the Nutell, tutt the Nutell for me."

As expected, Adamo led Eva astray, and God gave them two choices. They could continue in Paradise without Nutella. Or, "you can take the Nutell, no problem, but for you is the cacciation out of the Paradise, you will soffer, you will have to lavorar with the sudor of your front . . ."

There was no contest, of course.

Cassini offers other *racconti*. A poem called "Weight Watchers Blues" bewails life without Nutella. A Quixote tale in sort-of Spanish speaks of Dulcinea. Her name, the text explains, means 50 percent sugar, 7 percent cacao, 12 percent hazelnuts, and the rest, soy lecithin and natural aromas. In a fractured fairy tale, with a title that translates to "The Dwarves Are Many More Than Seven," Sleeping Beauty has needle tracks. Only the strongest drug of all—you guessed it—can save her.

Essentially, the little book's message can be summed up by the end of the opening story of Creation: "But the final pensier of tutti noi is 'It's meglio faticar and soffrier with the Nutell piutost che the Terrestr Paradise senz the Nutall.'" In clear English: Everyone's final thought is that it is better to toil and suffer with Nutella than to live in earthly paradise without it.

Cassini was hardly exaggerating. During the American invasion of Iraq, early in 2003, an Austrian television crew found itself stuck in Baghdad, robbed of just about everything by a gang of roving looters. Editors in Vienna made an urgent appeal to the U.N. High Commissioner for Refugees office in Jordan. They asked the UNHCR to find some way to get them the barest essentials of survival: a sizable stack of U.S. dollars, a Thuraya satellite phone, and a jar of Nutella.

# Chapter 15

# BODY AND SOUL

E ver since the overwrought guesswork in the fifteenth century, chocolate has suffered from extreme prejudice. Common wisdom still has it wrong: it makes you fat; it gives you pimples; it corrodes your dental work. But modern science is clear, nutritionally, psychologically, and pharmacologically. Chocolate is not bad for you. In fact, strong evidence suggests it may be very good for you.

Candy bars are not necessarily part of the deal. The sugar and God knows what else in each particular product make their impact on the body, for better or worse. But the food of the gods is also happily suitable for mortals.

Recent findings come as no surprise to specialists who have watched a sizable shelf of evidence build over the generations. In a weighty tome published by the International Cocoa Organization and the International Cocoa Research and Education Foundation, twenty-nine specialists delve into every component of *T. cacao*. The book—*Chocolate and Cocoa: Health and Nutrition*—looks at cardiovascular effects, diabetes, allergic reactions, gastrointestinal functions, psychological aspects, and just about everything in between.

John R. Lupien of the U.N. Food and Agriculture Organization in

Rome summed up the findings in an overview. "From a nutritional perspective, chocolate, like every other food, is neither good nor bad per se," he concluded. "In general, when consumed as part of a balanced and varied diet, chocolate can be both a source of nutrients as well as pleasure, and can be considered as being part of a healthful, wholesome diet. This is especially true in light of the contribution that the enjoyment of one's food makes to overall well-being."

Beyond question, Lupien declared, "cocoa is a veritable storehouse of natural minerals, more so than almost any other food item." He added some examples. Chocolate is a major source of copper in the North American diet. Its antioxidants protect against low-density lipoprotein (LDL) oxidation in cholesterol and help to alleviate stress. Allergies to chocolate are rare.

Some naturally occurring phytochemicals may excite the brain, he wrote, but the amounts are small. For the appeal of chocolate, Lupien offered an overriding opinion among researchers: "The most plausible explanation is in its sensory characteristics. It simply provides a unique and wonderful sensory experience, extending far beyond taste. Not only that, it somehow has the ability to provide an overall feeling of well-being, which in itself is beneficial to the consumer."

Poring over the various findings, I saw old myths exploding, one after the other. Although cocoa butter is fat, it is one-third stearic acid, which does not boost cholesterol; one-third oleic acid, the same monounsaturated compound found in olive oil; and one-third palmitic oil, which does not raise cholesterol. Cocoa has some caffeine, but a cup of it comes to 20 milligrams or less, half as much as tea. Coffee has 115 milligrams.

Tooth decay is another bad rap. Plain chocolate, though sugary, clears out of the mouth too quickly to do much damage. Some substances in chocolate may actually slow the bacterial growth that causes plaque and cavities. This is not necessarily true for, say, a sticky Baby Ruth.

David Benton, a University of Wales psychology professor, contributed a paper to the book entitled "Chocolate Craving: Biological or Psychological Phenomenon?" He started out with a respectful whack at a book by Debra Waterhouse, *Why Women Need Chocolate,* which invoked the effects of serotonins and endorphins, along with phenylethylamine, theobromine, and magnesium.

"In reality," Benton wrote, "any certainty concerning the basis of chocolate's popularity is unjustified; it has been subject to relatively little scientific attention." And later, like Dr. Chantal Favre-Bismuth in Paris, he noted: "This review has produced little, if any, evidence to support the suggestion that chocolate craving reflects a biological need that is satisfied, in a drug-like manner, by some constituent of chocolate." That is, it is not addictive.

Benton's summary seems to suggest that Waterhouse may not be wrong. Chocolate is by far the most commonly craved food, he noted, particularly by women before menstruation. He offered two explanations. One is the pleasant taste. The other is that chocolate triggers physiological mechanisms, which may include increased serotonin production, released endorphins, and the action of methylxanthines, phenylethylamines, and magnesium.

Louise Burke, a nutrition specialist at the Australian Institute of Sport in Bruce, Australia, confirmed what just about any athlete seems to know instinctively: Chocolate bars are an excellent way to fuel up before, and during, intense activity. Afterward, the fast clean hit of carbohydrates in chocolate helps the body to restore itself. But, Burke cautions, eating chocolate is not such a great idea during hot summer sports. The stuff melts all over the place.

A thoughtful study by Nicholas Jardine delves deeply into molecular structures in a paper entitled "Phytochemicals and Phenolics." As a staff member of Nestlé's research and development center in York, England, Jardine has an interest in finding good news. But as a careful scientist, in the end he came up with more questions than answers.

Jardine dealt at length with flavonoids, naturally occurring antioxidants. A number of these appear in cacao. In fermented cacao, the flavonoid found in greatest concentration is epicatechin, which other research has shown to have a possible role in preventing cancer. And that is just for starters. With diagrams and formulas, he showed how other flavonoids in cacao work to fortify the circulatory and central nervous systems.

"Underlying the pathologies of many human diseases are metabolisms which depend on oxidative reactions," Jardine said in his summary. "On the other hand there is also considerable epidemiological evidence that plant materials have protective effects against many of these diseases . . . It may be speculated that plant materials that are rich in antioxidants are also beneficial to human health."

Because of what he called "large and tantalizing gaps in our knowledge," it was too soon to draw irrefutable conclusions. But he ended with promise: "Yet we know already from early work with cocoa—raw and fermented—that it has a high content of antioxidants. Cocoa is conceivably a treasure chest of compounds with potentially beneficial effects on human health."

Scattered research points toward the same thing. During 2003, a German study published in the *Journal of the American Medical Association* divided thirteen adults with untreated, mildly high blood pressure into two groups. One group ate a daily three-ounce bar of dark chocolate, which is rich in polyphenols, as is red wine. The other group had white chocolate—that is, cocoa butter with no ground nibs. After two weeks, doctors noted a marked drop in blood pressure among the group that ate dark chocolate.

As I sought out data on chocolate, similar sorts of studies began to pile high on my shelves. The most comprehensive was a doctoral thesis by Myriam Chapelin of the University of Montpellier in France with the supporting stamp of the Cacao Program at the prestigious French International Center for Agricultural Research and Development, CIRAD. She entitled her work "Cacao, Chocolate and Derivative Products: Nutritional and Pharmacological Aspects."

I examined its five hundred pages after a two-hour talk with her adviser, Émile Cros of CIRAD. Of all the savants I encountered on the chocolate trail, Cros was the master guide. Gruff, sardonic, and perfectly happy to wear old khaki shorts to a fancy French office, he exuded confidence. Equally at home in Venezuelan rain forests, American laboratories, or French dining rooms, he had a wide perspective.

And, both independently funded and fiercely attached to scientific objectivity, he had nothing to sell.

"It's all here," Cros said, handing me Chapelin's five-pound document, as detailed as a space shuttle owner's manual.

In a review of American and European research, Chapelin adds perspective to well-trod ground. Cacao is an antioxidant on the order of red wine and green tea, as well as a source of vitamins and minerals. Its fats are easily digestible. Although it is regarded as a possible source of food allergy, instances are rare; in France, the allergy affects 15,000 people, mostly children, in a population of 60 million.

Chapelin also examines intriguing new evidence. She reports, for instance, that doctors at Princess Margaret Hospital for Children in Perth, Australia, have perfected a "chocuhaler" for young asthma sufferers. Not only do xanthines in cacao have a dilating effect on bronchial passages, according to data she cites, but the microdroplets of milk chocolate taste good.

Chapelin's conclusion makes no sweeping catchall statement. Instead, she lists each of the known components of chocolate and examines its effect on the brain and the body. She goes on for pages, examining molecular change reactions, hormone receptors, and neurological function. In a balanced approach, she cautions against exaggerating positive effects.

To conclude, she cites a three-hundred-year-old treatise by a doctor she identifies only as M. Duncan, whom she quotes as saying (in my retranslation of Chapelin's French): "The good and bad testimony rendered over chocolate is based on healthful effects for those who use it well and harmful effects for those who use it badly . . . Those who assign themselves the task of decrying it are no more balanced than those who praise it too well, and they charge it with many evils of which it is innocent."

I later found extracts from the book by Dr. David Duncan, published in 1705, with the catchy title *Wholesome Advice Against the Abuse of Hot Liquors, Particularly Coffee, Chocolate, Tea, Brandy and Strong Waters*. In it, Duncan indeed stresses the salutary effects of chocolate. But, he warns, Satan lulls people into believing it can do no harm.

*J*n 2004, fresh findings heaped yet more authority on upbeat conclusions. Researchers at the National Academy of Sciences' 2004
Cocoa Symposium in Washington spent a day discussing the ways
in which chocolate has—or might have—beneficial effects on the human body.

Dr. Norman Hollenberg, professor of medicine at the Harvard
Medical School and director of physiological research at Brigham and
Women's Hospital in Boston, reported on years of work among isolated Kuna Indians on the San Blas Islands off Panama. Sixty years
ago, a physician in the Canal Zone noticed that age did not raise blood
pressure among the Kuna and that hypertension was very rare. Yet the
people there ate more salt than most people do. Hollenberg found this
was still true. He attributed the phenomenon to a local flavonoid-rich
cacao the Kuna drink in quantity.

"These flavonoids are the same as those in red wine, tea, and
onions—all of which have been claimed to display cardiovascular protection," he said. "In vitro, these flavonoids mimic the actions of
acetylcholine on isolated strips of vascular smooth muscle, inducing
vasorelaxation."

Hollenberg wrote about his work in the December 2003 issue of
*Journal of Hypertension*. At the seminar, he focused on evidence that
cacao with a flavonoid called flavanol can help increase blood flow to
the brain and extremities. This, obviously enough, suggests good news
for the elderly and the diabetic.

In Panama, Hollenberg observed twenty-seven healthy Kuna, aged
eighteen to seventy-two, for five days. Each consumed a cacao drink
containing nine hundred milligrams of flavanols. With a finger cuff, he
measured their blood pressure on the first and last days. On the fifth
day, he reported, the subjects showed "significant improvement" in the
blood flow as well as in the endothelial cells, which line blood vessels.

His preliminary finding was that flavanols helped to regulate the
synthesis of nitric oxide, a compound that aids in maintaining blood

pressure and flow in the endothelial cells. Flavanols might also help dilate vessels and prevent platelets from impeding blood flow.

When Kuna moved to cities and switched to commercial chocolate, Hollenberg found, their blood pressure tended to rise. Commercial processing lowers the flavonoid content.

If most chocolate now on the market could not be called a health food, he told the seminar, a change seemed imminent. "We are well beyond the beginning of this, but we are nowhere near the end," he said. "It's coming."

Hollenberg, who spent seventeen years as an editor of the *New England Journal of Medicine*, is a giant in his field, not given to exaggeration. And in the abstract of his paper, he concluded: "The range of disease candidates for examination is extraordinary. Atherosclerosis, hypertension, diabetes mellitus, vascular dementias, preeclampsia, and progressive renal disease all leap to mind. The next several years promise to be very exciting."

The National Academy of Sciences seminar was sponsored by the National Institutes of Health, the U.S. Department of Health and Human Services, and the University of California campuses at Davis and Santa Cruz. It was heavily underwritten by Mars, Inc., which has pumped money into research for more than a decade. Mars began focusing on flavonoids after a study two years earlier suggested that the chocolate in a bar of its Dove brand showed promise in improving blood function.

Harold Schmitz, director of science at Mars, said research shows that controlled growing, fermenting, roasting, and processing could produce a more healthful chocolate. He said Mars had spent well into the seven figures to support research; he did not specify how much. As a private company, he explained, Mars need not justify its research costs to investors.

Mars patented a cocoa-making process, Cocoapro, which the company supplied to Hollenberg's study. The company was testing the use of Cocoapro in such products as Dove bars and M&M's, as well as CocoaVia, which was offered initially only via the Internet.

Consumer groups are often skeptical of research sponsored by industries and companies, but Mars-backed findings have been published widely in scientific journals.

Dr. Carl Keen, who chairs the nutrition department at the University of California at Davis, has reported in several studies that certain cacao could supply important amounts of flavanols, with healthful effects on the heart.

In 2002, Keen wrote in the *Journal of the American Medical Association* of his study among eighteen volunteers who ate twenty-five grams of flavanol-rich dark chocolate. Blood tests before and after showed the chocolate substantially reduced platelet reactivity. As blood components became less sticky and less prone to adhere to vessel walls, Keen reported, the risk of blood clots was reduced and blood could flow freely through the circulatory system.

Hollenberg added a cautionary note in his remarks to the seminar. Like vitamins, he said, these experimental chocolates are likely to have differing effects on individuals. What is good is not always good, he said. "It depends on who you are."

A range of papers explained other studies which pointed toward the healthful benefits of cacao. But Philippe Petithuguenin, the director of France's CIRAD, added a final thought to the conference: "I hope we do not solve all the mystery; we need a little mystery in life."

After everyone went home, I talked with Schmitz. He was—how else to put it?—jazzed. At thirty-eight, he had spent nearly eleven years doing research for Mars. It was his first job since earning his doctorate in plant science at North Carolina State. Every year, he said, the news got better and better.

"Look, I don't think that chocolate is going to save the human race," he said, "but it shows great promise for blood flow and function, for heart diseases which decrease the quality of life." And, he added, who knows what else? Schmitz was thrilled to see the headline that the specialized periodical *Science News* put over an account of the seminar: "Prescription-Strength Chocolate?"

Like most scientists, he was careful to measure his words, and he injected notes of caution. But he has done a lot of different research into foods. This time, he said, the promise is almost palpable.

"Chocolate is one of the weirdest, most gratifying fields of research," Schmitz said. "The usual course is that something looks good at the beginning, and then it falls on its face. Chocolate just keeps going from strength to strength. And I'm hopeful that will continue. Cocoa has had such a long history of use that I think we would know any negatives by now. I'm knocking on wood as I say this."

The 2004 Cocoa Symposium also looked at ways to combat disease in cacao and to encourage new plantations in order to slow damage to tropical forests. Along with the U.S. Department of Agriculture, the World Bank, and the Smithsonian Institution, among others, private researchers are targeting pests, funguses, and viruses.

"Let's be honest," Schmitz said. "Nobody is going to do good here if the point is only to do good. Companies like us need a stable supply of cocoa. Chocolate is like other commodities, and you have to respond to the good old demand. But while coffee seems to stabilize, the demand for cocoa is increasing."

The basic philosophy of Mars, Inc. echoes the smaller-scale ideas of Claudio Corallo: help producers to grow a better crop. And if the growers can earn more, everyone gains. "The focus before was always yield, yield, and yield," Schmitz said. "Now people are realizing that conditions and quality are important, and there are new opportunities for public-private projects."

Eager as he was to share his findings, Schmitz laughed off pointed questions. When asked about the "seven-figure" research, he said, "Well, seven figures, plural." With that, he chuckled. "It's true, we're a secretive company," he said. "But we found it is in everyone's interest to work together when possible. We are behind at least seventy articles in scientific journals. If we didn't attempt to interact, what would be the point?"

Within five or ten years, Schmitz said, he expected scientists to come up with new disease-resistant strains of *criollo, trinitario,* and *nacional* trees that would be able to bring back lost flavors from the past.

That is one direction, and there are others.

Late in 2001, a researcher at the Worldwatch Institute in Washington looked at cacao from a new perspective. In the institute's magazine, *Worldwatch,* Chris Bright argued that earthlings could satisfy their collective soul by saving rain forests that sustain their planet. His article was entitled "Chocolate Could Bring the Forest Back."

One goal of scientists and marketers alike is to expand new production areas in Africa and Asia. But another is to rescue old cacao heartlands. Great biomes are threatened by the collapse of long-established plantations and so are the socioeconomic systems they once supported. And a principal concern is Brazil, where vast plantations were all but wiped out by the virulent fungus known as witches'-broom.

Bright went to Bahia, Brazil's chocolate state, where 85 percent of the country's cacao crop now grows. At its peak in the 1980s, Bahia alone produced nearly 400,000 tons, one-quarter of the world's cacao. These days, a bit player, Bahia comes up with only 100,000 tons a year. That is below 4 percent of world production.

The problem dates back to colonial monocultures. Portuguese settlers cleared vast tracts of tropical forest and cut away secondary undergrowth to make room for cacao trees. When pests struck, they attacked with a vengeance. Wide unbroken expanses of the same variety of vulnerable plant are perfect targets for infestation.

Cacao trees were planted so densely in Bahia that they once touched each other. They covered many thousands of contiguous acres. Any fungal spore in the air quickly found susceptible tissue, either a young pod or a bud on any of millions of trees. An infected fruit pod is almost certainly ruined, its beans rotted inside. But in a bud, an ominous broom-like cancer grows, sapping strength from the tree. The broom dies, leaving a bouquet of pink flowerlike basidiocarps. And each of these will release up to 90 million new fungal spores.

Conscious of its vulnerability, Bahia enforced a strict quarantine on cacao from Amazonia. In 1989, fungus appeared on a Bahia farm. Authorities quickly isolated the outbreak, sprayed fungicide on a five-hundred-acre stand, and then burned the trees. But apparently workers had already cut branches from infected trees and thrown them in a nearby river. When witches'-broom surfaced again at another farm, it was beyond anyone's control.

Bright's intriguing thesis is complex, requiring large-scale action linking public funds with private marketers. But his main point is simple. Carefully placed cacao trees in the protective shelter of a high canopy of hardwoods could restore profitability to the rain forests. Instead of clearing the trees for beef ranches and farmland, the trees could be re-planted and made to pay for themselves.

The argument offers intriguing possibilities all along the equator. Deforestation is a calamity almost beyond belief in Ivory Coast. For decades since independence, loggers have cut down and sold tropical hardwoods, leaving mostly scattered fringes in the cacao regions. In Asia, timber cutting, along with dramatic forest fires, threatens Borneo and other parts of Indonesia.

As Bright says, the crisis is at its worst in Brazil. If conservationists can protect rain forests with something as lovable as chocolate, he concludes, it would be a triumph for the human soul.

*M*ore than the soul, most researchers are at work to find ways cacao can comfort the body. From the earliest times, Europeans realized what cocoa butter can do for the human organism, inside and out. At first, chocolate was sold largely by pharmacists. In recent years, the modern-day trend has turned sharply toward using cacao in cosmetics.

A whiff of Coppertone on any beach attests to the popularity of cocoa butter in tanning lotions. The chocolate spa at Hotel Hershey in Pennsylvania is more than a tourist gimmick. Apart from what cocoa butter actually does, the familiar aroma and the pleasant thoughts that inspires add to its overall attraction. Beyond that, however, it is a chemical treasure trove. Cosmetics makers' demand for cocoa butter is the principal reason for the European Union war over allowing cheaper substitutes for cocoa butter in chocolate making.

At the Salon du Chocolat in Paris, visitors beat a path to see a hot new line offered by The Body Shop. Cocoa butter starred in a full range of products, from moisturizer, lipstick, and hand lotion to creamy body wash.

But that was just a start. Each year, the salon's organizers issue a background paper on new trends in chocolate. For 2003, they summed it up with a favorite French term: *le well-being*. There were some novelties, such as various types of bags for carrying a day's dose. Or Boucheron's new line—a twist on Jean-Paul Hévin—of jewelry that looked like chocolate.

Mostly, there were chocolate body care and makeup products. A dozen different companies offered innovations. Biotherm's Celluli-Choc, for example, a cacao-based gel, is supposed to help take off weight.

Dior came out with Bitter Chocolate lipstick. Peggy Sage has fingernail polish in rich cocoa-brown. And then there were hair products, lotions, massage oils, air-perfuming sprays, and eaux de toilette.

A few adventuresome cosmetics houses have toyed with perfumes. But I found no one who had managed to capture the essence. Mandy Aftel, a Berkeley diva of scents, tried to make some for Scharffen Berger and, her friends report, ended up wishing that she hadn't. Perhaps the answer is simply eating enough chocolate so that its delicate nuances escape from the pores.

The more I researched, the more evidence I found to take me further along the same circular track. Yes, chocolate is good for us. Scientists, however, are still arguing about just how good for us it is. Answers will come slowly and steadily, as the chocolate industry realizes the commercial benefits of supporting laboratory research. But most likely, there will always be asterisks noting provisos and disclaimers in the findings.

I put the question to the family genius, my niece Randy Gollub, a brain researcher at Harvard. She referred me to J. K. Rowling. Sure enough, Harry Potter's professors at Hogwarts Academy stuff him with chocolate, the only substance capable of warding off life-sucking Dementors.

For me, the concluding word came from Dr. Marion Nestle, former head of the department of nutrition at New York University. Her books on the politics and health effects of food are fundamental to the way serious-minded Americans look at their diet. She carefully monitors all the studies and compares findings to track new trends in thinking.

Nestle concurred with an evolving general belief. Yes, she said, chocolate was a source of antioxidants, among a lot of other things. I grilled her on the possible bad news. What about overindulgence? Were there negative aspects that industry-sponsored research failed to find? Finally she gave a short laugh and threw up her hands.

"Look, the truth is that the quantities involved are so small that you don't take in enough chocolate to make a difference either way," Dr. Nestle said. "What's the point of overanalysis? Just eat the stuff and enjoy it."

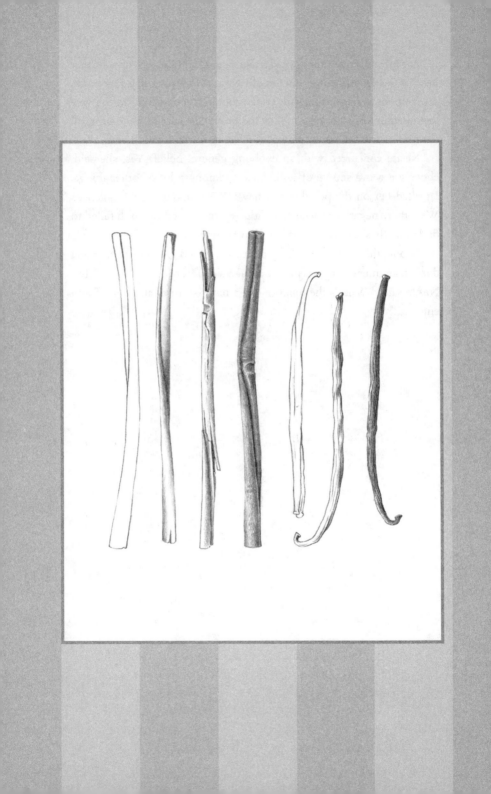

# Chapter 16

## CHOCOLATE SOLDIERS IN THE AMERICAN REVOLUTION

"Hey, I just bought a chocolate factory," Steve De Vries said, as much to himself as to me. He chugged some more of his long-necked Costa Rican beer and broke into a silly grin. "That's kind of a high." Considering that a few years earlier he was blowing glass in Denver and didn't know a cacao bean from a corn nut, I could understand his glee. And judging from what he already produced with an old wheat grinder, a bread oven, and some battered pans in his kitchen, his grand plan made perfect sense to me: "I'm going to make the best chocolate in the world."

Burly and lovable with a black mustache and bottle-bottom glasses, De Vries is a sort of cocoa-flavored Will Rogers. He manages to like just about everyone he comes across. Anything he tries seems to work out right. By the time he had his fill of glassware, he was a star. He shipped bathroom sinks to elegant homes in Milan, and his art pieces were sought by collectors.

When he sold the business, he went to Costa Rica to relax. "I'm good for about three hours on the beach, and then I get bored, so I started looking around for something else to do," he said. "I heard they grew cocoa down there, and I liked chocolate. I thought I'd see what I could learn." He hopped on a bus to the coast and then, asking around, kept taking buses. Finally he ended up at the door of a man who grew a few acres of cacao. "He showed me around, and we went to town for dinner and played dominoes all night. That was all it took."

He went home to Denver with a sack of cacao beans and started messing around in his kitchen. The processes, he said, were not much different from making miracles with molten glass. All one needs is a good thermometer and a solid foundation in physics and chemistry. Also, Steve failed to add, a touch of genius.

Steve decided to attack chocolate making from the ground up, starting with cacao trees. By the time I met him, he had already scoured southern Mexico to find rare *criollo* plantations and had trekked to Chuao in Venezuela to make friends in useful places. He had cruised industrial fairs in Cologne and Düsseldorf. At the New York Fancy Food Show, he met Chloé and recognized a kindred spirit. After she told me about his excellent chocolate adventure, I called him. He was headed back to Costa Rica to perfect his Spanish so he could buy beans the old-fashioned way. I caught a plane and joined him.

On the way down, Steve had stopped for a few hours in Mexico City, where he bought his factory. He had found a small industrial producer with some hand-me-down equipment. It was all there: roaster, *mélangeur*, refiner, and conche. With some grunt-work disassembly and heavy trucks, he could transfer the plant to Colorado. Negotiations went on through his agent. As we sat in a hotel courtyard, he got the call. It was a done deal.

"I don't even want to tell you what I paid for it," he said, still wondering if he should have upped the seller's asking price just to ease his conscience. "Oh well, at least they made more than if they had to break it up and haul it out of there." Mainly, he loved the idea of cranking new life into old Mexican machinery.

Listening to Steve spin out ideas, I thought of Claudio Corallo in Príncipe. Their approach was the same. Just because things had been done the same way for three hundred years did not mean there was no margin for improvement. Like Claudio, Steve challenged each assumption and retested every step of the process. Both experimented with roasting times and temperatures. Each deconstructed the basic science to find the hidden keys. Steve, like Claudio, decided the answer was simplicity and purity. Careful balance was essential so that good flavors did not escape with the bad.

Steve and Claudio shared a basic philosophy: Cacao farmers had to be helped to do better, and rewarded for turning out an exceptional crop, if anything good was to be expected further down the line. And both had the same realistic notions about humans as they did about trees.

"It all comes down to a simple matter of good business," Steve said. "Good producers work hard to grow something they know has a higher value, and the buyers should pay for it. That way each has an incentive, and the result will be better beans to make better chocolate."

As a hardheaded humanitarian, he is dubious of the popular Fair Trade movement. The basic principle is for buyers in the industrialized world to pay poor farmers more for their primary products than the arbitrary, imbalanced prices set by commodity markets.

Fair Trade is particularly active with cacao, and is often supported by the same people who champion organic plantations and harsh measures against Ivory Coast for using, according to popular but overblown allegations, child slave labor.

"The idea is great, and if more money actually gets to the farmer, all the better," Steve said. "But I'm leery about any program that relies on the goodwill of people in richer countries, which can change overnight. Farmers have to make commitments and plan their own lives on what they expect to earn. They're in business, and there should be no question of charity here."

If the chocolate world goes the way he thinks it will, he is convinced that the balance will work itself out just fine on its own. As more buyers demand better quality chocolate made from "flavor beans," manufacturers will have to look beyond their regular bulk cacao suppliers in West Africa and Asia. This will bring premiums to encourage the more careful producers. But it may also get ugly.

Early on, in fact, Steve had a foretaste of his theory in action. Following his nose and asking the right questions, he found an aging Mexican woman growing *criollo* beans at a small plantation in Tabasco. Hers was one of those juicy family stories, with crossed love affairs, mysterious deaths, and intrigue among the trees. Chloé happened to mention the place later in a conversation with Pierre Marcolini. Those were the beans that Marcolini quickly tracked down and locked up for the next five years.

When I left Steve in Costa Rica, he was about to spend a month with a family to work on the nuances of Spanish. If he was going to make the world's best chocolate, he would start by cultivating the world's best farmers. Then he set out with maps and old texts in hand to prospect rich new lodes as yet undiscovered by the great chocolate rush of the new millennium.

The next time I saw Steve, he handed me a couple of Ziploc bags with all the ceremony of a dope dealer offering up the good stuff. He had roasted, refined, and conched beans from Tabasco and Costa Rica. With cooking pots and his thermometer, he alchemized them into chocolate. One sample was awful, with a bitter undertone that masked everything else. A second was pretty good. The third was terrific, a subtle blend of berries and floral notes that lingered on the palate.

He had already given samples to Chloé. She spit out the first and pushed aside the second. But she loved the third. "In five years, we're going to be hearing about him," she reported. "If he perfects his process and keeps on like this, he'll be up there with Valrhona and Pralus."

Steve, though still disappointed at losing his secret source to Marcolini, took some pleasure in an e-mail Chloé later sent to the Belgian entrepreneur. By then, Marcolini had marketed his Mexican *criollo* chocolate with great fanfare. But, Chloé told him, it was nowhere nearly as good as what Steve had concocted in his kitchen.

I put Steve in touch with Janine Gasco, an anthropology professor at California State University, Dominguez Hills. She had repeatedly roamed Soconusco, the Aztecs' old cacao heartland in the Mexican state of Chiapas, in search of original *criollo* plantations. She found impoverished growers desperate for someone to help them market their beans. Jan took Steve on a grand tour, and he sent me one of his typically cryptic e-mails: "Much better than expected." Steve nearly had a heart attack when he missed the intended humor in my reply: "Great. I can't wait to tell Marcolini."

Besides looking for beans, Steve set himself on a mission to inspect every technological innovation and mechanical novelty to appear on the market. He sniffs his way through industrial fairs in Cologne like a pig after truffles. He knows all there is to know about tolerances, particle sizes, and temperatures. Despite his easy humor, his interest is so intense that he sometimes scares people who sense possible future competition.

Steve, like a kid without limits, just cannot get enough. Once we visited the Chocovic factory in Spain and came across century-old handwritten recipes for the company's first chocolate blends. He handled them with reverence. Soon after, he sent an e-mail:

> Paging through those recipes gave me an intense déjà vu. When I was nineteen I toured basically all the museums in the U.S. with American Plains Indians collections and got into the vaults to view and photo-graph bead, feather and leather work . . . It also gave me the feeling that this is what I want to do. Not into the past, but the idea that 100-plus years ago it was fairly common for people to know that they wanted a chocolate with a little more Caracas, or Fernando Po, [im-plies] a connection and recognition of the possibilities that today are virtually nonexistent, but would be beneficial for both the producers and consumers.

Chocolatiers were exploring similar possibilities today, but I had been with Steve in the Catalonian hills, and I knew what he meant. A certain spirit infused those recipes. There was no hint of marketing or fad or hype. Those old guys just wanted to make killer chocolate.

Everything about Steve runs counter to the old-world mold that has produced so many European chocolatiers. He grew up in a ranch house on the Colorado-Wyoming border, where his father was a ranch herdsman. He was the entire first grade at a one-room schoolhouse to which most kids rode on horseback. His family moved to Steamboat Springs, then Denver, where gourmet cooking or fancy pastries were seldom on the menu.

When he eventually threw himself into chocolate, he did it just as he had mastered glass art, quantum physics, and each of his other vari-ous interests. "I had some training in school," he said, "and I can read." Steve asked questions of everybody who might know something useful. And he answered frankly any question asked of him.

"I don't get all this secrecy among chocolatiers," he said. "You see the same thing with some glassblowers. A guy learns a certain technique, and he is afraid to share it with anyone. Think about that. He never picks up anything new. If someone refuses to talk to me about his work, that means he not only thinks he is smarter than me but that he is smarter than everybody in the world. How else do you learn to do better than by sharing thoughts? Guys like that have to come up with everything by themselves. That's stupid."

Steve's studies in agronomy confirmed something he had suspected from the beginning. The chocolate world's obsession with *criollo* has little to do with scientific reality. The pre-Columbian tree that Mayans and Aztecs worshipped has undergone five centuries of botanic drama. Neither particularly hardy nor productive, it picked up untraceable mutations and influences over uncounted generations. In each new terroir, it adapted to different soil compositions and weather patterns.

"I would rather talk about 'very *criollo*' or 'not-so *criollo*,'" he says. "You can still find some of the original characteristics and flavors, but very few pure *criollo* trees exist anymore, anywhere."

As usual, he was right on the money. Later I visited the prestigious institute of tropical agriculture, CIRAD, in Montpellier, France. Experts there had come to the same conclusion, proving it with elaborate gene research. Botany works that way.

One assumption that Steve challenges is among the most basic: Why should cacao be grown on the equator but made into chocolate only in Europe or America?

"That makes about as much sense as growing grapes in southern France and then sending them to another continent to make wine," he said. "Maybe that was necessary back before air-conditioning allowed people to cool down finished chocolate to keep it from melting. But why now? People do it that way because they've always done it that way. It isn't logical, economically. Why add all the shipping costs and stress on the beans? Also, there's an implicit cultural assumption I don't like: We can do it better in developed societies."

Steve likes to muse about pioneering equatorial chocolate factories. He wants to bring industry and expertise to poor economies, where both are desperately needed, while correcting an imbalance with roots in a colonial mentality. However he might pretend he is merely a capitalist in search of good business, he is the sort of guy who would end up as godfather and unofficial uncle to half the kids in the province.

But all of that is in the down-the-road stage, and Steve does not like to get ahead of himself. He had his kitchen in Denver in which to experiment. He was hard at work refitting his cast-off Mexican equipment and adapting it to a new age. Things would happen in their own time, and he would be ready.

We discussed this yet again when he visited me in France. Each time I took him to some sophisticated chocolatier's showroom, he fidgeted nervously. "This is the roof, and I'm still in the basement," he said.

"I'm just not goal oriented," he explained. "I like to take things one step at a time and see how they develop. Frankly, after selling my glass business I could probably get by without working again. But who wants to do that? I'd much rather make the best chocolate in the world."

When I first met Steve, a remark like that sounded like an idle, if amusing, boast. After looking at how chocolate making had developed over the years, however, it seemed perfectly possible. European masters had taken early processes to a high art. But the pressure of mass production and competition limited their old creativity. The cultural strictures of haute cuisine tended to block out new ideas in favor of the tried and true.

Why couldn't new-world iconoclasts, unburdened by romance and traditions, find some better way?

As it turned out, Chlöe was wrong about Steve. It would take much less than five years for the world to hear about him. Unsatisfied with his Mexican equipment, Steve kept looking. He followed a tip to Hamburg, where, in an ornate barn built in 1635, he found treasure. Four of those same *Langschieber* longitudinal conches that Sepp Schoenbacher used at Felchlin sat dusty and forlorn in a corner. They had served nobly for eighty years at Suchard's original plant in the Swiss Alps before being retired eighteen years earlier. After complex negotiations, Steve packed them off for a new life in the Rockies.

This was in 2004. Steve had already moved into a 2,500-square-foot space just south of Denver's high-rise downtown. He battled over zoning, health inspections, and building codes. In his home kitchen, he worked his Mexican and Central American beans to fresh glory. And in the meantime, he scoured the world's libraries for chocolate lore.

"Lately I've come to view chocolate as an overly industrialized food," he e-mailed me after a stop in Amsterdam. "Virtually all the changes in production techniques in the last hundred years have as their goal faster chocolate, more uniform chocolate, greater quantities of chocolate, and longer-shelf-life chocolate."

The last machine that actually made better chocolate, Steve said, was that good old 1887 *Langschieber* conche of Lindt's. "Around the turn of the century," he added, "all the factories had warming cabinets where the chocolate could 'rest' for a couple of days between steps (before lecithin). Both cocoa butter and lecithin were used to lower the viscosity and get it through the factory faster, not to improve the flavor."

A book he found entitled *Cocoa and Chocolate, 1765–1914,* by William Gervase Clarence-Smith, made the point. In 1893, the author calculated, a chocolate-factory worker had to put in sixty hours to afford the retail price of a half-kilo of the product he made. By 1913, he could buy the same amount of chocolate for just over one hour's work.

With his new old equipment in place, Steve decided to start small. But, he figured, he could build up to eighty tons a year as the market developed.

The first signs were encouraging. When Steve stayed behind on that Costa Rica trip we made, he tracked down a Dutch master grower named Hugo Hemmelink. His cacao, basically *trinitario* with strong traces of original *criollo,* was dried in the sun. "A lot less acid and no weird off tastes to get rid of," Steve reported. He brought home 1,200 kilos of beans.

Midway through 2004, Steve made two trial batches of chocolate, each with 75 percent Costa Rican cacao solids. A friend in Berkeley sent some of it to Leonard Pitt, a Bay Area writer and actor, who organized a monthly tasting for his California Dreamy Chocolate Club. Steve's two entries came out first and second, the best rating 43.5 out of a possible 45. Valrhona's 64 percent blend scored 37. "Steve's chocolate was tops," Pitt said. "It had a fruitiness, a richness, with flavors that seemed to go away and then come back again. Nothing else was like it."

By the end of 2004, Steve was doing more than experimenting. De Vries Chocolate, made in Denver, was ready to take on the world.


*D*uring 2003, San Francisco reincarnated its Ferry Building, an architectural jewel that for decades had been hiding as a workaday boat terminal. Farseeing developers ripped away false ceilings and scraped off coated grime. Long-forgotten tile mosaics and fancy woodwork were brought back to life from an age when people seemed to care more about their surroundings.

The best sort of merchants moved into refurbished spaces. It was a mecca for food lovers, with everything from cheeses and teas to tableware. Book Passage, the Marin County readers' haven, opened a branch just off the wooden wharves. And the old Farmer's Market, which once huddled tentatively each weekend on a parking lot out front, found its own home back where shoppers could watch ferries slip in from points north and east.

Among the new shops, I spotted Nan McAvoy's. When I had last poked around the Bay Area for literary purposes, I was after olives, not chocolate. Producers of the best European oil, back then, were amused at the California olive rush. There were some interesting players. McAvoy, for instance, had to sell her interest in the *San Francisco Chronicle* because of a family feud. So she went into the olive-oil business. With a flamboyant Tuscan adviser, a converted dairy farm on rolling hills near Petaluma, and Italian trees imported by the thousand, she created a world-class California oil. Could someone else's chocolate be far behind?

Just down the tiled floor from Nan McAvoy, a masterful chocolatier named Michael Recchiuti was offering ganaches and *pralinés* to rival the finest French bonbons. I had stumbled upon Recchiuti a few years earlier at the open-air Green Street market in San Francisco. From the bouquet wafting on the Bay breeze, it was clear he was no weekend amateur. After a quick sampling, I went to check out his shop in a modern warehouse between the Mission and the waterfront.

Recchiuti (pronounced *re-KYOO-tee,* as his brochure points out) takes a European-type approach. Trained as a pâtissier in Philadelphia, he knows he can buy good chocolate base. His skill goes into turning that into delicate finished masterpieces. The chocolatier's brochure says it simply enough: "We fuse classic French techniques with a global palette." I am not sure if he has misspelled *palate* or is likening his work to a painter's art. Either way, it works.

One by one, he handed me small squares in that game of "Try this!" that I came to love among chocolatiers.

I tasted a mix of star anise and crushed pink peppercorns infused into semisweet dark ganache. To soften the impact, it was enrobed in 41 percent milk chocolate. For a touch of art, it was topped with a dab of Venezuelan white chocolate. The palette ranges from cardamom and sesame nougat, Provençal lavender, Piedmont hazelnuts, lemon verbena, spring jasmine tea, to honeycomb and barley malt, among a lot of others.

I looked for a *palet d'or* and found instead a *force noir*: dark ganache flavored with a vanilla bean.

The Rose Caramel is sweet, swirled with rose petal–geranium oil. Another caramel, Fleur de Sel, is laced with fine sea salt à la Henri Roux in Quiberon, France. But Recchiuti's signature piece is Burnt Caramel, dark and smoky, blended with extra-bitter chocolate ganache.

The three-layer house sampler contains four varietals, numbered so they can be tasted in order of their power. L'Harmonie, which is nutty and floral, blends cacao from the Caribbean, South America, and Central America. Then there are Venezuelan and Colombian varietals, the first from trees in the Sur del Lago region below Lake Maracaibo, and the second from the Chucurreno region of Colombia. The big finish, Ecuador Varietal, is *nacional,* with its strong persistence of flavor, its rich coffee color, and its earthy, tobacco-smoke tones.

Besides his deft hand with chocolate and his artist's eye, Michael has a natural head for business. He figures out what people want, and then he finds a way to make it in a way that suits his own standards.

Michael's Italian grandmother taught him to bake when he was five. At eleven, he took up chocolate, about the same time he developed a passion for vibraphones and drums. Art followed. He apprenticed as a chef, working with Frenchman Alain Tricou, who pitched up in Philadelphia when his boss, the Shah of Iran, was overthrown. Michael moved to San Francisco where he and his wife, Jacky, opened Recchiuti Confections in 1997.

When I saw Michael again in 2004, he had launched a line of s'mores, that old campfire treat of marshmallows, graham crackers, and melted chocolate. He used rich dark chocolate, creamy homemade marshmallow, and freshly baked honey grahams. They were as far from what I remember from Boy Scout days as Jean-Paul Hévin's "Nutella" was from the industrial jarred stuff.

A fresh round of "Try this" produced his favorite: a tarragon-laced ganache with a strip of candied grapefruit peel hiding in the *enrobage*. A sweet rush of anise is cut by a note of bitter citrus.

By the time of my second visit, Michael had been discovered at the age of forty-four, a mixed blessing. "My God, I don't know how I'm going to do it," he moaned, as he sat down for a Japanese tea before beetling off to yet another appointment.

His chocolate could be found, for example, at a Whole Foods Market in Sebastopol, but it was displayed just above the stinky cheeses. New York specialty shops clamored for his chocolates, which posed the usual problems of delivery and of relying on people with limited chocolate experience to make sure the ganache stayed fresh. Some of his products showed up in the Williams-Sonoma catalogue, turbocharging his volume. He wanted to meet the new demand but without losing his ability to put his personal stamp on everything he produced.

*The Wall Street Journal* declared him the best chocolatier in America in 2003, without warning him, and his little lab was swamped with thousands of orders.

But, I sensed, Michael's moan carried no discouragement behind it. He reminded me of Patrick Roger back in Sceaux. It really would not matter how many people clamored for his chocolate. In the end, they would just have to hold on to see where his art took him. And whatever he produced, it would be worth the wait.

In the spring of 2004, Michael and Jacky pitched up in Paris bearing gifts. In fact, they bore so many gifts I was troubled by the dilemma all reporters face: What do you accept from a source about whom you intend to write? The answer is usually simple. Nothing. But when writing about chocolate, you have to sample a very broad range. Insisting on principle can border on rudeness, like taking out your wallet in a winemaker's cave. Some chocolatiers are overly public-relations minded; one must put down one's foot. With some others, every bite is purchased. But Michael is something different entirely.

Although his belly does not jiggle, his beard is more Yasir Arafat than long and snowy, and he never wears white-cuffed red suits, Michael always reminds me of Santa Claus. I decided that if I was a helpful guide, I could wolf down contents from his sack with a clear conscience.

One by one, we hit my favorites. Patrick Roger, in the midst of a crush, came out for two minutes to say hello. An hour later, I had to drag the two kindred spirits apart. Jacques Genin, equally busy, also sniffed a fellow genius. By the time we left, they were cooking up joint projects. Chaudun, in his hermit mode that morning, stayed in the back. But Michael was amused to find exact copies of the folded boxes he had designed nearly a decade ago. He had sent Chaudun some boxed samples. At Jean-Paul Hévin's, a saleswoman glanced at Michael's attire and wrote him off as a routine schlepper. The master was out.

We skipped La Maison du Chocolat because Michael had been there. Directors thought so much of his chocolate that they had once flown him to Paris and offered to buy him out in order to close him down. Anyone making such good stuff in America was bad for La Maison's image.

Mostly we sat on my deck, talked chocolate, and worked away at his stash. My favorite was a bar made of 85 percent South American cacao so expertly blended that it had no tinge of bitterness. "This is what we take with us to the movies," Jacky said. "You just keep eating it." But there was also that honey *praliné* bar.

Michael talks happily for hours about chocolate with disarming bluntness. Does La Maison really freeze its chocolate before export? Well, he said, he saw a gigantic freezer room that hosts tried to hide when he visited the place. Anyway, he said, the test is simple enough. If chocolates have been frozen, the sugar crystallizes and *couverture* flakes away from the ganache.

European *couverture* is smoother, he explained, because chocolatiers use invert sugar, which has a different molecular structure than the ordinary stuff. The ganache emulsifies into a rich, creamy texture. I quizzed him on the fine points of chocolate bloom, the grainy white fat particles that form with temperature change. It does not make chocolate inedible, but it blunts the fine edges of flavor.

During their ten days in France, I saw Michael and Jacky often. His cell phone was on, but it seldom rang. When crises arose back home, his people dealt with them. Suppliers clamored for his products, but he was in no great hurry.

"We want to grow, but we don't have any desire to let things get out of hand," Michael explained, leaning back to catch some late-spring sunshine. "All we want to do is make really good chocolate and enjoy ourselves."


*M*y northern California travels turned up two extremes in scale, little and big, which showed that finding good chocolate need not involve a plane trip to Europe.

Richard Donnelly, down the coast from San Francisco in Santa Cruz, is not into the art and poetry of it all. He wears a leather motoring cap and works in a cluttered back room which, at holiday times, resembles the scene of some grisly accident. Before my visit, he stuffed a hunk of white gauze in my hand; only later I figured out it was meant as a net to keep my unruly hair from falling into open vats.

Like Recchiuti, he buys the best chocolate base he can find, and with it he creates good chocolate for a fiercely loyal clientele. He loves to innovate and push the limits. For a small group of chili-head customers, he creates a bonbon with Mexican chipotle peppers that ought to come in a flameproof box. He has a popular line of chocolate massage oil. Novelties aside, he is a craftsman with a broad range of French-style ganaches and *pralinés*. When he dispatches his products, he inserts a card warning: "Perishable. Don't wait. Your box contains handmade, preservative-free fine chocolates. Please open and enjoy within one week."

As a child, he always found chocolate too sweet and pasty. He tasted something better on a trip to France, so he went back to apprentice with French and Belgian masters. In 1988, he opened his shop in Santa Cruz.

In the United States, Richard said, quality chocolatiers face an uphill battle.

"Europeans are ready to pay the necessary price for good chocolate," he said, "but here people don't understand why it costs more than in a supermarket. I have customers who drive up in the latest Mercedes, who brag about the property they own all over the world. Then they look at my prices and tell me they can't pay so much. And it's not even that much. I tell them they can also buy a Yugo for less money than their Mercedes, but obviously that is not what they choose to do."

His chocolate is not cheap. A pound of Donnelly's chipotle bonbons sold for $65, more than La Maison du Chocolat charges in Paris. Still, Richard is doing all right. His brother, Henry, left his old career to come work with him. He had been a successful stockbroker until the ugly days when the bubble burst. When the market picked up again, Henry stayed with his brother. After all, what's money compared to the early-morning chocolate scent in that messy little kitchen?

$G$ary Guittard, in his vast hangar of a plant near San Francisco Airport, is no small operator. He has built his French-immigrant grandfather's chocolate business into a bustling enterprise in Burlingame.

Since the company remains in his family, he does not have to discuss its size or its turnover. With a polite firmness, he waves off such questions. Valrhona might be a reasonable comparison, he allows, although he is bigger. The See's Candies factory next door relies exclusively on his chocolate, and it is only one of his many customers.

Size notwithstanding, Gary takes his chocolate personally. He loves what he makes. Early in 2002, I made a note to find him after the *Los Angeles Times* devoted a long front-page piece by Melinda Fulmer to "varietal" and "estate" chocolates. It began: "Swishing the smooth, dark blend around in his mouth, Gary Guittard searches for the right words: 'Astringent,' he decides, 'with some floral notes.' Zinfandel? Or maybe Merlot? No, chocolate."

Eager to join the specialized chocolate rush, the company introduced its E. Guittard Founder's Reserve line, with beans from South America and Africa. "If people hear something is the strongest in the world, they want to taste it and say they like it," the article quoted Gary as saying. It added: " 'Right or wrong,' he says, 'it's got snob appeal.' "

That sounded suspiciously like a marketing gimmick. In Europe, some large producers had already seized on the phenomenon, offering chocolate bars that are up to 99 percent cacao. As lovers of fine chocolate discover, the point is not what isn't there but rather what is. If the chocolate is not selected for flavor qualities to replace the missing sugar, the result will be ghastly.

But then my intelligence network had turned up signs of Guittard's energetic search for good beans. He had found a producer in Papua New Guinea who seemed thrilled at his efforts to improve the quality and flavor of the cacao. I knew he followed research in Venezuela and had nailed down reliable supplies all along the equator.

I went to Burlingame and, hours later, emerged with cacao-colored smears across my chin. I had tasted better chocolate, but I was happy to see a big-time producer take such pride in artisan-type quality.

One after the other, we sampled products in the Founder's Reserve line. Gary's favorite was a blend of eight beans from different—and undisclosed—sources. It was good, but I sensed that astringent bitterness I associated with the baking chocolate I'd steal as a kid from my mother's pantry when in desperate need of a fix. But I liked the Sur del Lago, with *criollo* flavors from south of Lake Maracaibo. It had the floral bouquet and spicy notes of Chuao with no hint of wet saddle leather.

When Michael Recchiuti made that trip to Paris later on, his bag of goodies included vacuum-sealed bricks of Guittard's Sur del Lago. Although he used plenty of Valrhona, Michael also relied heavily on Guittard. In Burlingame, with a quick taste among many others, the impact did not hit me. But in Paris, as I gnawed away at that wonderfully clean and crisp bouquet of fast-developing and long-lasting tones, I fell in love with it.

After a while, we wrapped up in white and toured the plant. In terms of scale, Guittard resembles Valrhona. Both operations are scrupulously clean, with a feel clear of hustle and bustle. But they are as different as industrial-zone Burlingame and old-world Tain l'Hermitage.

Guittard's chocolate works was geared for big business. Its assembly line of monster winnowers and refiners and tempering vats reminded me of a Ford factory turning out pickup trucks. Much of its chocolate emerged in ten-pound blocks for industrial customers. Valrhona, in contrast, seemed more like a blown-up version of a grand chef's kitchen. Odd-looking machines of varying sizes did a series of jobs, often to some mystifying purpose. Only when you understood the process did the logic become clear. Like in a restaurant kitchen, everything flowed in a single direction to produce a final artisan chef d'oeuvre.

In the end, I realized, style did not really matter. Both approaches were capable of turning out exceptional products. My sense was that Gary Guittard would love to dam his river of mediocre chocolate and, like his French counterpart, concentrate on small streams of real quality. But this is business. What matters is market demand.

*M*y happiest chocolate prospecting in the United States was on the West Coast. Friends had given me various addresses in New York and elsewhere around the country. I followed up on newspaper cuttings and bursts of enthusiasm in magazines. I found plenty of novel ideas, such as a former certified public accountant near Cincinnati who markets Chocizza, as in chocolate and pizza. She does not use pepperoni or tomato sauce, I determined, but I declined to look further.

As I was deciding where to explore further late in 2003, my e-mail inbox suddenly flooded with copies of a long *New York Times* article. Chocolate, it proclaimed, was the next coffee. Or olive oil. And it drew similarities with wine. That is, Americans were catching on and demanding quality. The enthusiastic writer offered a helpful list of places which she judged the best.

Clutching the article and a map of lower Manhattan, I made the tour. Before long, I saw that the comparison was apt, if perhaps unwittingly. A new breed of East Coast chocolatiers had captured the spirit that first infused West Coast olive-oil producers some years before. They devised imaginative packaging—from amusing to gorgeous—and attractive displays. Eventually, the more successful would get around to the product itself.

It was New York at its best. At MarieBelle, miniature paintings on each piece of chocolate cried out for tasting, at least for curiosity. But I decided against buying the custom-designed red and blue Italian leather box of forty-eight assorted chocolates. It cost $350. The ten-ounce tin of Aztec Hot Chocolate (from Venezuela) was only $17.

Posters around the shop showed different beautifully coiffed models, each with a perfect face—except for a disgusting red-rimmed white pimple on a nose, a forehead, or a chin. Each carried the same printed message: It's so totally worth it.

In conversation with a young man behind the counter, I remarked that, in fact, chocolate does not cause pimples; that was a myth. "Thank you!" he said, in a theatrical voice. "I keep trying to tell them that. Give this man a free sample." I laughed with him but, having already tasted the chocolate, I declined.

Before leaving, I found a happy surprise. In one corner, like a shrine, the shop offered a broad range of interesting chocolate bars. Along with the usual European suspects, I found El Rey, a line of extremely good chocolate bars from an eighty-year-old company in Venezuela. There was even the best of Enric Rovira, a Catalan chocolatier-artist with a small shop in Barcelona.

Nearby in SoHo, I stopped at Vosges Haut Chocolat. Headquartered in Chicago, the little company had made a splash in New York. Its owner, Katrina Markoff, is a strikingly beautiful woman with dark hair from her Macedonian bloodlines. She studied at the Cordon Bleu in Paris and apprenticed in pâtisserie at the Crillon. In a blast of panache during 2004, she took over part of Château Chenonceau in the Loire Valley to demonstrate her grand concept: "Deconstruct what you know about chocolate and open your mind to new possibilities."

At her SoHo shop, I tried my best to deconstruct. But after specialties such as wasabi- and curry-laced chocolate, too imaginative for my taste, I beat a hasty retreat.

Not far away, I found Kee Ling Tong, a Macao-born woman making another sort of product at her Chocolate Garden. The place was, literally, a hole in the wall. No fancy trappings, no broad range. Purchases were carefully fitted into simple white cardboard boxes. Kee's specialty is a crème brûlée truffle. I tried the dark chocolate ganache flavored with clover honey, green tea, and a hint of saffron. So what if the ganache was too creamy? I bought the rest on the plate.

Kee could make a dent in anyone's market, but the problem is scale. A customer such as Chloé could clean her out to satisfy a single day's fix.

*T*here was other good chocolate around. But I could see an overriding attitude toward chocolate in mainstream America. It occurred to me when I finally saw the film version of Roald Dahl's classic *Charlie and the Chocolate Factory,* with Gene Wilder.

When the lucky little band entered the inner sanctum and launched into its collective pig-out, I noticed what attracted each one. They gorged on frothy white cream concoctions, candy canes, gumdrops, and colorful lollipops. The fat kid tumbled into a chocolate river, but it was lighter than the brown water that many of us refer to as coffee. What fascinates so many people is more the idea of chocolate than the substance itself.

But then my last stop on the chocolate trail left me full of hope for the great awakening. I found Maury Rubin at City Bakery.

Rubin, with ducktails and a quizzical smile, came to the chocolate business through the back door. His previous métier was producer for Howard Cosell. He hustled from Super Bowl to World Series, barking orders to crews and trading wisecracks with the best-known lip on American television. One morning, he decided to shuck sports broadcasting, and he shut himself into his pastry kitchen with all the zeal of a medieval monk.

Maury went to France to study pastry-making and chocolate skills. Then he came home to bake, not as an exotic import who exuded mystique because of *r*'s rolled from somewhere in the back of his throat, but rather as a local guy who knew what his customers ate as kids.

He laughs at the idea that Europeans own the art of chocolate making simply because they act as if they do. "God knows, there is a lot of pretense," he said. "Sometimes it's really silly. Mostly, it is just boring. I have to admit I get great pleasure from taking the air out of chocolate snobs."

At City Bakery, you realize what ought to be obvious. No secret code to the chocolate arts comes as part of any genetic structure of a nation's people. Practitioners need not take themselves too seriously. Chocolate is fun. And yet excelling with chocolate requires technical ability as well as a sensitive palate and that indefinable alchemy.

However tempting the comparison might be, cacao is not like olives or coffee berries—and certainly not like grapes.

With olives, it is all in the fruit. A good oil maker learns to pick cleanly, press quickly, and stay the hell out of the way. Olive oil, in the end, is fruit juice. It develops its flavors rapidly and begins to lose them in a matter of months. Coffee involves husking and careful roasting. But it too is essentially no more than the direct result of what comes off the plant.

Grapes are far more complex. A winemaker's hand is nearly as essential as God's at every step of the way. In the end, well-made wine improves with age over years if not decades or even generations.

Chocolate makers need many of the vintner's skills, but they also blend in other components with differing chemical properties. And yet the best they can hope for is a product with a fraction of the life span of olive oil.

Cacao beans may have distinct characteristics the way grapes do, but their extreme sensitivity to conditions around them means that nothing can be taken for granted. The finest cacao can rapidly deteriorate toward inedibility, for instance, if smoke taints it while drying. When you see Médoc 1996 on a bottle, you know what to expect. Such assurances are less common with chocolate.

I had spent a lot of time with *fondeurs* who make finished bonbons from chocolate. But baking with it adds a whole new array of challenges.

"Anyone can turn out some excellent stuff as long as they're willing to throw away a lot of their mistakes," Maury said. The trick is to get things right on a regular basis. "No one can be a master chocolatier without unfailing consistency."

Consumers, he adds, must make a basic choice. They decide what they like and hope for no disappointment. Commercially packaged brands may offer more reliability but not much daring.

Maury opened City Bakery in 1990 and then spent four years working from 2:30 a.m. to 10 p.m. These days, he lazes in bed until 6 a.m. and sometimes takes the evenings off. It is still a seven-day-a-week job.

When I walked in, some obscure bluegrass group was torturing "Foggy Mountain Breakdown." Soon after, Johnny Cash droned on about jail time. It seems I had come in on Country and Western week in a New York hangout where even reliably terrific pastries and a relaxed atmosphere are not enough to ensure a full house. City Bakery, like nearly everyplace else in the city, is constantly evolving.

"A couple of years ago for no reason I could explain, I started to do more chocolate," Maury said. His thick, rich hot chocolate in a mug is still a bestseller, but now his range is wider.

The trend in America is shifting toward good chocolate, no question about it, Maury said. Studies by the Chocolate Manufacturers Association quantify that. In 1991, only 15 percent of Americans preferred dark chocolate. By 2004, the figure was near 30 percent. But still.

"I would liken this to organic food," he concluded. "It is booming in the United States. Sales of good chocolate are growing at five times the rate of the conventional kind. A lot of people are better informed, more curious. Absolutely. But good chocolate still makes up only about one percent of the whole picture. We have a ways to go."

# Chapter 17

## CAMP CACAO

On a warm, bright summer Sunday, Parisian boat people lazed on their decks and sipped chilled white wine. Aboard *La Vieille*, however, it was hard labor worthy of Captain Cook's *Endeavour*. Claudio da Príncipe was in town from São Tomé, chocolate samples in hand. Steve de Vries had taken a train from Amsterdam, fresh from a tour of European machinery. Jacques Genin brought some of his morning's product. Chloé, unwilling to miss the gathering, had popped over from London bearing gifts. It was the end of my two-year stint in chocolate boot camp, and the gang was there to see I didn't skip a single push-up.

I had learned a bit. For instance, I equipped my old wooden boat with cooler bags and ice so Jacques's peppered mint ganache did not melt into dark brown soup. It was no longer necessary to question Chloé, yet again, on the subtle nuances of the Manjari *longueur en bouche*. But as I listened to my various mentors argue away the afternoon, I finally caught on to the basic point of it all. With chocolate, there are no straight answers. There are only strongly held opinions.

In the end, not much has changed since Columbus tossed away those cacao beans half a millennium ago. It comes down to the most simple of questions. What do you like? What else have you tried? If after tasting Caraïbe you still prefer Cadbury, no shame in that. Just watch your back at the Salon du Chocolat.

There are few enough real experts; in any case, no one can speak for someone else's palate, let alone past life associations. If you like Hershey, count yourself lucky. If you crave Valrhona's best, mortgage the house if you must. Life has few enough pleasures.

Claudio was first to show up and last to leave. He spent hours on deck in baggy shorts and sandals. At a casual glance, he looked like the other Sunday afternoon schleppers with nothing but Sancerre and suntan lotion on their minds. We all knew better.

Claudio's eyes missed nothing as he kept up a steady patter about mysteries on the Seine that had puzzled me over the years. That huge Bateau-Mouche left no wake, for instance, because of furrows designed into its split hull. His hands never stopped moving. As he talked, he retied the silly knot I had on my marlinspike lanyard, and he spliced every rope on deck.

From time to time, Claudio seized my notebook to sketch out what he wanted to explain. On one page, he drew an elaborate coiled still to show how he made cacao brandy. On another, he depicted the steel ridges in a Lloveras Universal machine he had purchased for lack of anything better; from the design, he knew the thing would produce hot spots that could singe his precious nibs. I saved them all. One day, the museum at Vinci will want them.

Mostly, however, Claudio mused about roasting cacao beans. He was the farmer of the bunch, and he knew from handling coffee berries how crucial it was to get things right. With too little heat, flavors stay locked inside. With too much, the beans are toast. He was obsessed with roasting, and no store-bought machine would satisfy him. There had to be a better way, he knew. He also knew that some morning at 5 a.m., it would come to him.

Late one night, long after the Andalusian *pata negra* ham and deep into grappa, Claudio reached a high philosophic plane. "Why are people so jealous of their secrets?" he asked. "It is because there are so few secrets. The big secret is to have everything in balance, the trees, the beans, the final product. Everything must be well executed. If you do that, it is hard to have bad chocolate. If you don't, it's impossible to have good chocolate."

Steve, the self-taught technician, blew in at the last minute. He had been wrestling with heavy metal so he could move beyond grinding beans in his kitchen with a flour mill. Catalogues littered the deck table. Steve had traipsed faithfully to every industrial fair in Europe and America, and he had scoured the Net until his eyes ached. The machinery he bought in Mexico and Germany was a start, but his goal was to produce the best chocolate in the world.

Jacques, who to my mind already produced the best chocolate in the world, listened closely to the others. Actually, he only made chocolates— ganache and *pralinés* from Valrhona base. He had never seen a cacao tree or roasted a bean. And he was fascinated to hear about basics.

He lit up when Claudio produced a Perrier bottle whose contents seemed closer to those of a Molotov cocktail than to a flask of fizzy water. It was his distilled mucilage from cacao pods, powerful enough to strip varnish and yet incredibly tasty. Jacques finished the bottle and waited for another.

Before long, Jacques had arranged for Claudio to ship him a load of São Tomé's finest nibs. "I don't know what I'll do with them," he said, "but I think you'll like it."

Claudio nodded agreeably, but I was pretty sure he wouldn't like it. He prefers his chocolate rough, flavorful, and straightforward. Sophisticated French art forms, he believes, are best left in the Louvre.

Just that morning, I had taken Claudio and Steve to Michel Chaudun for a taste of his hallowed *chocolat aux éclats de fèves*. Both turned up their noses. Each had a different idea for doing it better. "It's over-roasted," Steve said, "but you notice I'm eating it." In fact, I noticed that the whole sack was empty within minutes.

Then we stopped to see Jean-Paul Hévin's jewel-like creations. Claudio stuck with the fruit jellies, and Steve passed on everything. The high-fashion folderol, coupled with the saleslady's scrutiny as she determined whether we were worthy enough customers, troubled their spirits.

Back at the boat, Chloé beamed as strong opinions, and no answers, flashed across the table. It was a curious Babel. We spoke nine languages among us. But neither Claudio nor Jacques knew English. Steve had Spanish but no French. No matter. Chloé's little clutch of protégés had clicked. They covered the gamut from inspired grower to focused dreamer to master doer.

As an appetizer, we passed around chocolates brought aboard in Ziploc bags, Tupperware, tinfoil, plastic sacks, or original fancy wrappings. We were mixed on Steve's Felchlin from Switzerland. Steve liked it. So did Chloé, sort of. Claudio offered: "Mechanically well made, but you can't say it's exciting, like a great wine. It's like an old lady with a face-lift."

Chloé had some Domori, made by an Italian near Genoa with an attractive Web site and a flair for overstatement. His label for Gem read, "I split the elements, the different cacao varietals into a refined mass, and cane sugar with crystals; Gems in the pre-Columbian gold." This time, we all agreed with Claudio's judgment. He made a face and pitched his piece of chocolate into the Seine.

But there was also a box from Enric Rovira that Steve and I had brought back from a trip to Catalonia. Rovira seemed to be completing a circle after five hundred years. Spaniards brought beans to the Old World, and they lost control of them to the Swiss, Dutch, Englishmen, and Frenchmen who mastered chocolate. Now a Spaniard—okay, a Catalan—was taking chocolate into space. Rovira, more gifted as an artist than as a chocolate maker, had crafted his Planetary Collection. In his solar system of superb, shiny globes, each planet was filled with a different ganache and hand-painted to look like new worlds.

Who knows whether it was dopamine, phenylethylamine, chocolate-triggered memories of childhood, or simply the rocking of an old English boat on an older French river in the company of friendly cacao lifers from a lot of different places. It didn't really matter. My original plan was to follow the chocolate trail to its end. Happily enough, I discovered, there is no end.

After a while, I grilled fat Argentine steaks on the barbecue. Jacques, who was due for heart surgery in three days, ate two of them, bloody red and liberally doused in coarse salt and olive oil. We wolfed down a bowl of corn on the cob and a bucket of salad. Next came the cheese, most of which Claudio finished with great wads of good bread.

And then it was time for dessert. You can probably guess what flavor.

# Acknowledgments

That was no exaggeration; I was a chocolate ignoramus. Except maybe at dessert time (or often during any day, mornings and late nights included), I never thought much about the stuff. John Glusman, my editor, and Geri Thoma, my agent, had the confidence to think I could fill a book on the subject. But I couldn't have come close without Chloé Doutre-Roussel.

Generosity poured in from all sides. Aodaoin O'Floinn covered my back. Hadley Fitzgerald sent books, wisdom, clippings, and energy. So did Gretchen Hoff, Willis Barnstone, Phil Cousineau, and Barbara Gerber. Louis and Paul Kay, and their parents, showed me some basics. David Lebovitz was generous with prodigious knowledge and time despite work on a book of his own. Sophie Body-Generot and Kerrin Feldman got me started. Olivia Snaije, Daphne Benoit, Ariane Troujman, Cecile Allegra, Linda White, Pan Kwan Yuk, Jerome Delay, and a lot of others helped along the way. The aid of Claudio and Steve and other chocolate masters is evident in the text.

Above all, of course, there is Rose, née Jeannette Hermann, who fed the process, from start to finish, and then helped clean up the mess.